STRIKE AND HOLD

Other Notable World War II Titles from Brassey's

The Story of World War II, by Henry Steele Commager

Spitfires, Thunderbolts, and Warm Beer: An American Fighter Pilot over Europe, by Philip D. Caine

Desperate Deception: British Covert Operations in the United States, 1939–1944, by Thomas E. Mahl

The Road to Victory: The Untold Story of World War II's Red Ball Express, by David Colley

Nuts! The Battle of the Bulge: The Story and Photographs, by Donald M. Goldstein, Katherine V. Dillon, and J. Michael Wenger

STRIKE AND HOLD

A Memoir of the 82d Airborne in World War II

T. Moffatt Burriss

Brassey's

WASHINGTON, D.C.

Library of Congress Cataloging-in-Publication Data

Burriss, T. Moffatt.
    Strike and hold : a memoir of the 82nd Airborne in World War II /
T. Moffatt Burriss.—1st ed.
        p.   cm.
Includes index.
ISBN 1-57488-258-9 (alk.) HB
    1. United States. Army. Airborne Division, 82nd.   2. Burriss, T. Moffatt.
3. Soldiers—United States—Biography.   4. World War, 1939–1945—Aerial
operations, American.   5. World War, 1939–1945—Campaigns—Western
Front.   6. World War, 1939–1945—Personal narratives, American.   I. Title.

D769.346 82nd B87 2000
940.54′4973—dc21

00-030411

ISBN 1-57488-348-8 PB
Printed in the United States of America on acid-free paper that meets the
American National Standards Institute Z39-48 Standard.

Brassey's
22841 Quicksilver Drive
Dulles, Virginia 20166

Designed by Pen & Palette Unlimited

First Edition

10 9 8 7 6 5 4 3 2 1

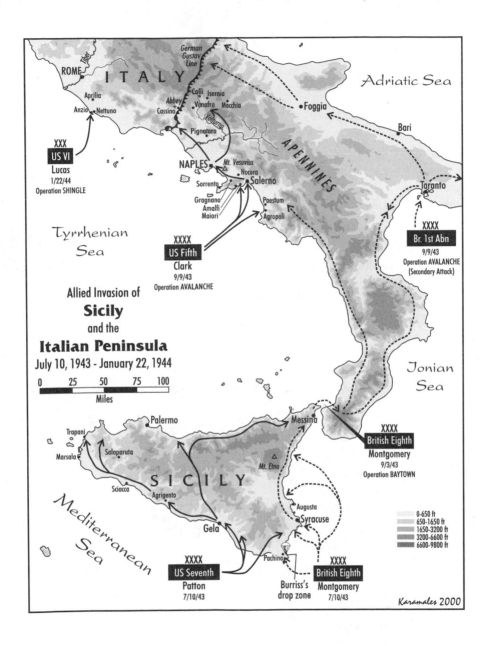

Allied Invasion of
Sicily
and the
Italian Peninsula
July 10, 1943 - January 22, 1944

0   25   50   75   100
Miles

ROME

ITALY

Aprilia

Anzio Nettuno

Tiber

Colli Isernia

Abbey Venafro Macchia
Cassino

Pignataro

Volturno

German
Gustav
Line

Adriatic Sea

Foggia

Bari

APENNINES

XXX
US VI
Lucas
1/22/44
Operation SHINGLE

NAPLES Mt. Vesuvius

Sorrento Nocera
Salerno

Gragnano
Amalfi Paestum
Maiori Agropoli

Taranto

*Tyrrhenian
Sea*

XXXX
US Fifth
Clark
9/9/43
Operation AVALANCHE

XXXX
Br. 1st Abn
9/9/43
Operation AVALANCHE
(Secondary Attack)

*Ionian
Sea*

Palermo

Messina

Trapani

Marsala Salaparuta

Sciacca Agrigento

SICILY

Mt. Etna

XXXX
British Eighth
Montgomery
9/3/43
Operation BAYTOWN

*Mediterranean
Sea*

Gela

Augusta
Syracuse

0-650 ft
650-1650 ft
1650-3200 ft
3200-6600 ft
6600-9800 ft

XXXX
US Seventh
Patton
7/10/43

Pachino

Burriss's
drop zone

XXXX
British Eighth
Montgomery
7/10/43

Karamales 2000

Contents

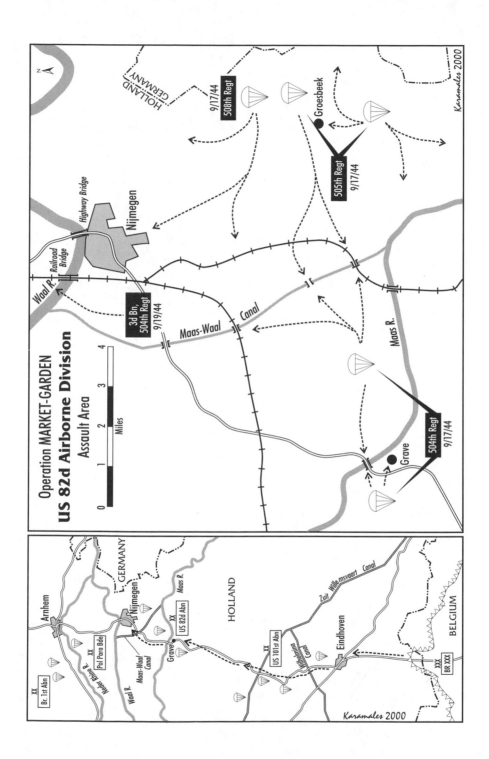

Preface

Over the past forty years, my children have frequently asked me to tell them about some of my war experiences, and I have. In recent years, they have insisted that I write down some of the stories for their children and grandchildren. Finally, I consented.

After I started writing, however, I soon found that I could not do it alone. To do justice to my unit and to my comrades, I needed input from them. Every man saw the war through a different set of eyes. Even though he might have been a few feet or a couple of hundred yards from me, his experiences could be totally different. So I wrote a number of my fellow officers and the enlisted men who served and asked that they write an article about one or two of their most memorable experiences for inclusion in the book. Several did, and they have been included, with minimal editing for stylistic consistency.

I wish there were some way to give appropriate credit to every man and officer who served in my unit, but that would be impossible. I served 3½ years (2½ overseas) in Headquarters Company, 3d Battalion, and I Company, 504th Parachute Infantry Regiment, 82d Airborne Division. In my opinion, no finer combat unit ever existed. Every man was a volunteer and committed to being the best fighting soldier in the U.S. Army. We were told that we were the best and trained to be the best, and we felt that we were the best. Few, if any, units had as much frontline duty as we had. I was fortunate and proud to serve in such a fine outfit.

We had a threefold mission: defeat the enemy, preserve the peace and freedom of our nation, and get back home to our loved ones. No one shirked his duty, and no one backed down. Many gave their lives. Our casualty rate was tremendous, and the hardships we faced were unending. We did our part in winning the war and preserving peace and freedom throughout the world.

To me, one man stood out above all others—Capt. Delbert Kuehl, the Protestant chaplain of our regiment, a true man of God and a brave soldier. He was everywhere, in the thick of battle or at the aid station, giving comfort and help to those in need. Through him, I dedicate this book to all the officers and men of the 3d Battalion of the 504th.

I also dedicate this book to my first wife (now deceased), Louisa Hay Burriss, who kept the "home fires burning" and prayed me safely back home. And to my four children, John Hay, Moffatt Jr., Francis, and Louisa ("Weesa"), who encouraged me to write this book and who have been a joy to me over the years. And to my present wife, Jean Wheelwright Burriss, who graciously takes care of this old soldier.

Prologue

S ome soldiers do not like to think about the wars in which they fought. They bury the memories and try to live their lives as if they never had been in battle or killed enemy troops or seen their friends blown apart. Others come to terms with war by talking about it, reliving it—usually with men who've shared similar experiences.

Apparently, I fall into the second category. I have attended reunions of paratroopers who fought in World War II and, over the years, kept in touch with a number of men who were with me in Sicily, Italy, Holland, France, Belgium, and Germany. I have enjoyed going to these gatherings and corresponding with old Army buddies—now *old* in more than one sense of the word.

Reunions, however, did not fully satisfy me. As I grew older, I felt a stronger and stronger urge to go back to the locales where the battles were fought, to see the landscape, to feel the air, and to hear the sounds of each place. After fifty years, I figured that if I were going, I had better do it soon. Finally, in the summer of 1993, I decided to make the trip.

I did not have to go alone. My son Francis, by then forty-four years old, had heard me talk about Sicily, Anzio Beach, and the Waal River all of his life; he had become a student of World War II and was almost as anxious to tour the battle sites as I was. I was pleased that he wanted to make the trip.

In addition, my old friend Joseph ("Joe") Taylor, said that he would like to come along. Joe and I had known each other since grammar school days, had attended the same high school in Anderson, South Carolina, and returned to live in Columbia after the war. He had seen a lot of combat during World War II, as well, so he shared my interest in revisiting battlefields. Fortunately, he had fought in the same parts of Europe as I, so we were able to plan a route to accommodate both of us.

In June, we flew to Rome and caught a plane to Palermo, Sicily, where we rented a Fiat to drive around that huge island. Sicily had been the center of European culture during the twelfth century and, for a brief period in 1943, the center of the world's attention. Both Joe and I had landed there in July of that year—he as part of the seaborne forces that hit the beach at Gela and I as a paratrooper who had jumped from a plane near Pachino and Marzemimi and landed many miles off course. Fifty years later, we drove south from Palermo toward Gela—along the same route that the American and British forces had traveled—though back then we went from Gela to Palermo as we chased the enemy all the way.

Joe and I assumed that Sicily would have changed after half a century, that we wouldn't be able to locate the places we remembered. But the Sicilian landscape remained exactly as it had looked in July 1943. The countryside was an endless succession of vineyards, spread out in every direction and separated by dirt roads and rock fences. The grapevines, propped up on wooden frames, ran up steep terraced hillsides, spilled over the top, and poured down the other side. Now, as then, they were a rich green. As we drove along, I recalled the moonlit night when I had joined the British and chased Italian soldiers through those vineyards and down those roads. We had killed a lot of them and captured many more.

We even located the two-foot stone wall behind which I and two other paratroopers had lain, clutching hand grenades, ready to toss them when the enemy soldiers came closer. We had each thrown two grenades and then run for our lives as we left a road littered with dead and dying Italians.

"Are you sure this is it?" Francis asked.

"Pretty sure," I said, "but the vines were taller then. I guess the old ones died, and the farmer had to replant."

We stopped in the village of Pachino, which we had captured, and I saw the same little houses that I had seen then—stucco with terra-cotta tile roofs. Some of them were two hundred years old, and, in 1943 we had left them intact as we swept across the island. In fact, after fifty years, we saw no visible scars of war. Nature had long since covered our tracks.

Getting out of the Fiat, we looked harmless enough in our khaki pants and T-shirts, and the local people smiled and nodded. We tried to talk to them, but few spoke English. Some of them who did talk to us remembered when the Americans and British had come, but most were only children then and could recall few details.

The purpose of the 1943 invasion of Sicily had been to gain a toe-hold from which to invade Italy. Because both Joe and I had taken part in the invasion of Italy, which was mostly by sea, we traveled up the east coast of Sicily to Messina, where we drove our Fiat onto a ferry and made the short trip to the Italian mainland.

In 1943, we had made that trip in amphibious landing craft, while being shelled by artillery and strafed by machine-gun fire. Joe had come ashore at Salerno, and I had landed first at Salerno and then at Amalfi-Maiori. So we headed north along the highway to Salerno. After fifty years, Salerno was all but unrecognizable. We saw a few of the old stucco buildings huddled along the beach, but high-rises made of glass and steel had taken over the landscape like an invading army.

On leaving Salerno, we drove along a mountain road to Amalfi-Maiori on the Sorrento Peninsula. It was also a modern city, and the change was dramatic. The stucco and tile buildings were dwarfed by huge commercial buildings and apartment houses, but I still recognized the topography of the place—the wide beach, the valley, and then, suddenly, the mountains sweeping up to the top of the sky.

We then traveled to the Chiunzi Pass—during the war, we had called it 88 Pass—the gateway to Naples, the first major European city occupied by the Allies. Our forces had entered the city on 1 October 1943 and later landed at Anzio on 22 January 1944. Naples certainly looked different in 1993—a modern metropolis with late-model automobiles crawling along its streets. Fifty years earlier, it had been an old city, clearly on its way downhill after centuries of prosperity. The Allies had shelled Naples before entering it; when we first arrived there, some sections had been in ruins.

From Naples, we drove through Capua to Cassino and then to Anzio, which had not changed at all. Although we could not get to the beach where we had landed—it was now an Italian military base—we did visit the American cemetery, where many good men had been buried so many years ago. The cemetery was so large that it took one's breath away—row on row, rank on rank of white crosses that stretched as far as the eye could see. On the markers were names and dates.

The reception building had a directory; if you knew a man's name, you could find out which block and which row he was in. I knew the names of my men all right. I'd never forgotten them. I could recall exactly what they looked like, the sound of their voices, things they had said. I visited each grave in turn, put my hand on the cool stone, and read the name, birth date, and death date. Back when they were killed, the rest of us had no time to grieve, but fifty years later, as I stood beside each grave, I wondered why I had survived and they had not. Thinking about it, I was moved to tears.

As we had traveled through Capua, Joe had a faraway look in his eye.

"It was somewhere along here that I was shot by a sniper. Got my first Purple Heart. The bullet grazed my head and took off an eyebrow."

"When did you get your next one?" Francis called out from the backseat.

"It wasn't very long afterward," Joe said. "In early 1944, just north of Rome."

If Francis thought Joe was particularly unlucky, he changed his mind when Joe told him about the incident.

"I was leading a nine-man patrol," he said. "We stumbled into a minefield and somebody stepped on one. I got a piece of shrapnel in my shoulder. The other eight men were killed. After the Good Lord spared me that day, I vowed to spend the rest of my life helping other people."

And back home in South Carolina, Joe had become renowned for his public service, to which my missionary son Francis can certainly attest.

After leaving the cemetery, we drove up Mount Sammucro. Fifty years earlier, we had called it Hill 1205. When we reached the top, we saw the Monte Cassino Abbey, which had been blown off the mountain by our bombers in early 1944. During that famous moment in the European theater, I had watched the bombing attack and prayed that our planes would succeed before the guns inside the abbey blew us to bits. The abbey had been completely rebuilt—a replica of the one that our bombers had reduced to rubble.

During the war, Joe had been sent to Edro, a small village in northern Italy, where he spent the rest of his service time, so that was our next stop. During the 1940s, Edro had been a small resort village, as it still was—nestled in the green mountains and surrounded by a number of round, blue lakes where people were still boating and fishing.

Joe looked over the place. "They may have built a few additional inns," he said, "but that's about all that's different."

Then he told us about his affair with a beautiful Italian girl named Rita. We located the house where she lived—and where Joe had slept—and her brother remembered him. In fact, Joe talked to Rita on the phone, but he was not able to see her.

After fighting in Italy, I had gone through France and on to Belgium to fight in the Battle of the Bulge. We visited all those spots, as well as Cologne and Düsseldorf on the Rhine River, where my unit, I Company of the 504th Paratroopers, made an assault crossing in early 1945 near Hitdorf. Cologne, which had been nothing but a pile of rubble by the time we had crossed the Rhine, had risen out of its own wreckage to become a thriving modern city, one of the many examples of the miraculous West German economic recovery. In fact, the only building that I recognized on my return trip was the cathedral, which our bombers and artillerymen had spared.

We next went to Nijmegen, the Netherlands, the site of the famous Waal River crossing commemorated in a book by Cornelius Ryan, *A Bridge Too Far*, published in 1974. Of all the battle sites, this one stirred the most memories in me.

Operation Market Garden provoked controversy almost from the day that it was conceived. After the terrible Allied losses sustained at Nijmegen and Arnhem, it became even more controversial.

Nijmegen and Arnhem were right on the German border, and it was Gen. Bernard Law Montgomery's grand scheme to enter the Third Reich through the back door. When we had reached the Waal in September 1944, the bank had been green and covered with trees. When we returned in 1993, it was lined with plants and factories.

Though the south bank had industrialized, the city of Nijmegen seemed unchanged. We learned that the people in nearby Groesbeek maintained the Airborne Liberation Museum commemorating that action. When we arrived at the museum, we found ourselves looking at a huge mural depicting the event.

My son Francis stared at it for a long moment. Then, glancing at me, he asked, "Dad, was that the way it looked forty-nine years ago?"

"Yes," I said, "except I remember the bullets kicking up more water-spouts than you see in the painting. They were so thick, they looked like raindrops falling into the river."

A few feet away, a Dutchman, who had been staring at the same mural, turned to me.

"Were you involved in that river crossing?"

"Oh, yes," I responded.

"What is your name?"

"Burriss."

His eyes lit up.

"Could that be Moffatt Burriss?"

I couldn't believe my ears.

"How could you possibly know my first name?"

"Several of us have just collaborated on a book about the Waal crossing," he said, "and your name appears numerous times. I translated the book from Dutch into English. Would you like to meet the authors?"

We met with them the next morning. G. Thuring, F. Van Den Bergh, and L. Zwaaf were middle-aged Dutchmen who had been children during the war. For several hours, we discussed their book and our recollections of events that had taken place almost fifty years earlier. Then we went to the Nijmegen bridge and the nearby spot where we had crossed the river.

Nothing had changed. The bridge, with its humpbacked steel span, still looked as if it had been built with a giant Erector set, the river churning underneath, its waters dark and swift. The grass was still a rich green on the other side—flat for 900 yards, then rising suddenly to form a dike stretching out of sight in both directions.

The Germans had placed flak wagons, mortars, artillery, and machine guns along the dike and had fired down on us as we crossed the river and charged toward them across a flat, green pasture devoid of cover. Men had dropped on all sides, but no one had even slowed down until we had swarmed over the dike and killed or driven off the Germans manning the machine guns.

Later that day, our Dutch friends took us to see a memorial to the men of the 3d Battalion, 504th Parachute Infantry Regiment, who were killed in the crossing. Their names were cast in bronze. I recognized most of them and remembered the voices and faces that went with the names.

In front of the monument stood several vases of freshly cut flowers. I turned to the Dutchmen and pointed to the flowers.

"It looks like we came at the right time. What's the occasion?"

One of them smiled and said, "There is no special occasion. Every day, we keep fresh flowers here and at the other memorials. In fact, we bring schoolchildren here regularly so they will know the great price the Americans paid for our freedom."

We walked around town and saw the monuments to other units. Sure enough, there were newly cut flowers at each one. I was surprised at the strong sense of gratitude that the Dutch people felt for the men who had attempted to liberate their town and their country at such a terrible price. I couldn't help but wonder if Americans still felt as strongly about those brave men who never made it across the river and pasture.

As we were about to leave, one of the Dutchmen, pastor of the local church, called me aside and said, "Next September, we are having a fiftieth anniversary celebration of the liberation of Holland. We would like to invite you to attend. We are planning to reenact the crossing of the Waal. We would be honored if you would participate."

I accepted on the spot but wondered if they would expect me to jump, just as I had jumped on 17 September 1944. On 20 September 1994, the date of the reenactment, I would be two days shy of my seventy-fifth birthday.

After we left Nijmegen, Francis told me that he had found the scene strangely moving. "Dad," he said, "I couldn't help thinking that if you hadn't made it across that bridge, I wouldn't be here today, nor would my three children."

From the Netherlands, we drove on to Ludwigslust and Wobbelin, due south of the German city of Schwerin. My memories of Wobbelin were troubling. I had seen many men die in combat before we came to this spot, but what I saw there was the most horrifying sight of all. A concentration camp was stacked with corpses—bodies wasted away, skin stretched over bones, swarming with insects.

And the living had the same appearance, except for their haunted eyes, which stared at us in fear and wonder as we released them from their barbed-wire prison. Many were too far gone to survive for more than a few hours. We sent them off in stretchers to die in clean beds. The rest, we fed and medicated as best we could.

Then we discovered the mass grave, with hundreds and hundreds of bodies bulldozed under tons of earth. We forced the Germans to dig up all the bodies—every one—and rebury them in a nearby town square.

In 1993, the place where the concentration camp had stood was now a field waving in hay. In fact, I could not tell for sure where the barbed wire had been strung and the shabby buildings had stood.

In the town, we found a museum established by the Germans as a memorial to the dead. We also visited a monument erected over the graves of those starved, tormented people. Coming back to Wobbelin brought all that horror back.

I was glad when we left the place and headed for Berlin, our last stop. By then, the Berlin Wall had fallen, and we saw only its remnants. I had always thought it was a massive barrier, like the Great Wall of China, but, where we stood, it was only about eight inches thick.

The eastern segment of the city still reflected the failed policies of the communist regime that had governed it for more than forty years. Except for some of the older buildings, East Berlin was a giant slum. In fact, almost fifty years after the war had ended, we could still see the scars of war—gutted buildings, vacant lots heaped with rubble, and craters everywhere.

By contrast, West Berlin had been completely restored. That part of the city was prosperous. We could tell by the look of the shops, the way the people dressed, and the number of Mercedes-Benz automobiles moving along the thoroughfares. All of this new construction had been fueled by a dynamic economy, modeled on the free markets of the Western democracies, that, over the years, had shown only occasional signs of slowing down.

Francis had learned that the Berlin Marathon would be run the day after we arrived. Without telling us, he had entered the race. The route took the runners through the streets of what had been, until the reuniting of Germany, West Berlin. They ran down modern streets between glass and steel high-rises, many of them containing the corporate offices of Fortune 500 companies.

Joe and I watched Francis finish the grueling race. He was not the first to cross the finish line but by no means the last. I couldn't help but note the irony of the situation. Almost a half century earlier, before he was born, I had come to this country to kill its young men and to destroy its political regime. Now Francis was running races with the sons and grandsons of the men against whom I had fought.

On the plane back to New York, I thought about our trip, and I was glad that I had made it. The memories that I stirred up were bittersweet. I encountered a lot of dead faces along the way, men who had served with me and had been killed long before VE-Day. I thought of the years that I had been granted and that they had missed as they lay under identical white markers in European cemeteries. I had raised children, benefitted from postwar prosperity, lost my wife to Alzheimer's disease, married again, and lived to enjoy my grandchildren.

Many of the men who had died in the war were probably forgotten now, with fewer and fewer people still living who remembered what they looked like or even who they were. Soon enough, all of us would be gone, including me. The more I thought about it, the more I was determined to preserve what we had done together in these now-historic places and try to give them some small place in the memory of a nation less and less mindful of the sacrifices that they had made. The words haunted me: "Those who forget the past are doomed to repeat it."

So I decided to write a book—to tell everything of importance that had happened to me during World War II, and in so doing, to tell some of their stories as well—for their grandchildren and great-grandchildren and for mine. I also invited those who survived the war to tell their stories as well.

This is our book.

— 1 —

The Way We Were

By September 1940, half the world was at war. In June, the Germans captured Paris, France surrendered, and Marshal Philippe Pétain set up a government in Vichy. The Soviets occupied Latvia, Lithuania, and Estonia. In August, the Germans began to bomb Britain, first, airfields and factories and, then, the heart of London, where civilian casualties were high.

But even with these events occupying the headlines of the nation's newspapers, my mind was on other matters. After graduating from Clemson University in June, I had just begun my new job as a physics and science teacher at Orangeburg High School in Orangeburg, South Carolina. And, at the teachers' orientation, I spotted the cutest girl I had ever seen.

"Who is she?" I whispered to one of the other male teachers.

"Her name's Louisa Hay," he whispered back, "but they call her 'Squee.'"

She was a stunning brunette with an infectious laugh. I couldn't keep my eyes off her.

"Don't get any ideas," my friend said. "She's already dating Jack Padgett, the chemistry teacher."

"Regularly?" I asked.

"Regularly."

But I wasn't deterred. I made every opportunity to talk to her during the school day, and I finally asked her out. She accepted, but, for a while, she continued to see a lot more of Jack Padgett than of me.

It was a different world then. The Great Depression hadn't yet ended, and nobody had any money. My teaching salary was $85 a month, and I picked up an extra $30 for driving the school bus. In today's economy, $115 wouldn't pay for a night's lodging at a downtown motel. But, in those days, I lived at Mrs. Pike's boarding house for $25 a month, which included my room, clean sheets every week, and three meals a day. I had a roommate, a fellow Clemson graduate. A county agent, two secretaries, and one female teacher also roomed at Mrs. Pike's.

In addition to paying room and board, I bought a slightly used red Ford convertible, and my monthly payments were $22. Those were my big expenditures, so I had plenty of money left to spend on entertainment.

Those days, a typical date in Orangeburg consisted of going to the soda shop on the first floor of the Hotel Eutaw (located right across the street from Mrs. Bozard's boarding house, where Squee and eleven other female teachers lived). A fountain Coke was a nickel, and a bag of peanuts was a penny. On a wild night, you could spend twelve cents on your girl.

On some weekends, Squee went to Columbia, where her sister was teaching high school. I had an uncle who lived there, so when she visited her sister, I visited my uncle and took her out. That's when I began to cut in on Jack. I also dated other girls for awhile, but Squee and I began to see more and more of each other.

Courtship in those days was conducted under strict rules. For example, when Clemson was playing in the Cotton Bowl, I asked Squee to go with me. Her friend Mary Carey was also going with a Clemson boy, and the four of us decided to go. However, we settled on the Sugar Bowl in New Orleans since Dallas was so far. Even though Squee was twenty-two years old and living on her own, she felt that she had to get permission from her parents to make the trip. They were members of the Presbyterian Church US. Her father was an ordained minister, and her mother once had been an Associate Reform Presbyterian (ARP) medical missionary in Mexico. Fortunately, I was also an ARP, so her mother said that Squee could go.

Clemson won their game. On our way back, we stopped in a restaurant in Tallahassee. As we waited for our food, Mary's date had an idea, "Let's order a bottle of champagne to celebrate Clemson's victory."

Neither Squee nor Mary drank—and neither did I, but we decided it wouldn't hurt if we raised our glass in a toast and took just a sip of the champagne. When the waiter opened the bottle, the cork made a loud pop, hit the ceiling, and bounced back into a metal chandelier, then ran round and round. By the time it came to rest, everybody in the restaurant was looking in our direction.

The South was one big community back then. Everybody knew everybody else. A couple at one of the restaurant tables came from Morristown, Tennessee, Squee's hometown. A few days later, she received a stern letter from her parents. I think we finally convinced them that we were merely toasting the team with a tiny sip, but it was a hard sell. Drinking wasn't as socially acceptable in 1941 as it is today.

In those innocent times, we enjoyed dating as much as young people do today, perhaps even more. The automobile was changing some of the rules. Squee's mother never would have been allowed to travel across the country with a young man, but the rest of the rules were still intact. For example, there were no unchaperoned overnights, but we did have house parties. Near the end of the year, Mrs. Bozard invited the teachers in her boarding house and their dates to join her in the mountains of South Carolina for a weekend party. She was the chaperon, and we all behaved ourselves.

That Sunday morning, 7 December 1941, Squee and I were sitting on a sofa and talking to each other, barely aware of the other couples moving in and out of the house. Someone switched on the radio, the chief form of home entertainment in those days, and a voice broke through the static to say that the Japanese had just bombed Pearl Harbor, that the United States was about to go to war.

"Where's Pearl Harbor?" someone asked.

"In the Philippine Islands," someone else replied.

Squee turned white.

"My brother," she said. "He's a second lieutenant in the Army. He just landed in the Philippines last week."

"He's probably OK," I said.

But the more we crowded around the radio and listened to the reports, the more obvious it became that our troops in the Philippines were marooned, that they couldn't be rescued from the advancing Japanese because our entire Pacific fleet had been destroyed.

One of the men said, "I guess I'll be called up. I have a reserve commission in the Army."

Then it hit me. So did I.

Shortly thereafter, the party broke up. Some of the girls were crying, and the rest of us were grim and tight-lipped. We drove back to Orangeburg in silence.

The next day, President Franklin D. Roosevelt gave his famous "A day that will live in infamy" speech before Congress, and the United States voted to declare war on Japan, as did Great Britain. Three days later, Germany declared war on the United States, and the line had been drawn in the sand.

The innocent days were over, the days when I had nothing more to worry about than whether to take Squee to the movies or for peanuts and a Coke at the soda shop. From that time on, the U.S. Army would tell me when and where I could see my girl—and almost everything else I could and couldn't do. Americans no longer had the luxury of ignoring the ominous newspaper headlines and turning to the comics. Everyone, whether military or civilian, would focus on winning the war.

It didn't take long for the Army to come after me. My orders arrived on 24 December, when I was spending Christmas with my mother back home in Anderson. I was scheduled to report for duty at Fort Benning, Georgia, on 9 January. By then, German U-boats were already patrolling the East Coast of the United States.

The day after Christmas, I drove over to Morristown to spend a few days with Squee and her family. Squee and I were serious about each other, but I still hadn't asked her to marry me. Now I had a new set of questions to consider.

I went back to Orangeburg High School for a week. On a beautiful sunny day, I got into my red Ford convertible, took one last turn around the practice field, and said good-bye to the students. All the girls swarmed around me and began hugging and kissing me. I put up absolutely no resistance. Then I drove away, waving as I went, and headed west toward Georgia.

— 2 —

Learning How to Kill

When I arrived at Fort Benning, I was immediately assigned to the Infantry School and placed in an officer's refresher course. There were two hundred of us in all. We were housed in long two-story wooden barracks, and we slept on metal cots less than three feet apart.

Each of us had a footlocker at the end of our bunks, in which we kept toilet articles, socks, underwear, shoeshine kit, brass polish, and whatever else we owned. We hung our uniforms on racks at the head of our bunks. Clearly, the Army expected us to learn to travel light.

Reveille was at 0500. We immediately hustled outside for physical training, which consisted of strenuous exercises that utilized every muscle in the human body. Then we had breakfast in the mess hall and went from there to classes, where we learned basic infantry tactics—sometimes from combat veterans and sometimes from training films. After the lectures, we sat outside on bleachers and watched demonstration teams execute some of the tactics.

Along more practical lines, we learned how to assemble, disassemble, clean, and maintain a variety of weapons. After simulated firing, we went out to the range and actually fired the M-1, the Browning automatic rifle (BAR), and the machine gun with live ammunition. We also practiced throwing hand grenades and firing mortars. Once we qualified on the various weapons, we learned to operate as a combat unit and worked with tank and artillery units.

Our training went on from 0500 until dark, six days a week and sometimes seven days. In all these activities, our instructors made it clear that our chief purpose in life was to lead men into battle and to kill the enemy. They reminded us that, in a matter of weeks, we probably would be in the field and be facing the Germans or the Japanese. In fact, on 26 January, shortly after I began my training, the first American forces arrived in Great Britain. Thinking about this grim responsibility inspired us to take our training more seriously.

Several times, as I sat on the bleachers and watched demonstrations of infantry tactics, I saw airplanes flying over a far field and tiny figures plunging out of a door on the side of the plane. Then the sky suddenly blossomed with parachutes. The men swayed gently underneath the silk mushrooms as they drifted to earth. One of the rides at the 1939 World's Fair had been a simulated parachute jump. From my perspective on the bleachers, it looked like more fun than being an infantryman.

One evening, I stopped by the parachute school unit, stuck my head in the door, and saw the familiar face of Leonard Almeida, an ROTC classmate at Clemson. He was a captain in parachute training school, and as soon as he realized that I was interested, he immediately tried to sign me up.

"This is the place to be," he said. "No draftees. All volunteers. We're an elite group, the greatest troops in the Army."

I was impressed. "What exactly do paratroopers do?"

"Paratroopers are sent on great missions—much better missions than infantry," he said. "You jump, capture the objective. Then the infantry relieves you, and you go on to the next mission. You never have to dig a foxhole and live in it for three months."

As it turned out, most of what Leonard said was untrue. The few times that we jumped on a mission, we stayed there until the bitter end. And if that meant living in foxholes, we lived in foxholes. As I recall, the big difference between paratroopers and the infantry in the field was the level of comfort. Infantry units brought along their own jeeps, kitchens, and hospitals. Paratroopers brought along only what they could carry on their backs.

One thing that Leonard said, however, *was* true. Officers in the paratroopers were paid an extra $100 per month. After making only $85 per month for teaching school, I thought this was an enormous benefit. So I put in an application to join the paratroopers.

In February, knowing that I'd be receiving this extra pay, I obtained a weekend pass, drove to Anderson, and bought a diamond ring. Then, I drove down to Orangeburg, where I slipped it on Squee's finger and asked her to marry me. As I'd expected, she said, "Yes." We telephoned her parents, who knew we had been going steady for months and expected that we would get married.

When her father answered the phone, Squee said, "Daddy, I have an engagement ring."

He said, "That's great, honey. Who gave it to you?"

"You know who," she said.

Her parents said they were pleased, though they must have had some reservations. Marriage was a serious proposition in the best of times, but the war introduced new considerations. After talking it over, Squee and I decided to have the wedding as soon as I finished paratrooper training. It was the same choice that many young couples would make during the following months, when it seemed as if a brief period of happiness was all that anyone could realistically hope to enjoy. We were both apprehensive about the future but happy with our decision.

I expected to go to parachute school in April, immediately after finishing my basic officer's training, but the orders were late in coming so I was sent to Camp Wolters in Texas. There, I was assigned to a basic training outfit as an instructor. After two weeks, my orders finally caught up with me, and I was shipped back to Fort Benning where I began my jump training in May. The training program lasted for only four weeks. The first week was physical conditioning—more calisthenics and running.

During the second week, we continued the body building but also learned to pack and care for parachutes. This was an important lesson because our lives would depend on how well we learned it.

Finally, during the third week, we learned the techniques of jumping and landing in parachutes. We climbed a 34-foot wooden tower, put on a harness that was hooked to a cable and a pulley, stepped off the platform, and slid down the cable. This training phase was designed to separate the sheep from the goats, and a lot of guys flunked out because they couldn't bring themselves to step out into empty space.

I had never been afraid of heights; otherwise, I would never have considered the paratroopers in the first place. In fact, I had done something similar to this cable exercise as a boy. I made a trolley by stringing a heavy wire from one tall tree to another. Then I attached a pulley, dropped a wire from the pulley, wrapped it around a stick, and, holding both ends of the stick, slid down the wire from one tree to the other. So, in this phase of the training, as far as I was concerned, I encountered nothing new.

The next tower was steel and rose 250 feet high. A machine lifted a parachute with a trainee strapped in it to the top of the tower and then cut him loose. He fell, then drifted, and finally hit the ground. This exercise gave us the true feeling of falling in a parachute and landing. In fact, because of pilot error, I later made a jump from a plane at about that same altitude, though I wouldn't recommend it.

During the final week, we jumped from an airplane. As strange as it might seem today, I had never been up in a plane, and the experience was as new and exciting to me as jumping with a parachute. In order to complete our training, we had to make five successful qualifying jumps. In these exercises, we packed our own chutes, so we were particularly careful. (Later, when we were making combat jumps, a special unit of parachute riggers did this job.)

We made these jumps from C-47s especially adapted for paratroopers. Inside, we sat facing each other on either side of the fuselage. A steel cable ran along the top center of the plane from one end to the other and was hooked at the front and rear. We each wore two chutes, the main chute on the back and the reserve chute on the chest. Dangling from the main chute was a *static line*—a web belt with a metal snap on the end. When the time came, we hooked our static lines to the cable running along the top of the plane, and, when we jumped, our chutes jerked open automatically. If, for any reason, the main chute failed, we were supposed to pull the rip cord in front and come down on the reserve chute.

The jump master for these qualifying exercises was an officer or a noncommissioned officer (NCO), who stood or knelt at the open door to watch for the landing area below. As the plane approached it, he shouted out the command, "Stand up and hook up!" Everybody immediately stood and hooked his static line to the cable.

Next, he said, "Check equipment." Everyone checked his spare chute and the main chute of the guy in front of him to see if anything was spilling out. Then, the jump master gave the command, "Stand in the door!" One by one, we came up and stood in the door, with our hands gripping both sides of it. As the jump master shouted, "Go!" and slapped each one of us on the rear, we jumped.

Later, during combat missions, we jumped in *sticks*—units of seventeen men. It took about ten seconds for a whole stick to go through the door. The longer the interval between individual jumps, the farther apart we landed and the more difficult it was to reassemble.

In this final training exercise, however, we jumped one at a time, three during each pass over the landing area. The plane circled around again and returned, and three more men went out.

My first two jumps posed no problems. As instructed, I came down with my knees bent and rolled to the side when I hit the ground. Then I got up, gathered up my chute, and walked over to a waiting truck. On the third jump, however, I sprained my ankle. I managed to get into the back of the truck without too much trouble, but by the time we returned to the bachelor officers quarters (BOQ), I could barely hobble.

"You better hope your ankle clears up by tomorrow," one of my buddies said. "If the instructor sees you limping, he'll ground you, and you'll have to start the program all over again."

"I can't do that," I said. "I'm getting married next week."

The next morning, my ankle was a little better; but it still hurt and I was limping badly.

As we were being driven out to the airfield, my buddy shook his head and said, "You'll never get away with it, not with that limp."

"I've got to try," I said. "You walk next to me, close enough so I can hold on to you. That way, maybe he won't notice."

We tried it. The instructor was busy with some paperwork as we approached the plane, and, with some help, I managed to struggle on board. When I heard the command, "Stand in the door!" I stumbled over and took my place as I held my breath.

"Go!" he said and slapped me on the rear. I'd gotten away with it.

On the last day, an officer assembled us and announced that we wouldn't be jumping because the planes were not available. I wondered if we'd have to wait another week. Then he gave us the good news.

"We can't hold you over," he said. "We've got another bunch coming in on Monday. But you've done well, so we're going to give you your wings anyway, after four jumps."

We cheered. We were paratroopers.

That Sunday, we went through a graduation ceremony and the colonel of our training battalion pinned silver wings on each of us. As we sat in metal chairs and listened to a speech, my mind was on other things. Squee and I had planned to be married the following week, but I hadn't been eligible to apply for leave until graduation. So I was waiting for the ceremony to end and someone to shout "Dismissed!" Then I was going to break from the group and run to battalion headquarters to apply for a two-week leave.

When that moment came, however, everybody had the same idea. With other guys all around me, it was like running in a marathon. We lined up at headquarters, and, one by one, new second lieutenants marched into Capt. Julian Cook's office, threw a salute, and gave the reasons why they wanted leave.

Captain Cook, the battalion adjutant, told each in turn the same thing, "Request denied. You're to report to Company C by 0800 hours tomorrow. Next."

The guy in front of me asked for two weeks, and Captain Cook shook his head. "Request denied. Report to Company A by 0800 hours tomorrow."

By then, I was sure my wedding plans were out the window. I had also planned to ask for two weeks, but I decided to try something more modest.

"I'd like to request a one-week leave, sir," I said.

"For what reason?" he asked.

"I'm scheduled to get married, sir."

He looked at me for a moment, then got up.

"Excuse me a minute," he said. He stepped through the door that connected his office with the colonel's. In a minute, he returned.

"OK," he said. "You can take two weeks off. We'll cut your orders while you're gone."

I thanked him and dashed out the door to call Squee.

We were married on 22 June 1942 in Morristown, with Squee's father performing the ceremony. After a reception, we drove to Knoxville to spend the first night of our honeymoon. We spent the next three days in Montreat, North Carolina, one night in Florence, South Carolina, and the last week in Myrtle Beach. At the end of the two weeks, we drove back to Fort Benning and moved into a small garage apartment. I had been assigned to the 3d Battalion, 504th Parachute Infantry Regiment, 82d Airborne Division.

The next day, I went to Battalion Headquarters and asked the adjutant what my duties were. Smiling, he shrugged his shoulders and said, "Nothing, until they assign troops to your unit."

"You mean I can stay at home?"

"That's right."

I couldn't believe it. Every day, Squee and I went to the Officers' Club, sat around the pool, had lunch, and enjoyed each other's company. This extended vacation lasted for almost two weeks. Then the troops arrived, and our life together drastically changed.

Our unit was taking intensive combat training, and I had to be in the field by 0430 or 0500. I was gone all day, and sometimes I didn't get in until 2200. Needless to say, at those times when I saw my bride, she was sound asleep.

Because I was gone all the time, Squee began to worry about being alone. In the beginning, we thought we were lucky to have our own apartment. Most of the other married couples were renting rooms in private homes. But the more I was away, the better a private home looked, with people there to look out for her. So we traded accommodations with our friends Ray and Ann Gillespie and moved into an apartment that was part of a home. We had our own entrance, but there was a family present in the house when I wasn't there.

These were extraordinary times, for civilians as well as for the military. People who had never rented out their rooms, and would never have done so under ordinary circumstances, opened their homes to the military in order to support the war effort. In Georgia, families drove down the streets to look for men in uniform and invite them to dinner, even though the soldiers were strangers from faraway states.

The war effort posed problems as well. Suddenly, things that one took for granted were no longer available—beef, coffee, sugar, silk and nylon clothing, and anything made of rubber. Many of these commodities came from other continents; with German submarines operating off the East Coast and Japanese submarines off the West Coast, imports dropped off. In addition, these products were needed to provide the troops with food, weapons, and transportation.

One of the first items to go was the automobile tire. The armed forces needed all the tires they could get for planes, half-tracks, jeeps, and other military vehicles. A few days after the United States declared war, new tires disappeared from Goodyear stores, auto dealers, and service stations. Eventually, synthetic rubber tires appeared, and recapping became big business. Meanwhile, Squee and I were stuck with my old Ford convertible, which had four bad tires. Every morning, I was up an hour early to look out the window and see how the car had fared through the night. If it was tilted to one side or the other, two tires were probably flat; if the car was level, four tires were flat. I spent an hour pumping air into them with a hand pump and hoped that I would make it to the base before they went flat again.

I was a mortar platoon leader. A platoon is typically composed of four squads, each led by a noncommissioned officer. As paratroopers, our job was to parachute into combat zones, assemble a mortar, and begin lobbing shells on the enemy. Of course, we carried rifles and were also expected to take part in infantry fighting.

When my platoon had filled up, it was time to begin combat training. As soon as I saw the men, I knew the mere presence of that gold bar on my shoulder would not convince them that I was qualified to be their leader. I was only twenty-three years old, younger than some of them and no more than two or three years older than the rest. They could tell just by looking at me that I wasn't a seasoned combat veteran. I had to earn their respect—and earn it quickly.

So I went into the barracks and told the men to load their back packs with whatever equipment they had—canteens, mess gear, entrenching tool—and to fall out in five minutes. "And be sure you bring your gas masks," I added.

When they were standing before me at attention and in full gear, I said, "OK, everybody put on your gas mask and follow me. We're going for a run." I put on my gas mask, too, and we started running down the road at a good clip.

It was deep summer, and the temperature hovered around 95 degrees, without the slightest hint of a breeze. After twenty minutes of running, the men were suffering. I figured I was in better shape than most of them, so I pushed myself to the limit. When I shouted "Halt!" and told them to remove their masks, some of their faces were bright red and others were deathly white. Then we started running again, this time without the masks. After we had been running for about ten minutes, I told them to stop again and put the masks back on. Then we ran some more. Finally, after an hour, we circled back to the barracks and stopped.

Years later, Bob Tallon of Dillon, South Carolina, a sergeant in my platoon, could still recall that run. He wrote:

> This was without doubt the worst exercise I had been through at Ft. Benning. Some of the troops didn't make it through to the end. This episode taught me that Lieutenant Burriss was one tough officer. He gained my respect by enduring the same training that he required of his men. He kept that respect through all the time we were together.

Of course, I didn't endure this torture merely to impress the troops. I also knew that the more I pushed myself and my men, the more strength and reserve we would all have when we got into combat. I was tough on everybody because I wanted all of us to survive.

We made a lot of practice combat jumps, and they were somewhat different from our first training jumps at 1,200 feet. Now, we were jumping at 600 feet. The reason was obvious. When we jumped into a combat area, we wanted to be in the air as short a time as possible so we wouldn't present easy targets for the enemy on the ground. At 600 feet, we were in the air only about twenty-five to thirty seconds. In combat, even that short amount of time can seem like an eternity.

Instead of the jump master timing the jumps, the pilot gave the signal. There were two lights above the exit door. As the plane approached the drop area, the pilot flipped on the red light and the jump master made certain that everyone was ready. When the pilot flipped on the green light, the jumpers went out the door.

By then, we were learning to jump in sticks—leaving the plane with an interval of less than a second between jumps. The greatest danger during these jumps was not parachute failure. This never happened during our training period. The danger was carelessness: not watching where you were going and becoming entangled in another chute, or landing in trees or wires, or hitting the ground improperly. Because everyone was new at this game, accidents did occur.

During one exercise, Capt. Melvin Blitch jumped out of the plane and was followed by a hefty lieutenant. The lieutenant came plunging down on top of the captain's parachute and sank into it, as if it were a silk pillow.

The captain shouted, "Get the hell off my chute, Lieutenant! That's an order!"

But the lieutenant's own chute, without any weight on it, had collapsed on top of him, and he had no alternative but to ride the captain's chute all the way down. The captain had no problem in landing, but as soon as he did, his parachute collapsed. The lieutenant plunged 20 additional feet and badly bruised his posterior. They laughed about it afterward, but it was a dangerous moment for both of them.

When a paratrooper sees that he is about to land in water, he follows a set procedure. When he's about 100 feet above the water, he unbuckles his leg straps, holds on to the risers until he's 10 to 15 feet above the water's surface, then drops free of his chute and lets it float away so he doesn't become entangled in the ropes and drown. One dark evening, we were practicing night jumps over a field close to the Chattahoochee River. Lt. Otis Danneman, of the Parachute Maintenance Company, jumped with his group and saw that he was quite close to the Chattahoochee, a very muddy river but one that was easy to see on a moonlit night. At about 100 feet, Danneman unbuckled his leg straps, and, at about 15 feet, he let go because he expected to plunge into the cool water. Instead, he hit a meandering dirt road that he had mistaken for the river and broke both ankles.

Another time, Lt. Francis Payne was leading his platoon in a practice jump on a field near the battalion area. Overly eager, he jumped his plane load too soon—right over the battalion command post. The buildings in that area were surrounded by trees, and Lieutenant Payne landed in the top of a tall pine and hung there, swaying back and forth.

Maj. Leslie Freeman, the battalion commander, walked out of the command post, looked up, and saw Payne.

"Payne, what the hell are you doing there?" he barked.

"It was chow time, sir," Payne said, "and I thought I'd drop in for a bite to eat."

They had to locate a tall ladder in order to climb up the tree and cut him down, after which he was chewed out for his mistake.

Soldiers were not the only ones who made mistakes. Civilians sometimes got in the act, too. One day, when we were scheduled to make a jump, Squee and another officer's wife decided to drive to the drop zone and watch us float down. It would be their first time to watch us jump. They piled into the red convertible and started out. The road to the drop zone circled the entire base. When they saw another dirt road that bisected the circle, they decided to take a shortcut.

As they bounced along the bumpy road, they suddenly heard a loudspeaker blare: "Cease fire! Cease fire!" Curious, they looked to their right and saw a row of giant targets. Then they looked to their left and saw a row of soldiers aiming their rifles. They had driven across the rifle range and were directly in the line of fire.

The voice continued, "Driver of the red convertible. You are in danger. Repeat, you are in danger. Turn around and leave the range immediately."

Even though they were 100 yards away, the recruits could see their long hair and knew that they were women, so they began cheering. Squee immediately turned the car around, and the two wives waved as they sped back down the road.

Some mistakes were more costly. In large military operations, hundreds and sometimes thousands of paratroopers are dropped simultaneously on a combat area. For this reason, it's very important that pilots hold their planes in perfect formation before and during jumps. Otherwise, the jumpers might collide with something or somebody before their chutes open.

We were transferred to Fort Bragg, North Carolina, to complete our combat training. While we were there, one pilot broke formation and flew higher than the rest of the planes. As a consequence, three of his men jumped and were swept into the propellers of a plane trailing at the proper altitude. We all took note of these three deaths. They illustrated the necessity to maintain strict discipline and to work together as a team.

None of my men was involved in that accident, but a near disaster hit closer to home. We had taken off for a practice combat jump in a 15-mph wind, the maximum at which we were allowed to jump. Hoping the wind would die down, the pilot flew around for an hour, but the wind picked up to 25 mph. According to regulations, the mission should have been scrubbed. Instead, someone gave the order to jump.

The plane was skimming the treetops as an exercise in avoiding enemy radar. As we approached the drop field, we were supposed to soar to 600 feet and bail out. Unfortunately, the jump area slipped up on the pilot. He started climbing and flipped on the green light button at the same time. We were only 200 feet above the ground. As jump master, I was the first one out the door.

I remember my chute opening, and I swung forward. On the backswing, I hit the ground—first on my feet, then my tail, and then my head. The impact was so great that it split the plastic liner under my steel helmet.

The wind caught my chute, and I found myself bouncing across the field at 25 mph. I was holding my rifle in my hand, so I couldn't reach up and grab the risers to collapse the chute. Finally I had to drop the rifle, something we were forbidden to do, in order to stop myself from being dragged to death.

Several of my men sustained serious and painful injuries as the result of the pilot's error. Two had broken ankles, and one, who landed in a tree, had several cracked ribs. We were lucky that no one was killed.

That was my only jump at 200 feet. We made several more jumps at 600 feet, however, including one at a demonstration for British Prime Minister Winston Churchill when he was touring the United States. Later, we received the word that he was impressed and looked forward to our arrival in England.

During this training period, I was summoned to Regimental Headquarters by Col. Reuben Tucker, the regimental commander. When I stood before his desk and saluted, he told me to stand at ease.

"Lieutenant Burriss," he said, "as you know, Maj. Gen. Matthew Ridgway is the commander of the 82d Division, which, until recently, wasn't a parachute outfit. The General is still down in Louisiana, and he hasn't received his jump training. He's coming up here tomorrow, and I want you to handle his training."

"Yes, sir," I said, awed by the responsibility.

"And Lieutenant, the General doesn't have time to do the full four-weeks' training. He'll be here one day only."

The next day, I took General Ridgway to the packing shed, familiarized him with the parachute, and showed him how to pack his chute. Then a jeep rushed us over to the 34-foot tower, where he jumped. Next, we sped on to the 250-foot parachute tower and finally out to the airfield, where we put a chute on him and took him up. I acted as his jump master and sent him out over the drop zone. As he hit the ground, several officers met him and pinned his wings on him. He stepped into a plane and was on his way back to Louisiana.

Months later, after the entire 82d had transferred to Fort Bragg, I was out early one morning to train my mortar platoon. General Ridgway came riding by the area on a white horse. When he saw us there, he rode over.

I shouted, "Attention!" and saluted.

He returned my salute and said, "Hello, Lieutenant Burriss. Good to see you again."

I was impressed. He had remembered me from that one-day jump-training course.

In September 1942, I was promoted to first lieutenant and became the Battalion S2 (intelligence officer), which meant more money and more responsibility. I was pleased that the Army had that much confidence in me.

Squee and I weren't able to find adequate accommodations in Fayetteville, North Carolina—a small town overwhelmed by the demands of war. The apartment we rented had no central heat, and the tiny oil stove was insufficient to keep the pipes from freezing. We had to draw water each night and keep it in the bedroom so that we could have coffee and brush our teeth in the morning. Sometimes, even that water had a cap of ice on it.

Squee was pregnant with our first child, which was due in June. Training kept me busy and away both day and night. Fortunately, Sara Shealy Carlisle from Squee's hometown was married to a supply sergeant in the 82d Airborne Division, so Squee spent most of her days with Sara.

Then, the inevitable happened. One day in March 1943, we were told that our unit was on alert. We were going overseas and could leave at any time. All leaves were canceled. Everyone was confined to the base. I couldn't even go home to be with Squee at night.

We did see each other again before I shipped out. Some friends, a married couple living on the base, invited Squee to visit them. We had a few nights together. Then, the word came down—we were on our way to fight the Germans.

— 3 —

Staging Area

On 10 May 1943, our ship chugged toward the port of Casablanca, Morocco. From the deck, we could see the distant white buildings that gave the city its name. They appeared to be made of fine, new marble. As we moved across the water and approached the dock, we looked down and saw the dark corpses of sunken French ships, resting on the bottom, their days of battle over.

After what seemed like hours, we were given the order to disembark. For many of us, it was our first time on foreign soil. On the dock, I told my platoon to fall in. With full packs on our backs, we marched through Casablanca and saw the same white buildings at close range. They were bleached and mottled, worn smooth by time, the sun, and the wind.

Casablanca, one of the best World War II movies, is still regarded as a classic; however, the city wasn't as romantic as the film. I remember the palmetto trees and the sand—sand that blew from the desert and made its way into our food, our shoes, our eyes, and our noses. The poor section of the city was filthier than any slum in America—and more dangerous. But, with its Moorish architecture and its exotic shops and restaurants, Casablanca was interesting and a cut above other cities in North Africa.

After marching for seven or eight miles, we pitched our tents on the outskirts of the city. We listened to the wind blow and the grains of sand sweep over the canvas during the night. When we awoke in the morning, everything inside the tents was coated with sand.

The Arabs swarmed all over us like roaches over food. They wanted to trade with us or, preferably, to steal. They were particularly interested in our sheets, mattress covers, cigarettes, and chocolate. For these things they offered trinkets and fresh food—dates, exotic bread, and meats of dubious origin. We had to post guards twenty-four hours a day in order to keep them from stealing everything we had. Theft was so common that we came to regard the Arabs with almost as much ill will as we did the Germans.

When we shipped out, a sergeant exacted revenge for all of us. We had already boarded a train when an Arab came to the open window and offered to buy a mattress cover—anyone's mattress cover. A sergeant obliged. The Arab handed the money through the window and clutched the mattress cover, which was partially hanging out the window. At that moment, as the train started to move out, the Arab tried to pull out the cover; however, the sergeant had tied one end to the seat. When the train picked up speed, it dragged the Arab along with it. He turned a flip and let go of the cover. Scrambling to his feet, he chased the train for a few moments, shook his fist, and cursed in Arabic. Most of the soldiers laughed and jeered at him because Arabs had cheated or stolen from virtually all of them during their stay at Casablanca.

At Oujda near the Algerian border, we were told to prepare for a practice jump in honor of Generals Dwight D. Eisenhower, Mark W. Clark, and George S. Patton, all of whom were in North Africa at the time. We would see more of General Patton when we arrived in Europe.

After a brief stay at Oujda, we moved to the Tunisian village of Kairouan on the edge of the desert. I recall flying from Oujda to Kairouan in the cool air of 10,000 feet. When we landed, the temperature was 135 degrees, the hottest day in the history of Kairouan. When we got off the plane, we thought we had stepped straight into hell.

In Kairouan, we lived in a tent city, with enlisted men sleeping in pup tents and pairs of officers sharing two-man tents. We were supposed to continue our training, but we couldn't move around during the heat of the day, so we trained a little at night—erecting sand tables (table-sized scale models of target areas made in what looked like sandboxes), setting up road blocks, and destroying enemy artillery. We were still playing at war, but here in North Africa, where bloody fighting had already taken place, the game became more and more serious. Still, it had its lighter moments.

Late one evening, on one of these mock missions, I was leading a patrol along the edge of the desert. Someone pointed up in the sky and said, "Look, there's a hawk."

The bird was flying so high it looked like a sparrow.

"Lieutenant Burriss, I'll bet you can't knock that hawk out of the sky," one of the men said.

I raised my rifle, aimed, squeezed off a round, and the hawk dropped like a rock. It was sheer luck. I would have missed on the next fifty tries, but from then on, the men called me "deadeye."

In addition to enduring the heat, we also had to eat C rations, which meant all our food was dehydrated or came out of cans, and it was heavily laced with preservatives. We had no fresh meat, no fresh vegetables, no ice, and—above all—no Coca Cola. Early one morning, an Arab came by and offered to trade me thirteen eggs and two ripe tomatoes for cigarettes and chocolate bars. I jumped at the chance. As soon as he left, I cooked all thirteen eggs and the two tomatoes in my mess kit, sat down, and ate them all in one sitting.

As for the Cokes, we were obsessed with the thought of them. During the heat of the day, the entire outfit talked about little else. At first, we simply prayed that a battalion truck would roll up one day, loaded with Cokes and ice. Then, when we realized this dream would never come true, we began to hatch schemes to get them ourselves and figured out a way.

Lt. Cal Campbell learned that his brother's Navy ship was docking in Bizerte, Tunisia, close enough for him to make contact and have a reunion. We knew, of course, that the Navy was well stocked with every kind of food, including syrup to make fountain Cokes. Several of the battalion officers arranged to commandeer an Army plane on a nearby base and send Lieutenant Campbell to Bizerte for a visit with his brother.

"Have a good visit," we told him, "but don't bother to come back if you don't have at least a gallon of Coca Cola syrup with you."

When he returned to the unit the next day, he was carrying a bottle of the syrup. So that was half the battle. Next, we had to figure out a way to carbonate the water. For a while it looked as if we might have to drink flat Cokes, but then someone came up with a great idea. Our life jackets were filled with tiny carbon dioxide cylinders that could provide the carbonation. This procedure, however, was easier said than done. What vessel would we use to hold the water?

"What about a canteen?" someone said.

"How would that work?" we asked.

The guy thought for a minute. "You could drill a hole in the cap of a canteen, a hole just the size of a cylinder, then shoot in the carbon dioxide from the top."

We concluded that such a plan would work, but we had no drill. Finally, we sent a driver and truck to an ordnance company 50 miles away, and one of its mechanics bored the hole. As soon as the driver got back, we grabbed the canteen, filled it with water, and plugged in a carbon dioxide cylinder. The canteen blew up.

The cap with the hole in it remained intact, however, so we screwed it on a second canteen and tried again with less water. This time, it worked. We had soda water. Now we could make warm Cokes, but we wanted the same Cokes available at soda shops back home— Cokes filled with ice. So we went back to the airfield and persuaded a crew to fly to Bizerte and get ice.

We brought the ice back to the camp in coolers, and six of us sat around in a circle and made genuine Cokes. We added ice, passed the canteen around, and every man in turn took a sip. Over the years, I've tasted fine food and expensive wine, but nothing since has measured up to that sip of Coke on the edge of a North African desert.

We knew we weren't in North Africa to fight the Germans, though a major battle had already been fought there. British forces, commanded by Gen. Bernard Law Montgomery, had defeated German Field Marshal Erwin Rommel at the battle of El Alamein. Montgomery's men had out-numbered Rommel's, and Montgomery had nearly twice as many tanks. The British commander would never forget how he won that victory. Throughout the rest of the war, he was reluctant to attack without the same superior odds. As best I could tell, his reluctance was catching.

For us, North Africa was the staging area where the Allies pre-pared for an invasion of Europe. Adolf Hitler and Benito Mussolini understood this fact as well as we did. Only one question remained to be answered. Where would we attempt to land?

I first learned of our destination as the result of something that Capt. Wylie Cooper planned and his conversation about it with a friend of mine. Cooper commanded the Parachute Maintenance Company, the unit that packed our chutes, and he had a problem, a private with the nickname of "Eightball," who was a chronic troublemaker. I knew Eightball from my Fort Benning days. He had been a particularly obnoxious physical education instructor. Then a sergeant, he had taken advantage of his position to bully the officers whom he was training. If he didn't like the way one of us was performing calisthenics, he pointed to the ground and screamed, "Give me ten!" and the officer would have to perform ten push-ups. A large, good-looking man, Eightball could have appeared on a recruitment poster for the paratroopers. He must have been in trouble constantly, however, because he had been demoted to private and assigned to the 504th Regiment, a combat outfit.

Cooper called in one of his lieutenants, my friend, and said, "We're going to be landing in Sicily shortly, and I've got to get rid of Eightball. I can't have him jumping with us. He'll screw up and get us all killed."

The lieutenant agreed but didn't know how such a thing could be managed.

"I have a plan," Cooper said. "We send him off on a mission just when we're about to leave. We make sure it's sufficiently difficult to keep him busy until after we take off. That way, he won't jump with us."

Sure enough, Cooper called in Eightball and outlined the mission. "We're short about five hundred endcaps for A5 containers," he said. "I need you to go back to Casablanca, round up the five hundred endcaps, and bring them back to this company."

The mission was the military equivalent of a snipe hunt. Cooper was convinced that Eightball would never locate the endcaps, much less do so during the few days remaining before we took off. Eightball swallowed the bait and headed toward Casablanca. Everyone who knew him breathed a sigh of relief.

Two days later, Captain Cooper looked up to see Eightball drive up in a command car followed by two trucks. The trucks were loaded with A5 endcaps. Cooper was stunned.

"How did you manage this in two days, Private?" he growled.

Eightball said, "Well, sir, I realized that nobody would pay any attention to a private, so I put on a major's uniform, commandeered a plane at the airport, and flew to Casablanca.

"I figured I might as well start at the top, so I went to the commanding general of the supply depot, told him this was a matter of extreme urgency, that we had to have these endcaps right away and didn't have time to requisition them. So the General said, 'OK, we can accommodate you.'

"He sent me back in this command car, with the two trucks following."

When I heard this story from my friend, I laughed and shook my head. I might not have laughed so hard had I known that one day Eightball would be reassigned to my company.

A few days before we took off for Sicily, I received some grim news. Squee had given birth to a baby boy, but the child had lived only a few minutes. She was fine, but the loss was devastating to me, particularly because I couldn't be with her. In addition to grief, I felt anger. I blamed the Germans for taking me away from home at this crucial moment, and I was even more determined to do what I could to defeat them and return to my young wife. The invasion of Sicily presented me with my first opportunity to fight the enemy so, instead of entertaining fears, I was eager to get on with the grim business of war. During our last two weeks in North Africa, we prepared to do just that.

We studied maps and made sand tables. Intelligence officers briefed us on the enemy's strength. They told us that the mission would be no picnic. They were expecting an attack, and we would probably encounter a good deal of antiaircraft fire.

The basic strategy was as follows: Paratroopers would jump at midnight, land behind enemy lines, disrupt enemy communications, and cause as much damage as possible. The next morning at 0500, a seaborne force would land at the city of Gela.

The parachute units assigned to make the jump were the 505th Regiment, commanded by Col. James M. Gavin (who later became our division commander), and the 3d Battalion of the 504th Regiment, commanded by Lt. Col. Leslie Freeman. General Ridgway, as division commander, headed the entire operation.

On the night of 9 July, we boarded C-47s with full combat gear, which included backpack with clothes and mess gear, canteen, M-1 rifle, knife, and hand grenades. This was our first combat mission—the day we had anticipated since we began training a year and a half earlier. The mission of our unit, the 3d Battalion, was to land near the high ground about 15 miles northwest of Gela. The 505th Regiment was to land several miles behind the beach area just north of Gela.

As we took off and Africa fell away from us, we could feel the variety of moods. Some men were anxious, nervous, and sweating profusely, despite the chill in the night air. Others were pumped up with adrenaline and eager to engage the enemy. Still others dropped off to sleep, as if tomorrow were just another day.

— 4 —

Paratroopers Don't Stop for Tea

Just as we reached the coast of Sicily, we ran into extremely heavy antiaircraft fire. The nervous guys sweated more profusely, the gung-ho types quieted down, and the sleepers woke up. We saw bursts of smoke all around us and heard the explosions. As a defensive maneuver, the formation split up. Our plane banked eastward instead of westward, and suddenly the red light came on. That meant ten minutes until jump time.

I gave the order, "Stand up and hook up."

Then, only a minute later, the green light flashed. I hadn't even given the command to check equipment, which was normal procedure, but we had no time. The green light meant that we were over the target area. If we didn't jump immediately, we would be too far away to carry out our mission.

"Go!" I shouted.

"Hell, I'm not even hooked up!" someone in the back shouted.

Ordinarily, it took ten seconds for the entire stick of seventeen men to bail out the door. Because we had no real warning, however, it took us longer. As I jumped, I knew that my men would be scattered over a very wide area, rather than bunched together. That would make reunion more difficult and would jeopardize the mission. (I later learned that three men couldn't jump because they were over water.

One, Lt. "Rosie" Rosenthal, made the pilot fly back over the jump area, but they still landed 15 miles from the rest of us.)

As soon as my chute opened, I looked around. It was a beautiful moonlit night, and I could see the landscape below almost as clearly as if it were the middle of the day. No one was moving down there, and I heard no gunfire as I dropped silently into a vineyard. I saw hundreds of vines, laden with ripening grapes, winding through trellises. I landed between two rows of vines, rolled, stood up, and checked to see if I was in one piece. Then, I disentangled my parachute from the grape-vines and laid it on the ground so that enemy ground troops wouldn't spot it in the daytime.

At that point, I proceeded to "roll up the stick"—that is, walk in the direction that the plane was flying—so I could reunite with the other members of my unit. After twenty to thirty minutes, I found two of my men, Lt. Forrest Richter and Pvt. Harry Gough.

Where were the other jumpers in the stick? We looked up the moonlit road adjacent to the vineyard but saw nothing. Crouching behind a two-foot rock wall, we looked at our map with a pin light.

"That must be the crossroads we flew over," Richter said.

"It may be," I said, "but we can't be sure. Where is that other road?"

As we were discussing our position in whispers, we heard voices down the road. A detachment of men was approaching. We couldn't tell whether they were German or Italian, but we knew they weren't Americans. We lay flat on the ground beside the wall. They were stumping along and talking in normal voices, their weapons slung over their shoulders. They had no idea we were in the area.

"Get your hand grenades," I whispered to the other two. I already had my grenade in hand. "When I give the order, we toss them!"

As the troops were passing on the other side of the wall, I whispered, "Now."

The three explosions came almost simultaneously, and pieces of shrapnel rained down on the vines behind us. We heard screams of pain and frightened yells from the wounded and dying men. Just by listening, we knew we had gotten a number of them. What's more, the survivors didn't know where we were located.

The night was silent except for the cries and groans of the wounded. Finally, after what seemed like an hour, we heard muffled conversation and then footsteps. The others, apparently confident that no one was still around, were coming after the wounded. When we heard them speaking to their comrades on the other side of the wall, we tossed three more grenades and explosions again shook the countryside. At that point, the few survivors took off running, and we ran back through the vineyard in the opposite direction.

That was about 0100, and we didn't see any more enemy troops until about 0500. We were digging foxholes, and apparently the sound had alerted them. Suddenly we heard the spitting of a machine gun and the whine of bullets over our heads. We dived into the foxholes. After a few minutes, I stuck my head up and a burst of machine-gun fire and lead whistled just inches over my head. I ducked back down. At that point, we were pinned down by both machine-gun and rifle fire. We were facing a much larger, better-equipped force. The adrenaline was pumping. This was combat.

I called over to the other two, "Well guys, this could be it. We've got two choices—stay and fight or make a run for it. If we stay and fight, they'll eventually overrun us, and if we try to escape, they'll probably gun us down before we take two steps."

While we were considering these grim options, we heard a huge boom that shook the earth, and then another and another. The shells were landing closer and closer to the enemy. Suddenly, we heard the sound of men running down the road. I stuck my head up and saw the enemy, in full retreat, scrambling wildly through vineyards, not even bothering to turn and fire. Behind them came another group, running as well. They were shouting. We listened to the shouts and recognized words.

"They're British," said Lieutenant Richter excitedly. Sure enough, they were. I could tell by the silhouettes of their brimmed helmets, which didn't quite cover their ears, the way American and German helmets did.

We waited until a group came near. Then we stood up and yelled to them, "Hey! We're Americans!"

Immediately, a huge blond sergeant and two scrawny enlisted men headed in our direction. When they came within a few yards of us, the sergeant stopped and abruptly brought his rifle to his shoulder.

"Look out, chaps! It's a trick! They're Krauts!"

By then, all three of them were aiming at us. We immediately raised our hands above our heads.

"We're not Krauts. We're American paratroopers."

The sergeant approached us cautiously, eyes darting back and forth. "Get their rifles. Get their grenades."

As the two scrawny men disarmed us, they clearly expected treachery at any moment. Then the three of them marched us over to their lieutenant.

"Three Kraut prisoners, sir."

"We're American paratroopers, Lieutenant," I said. "We were dropped in here last night shortly before midnight."

"No one told us about any paratroopers in this area," he said.

I suddenly realized the problem. I pulled out my map.

"Exactly where are we?"

He pointed, "Somewhere around here."

"No wonder," I said. "We're at least 50 miles from our drop zone. We bailed out too soon. We should have landed here."

I pointed to a spot, and the lieutenant nodded, "Yes, that's where they said you'd be."

I told him about the firefight we had.

"They were probably Italians," he said. "I'd guess they were on their way to reinforce the pillboxes along the beach."

We later learned that the troops manning the pillboxes had heard the grenade explosions and concluded that a hostile force had landed behind them. At that point, they abandoned the pillboxes to search for the enemy force, which consisted of three lost paratroopers. As a result, the British seaborne forces had landed without a shot being fired. Our diversionary attack probably saved the British landing forces many casualties. Although we were mistakenly dropped 55 miles from our target area, we did precisely what paratroopers were supposed to do in such a situation—wreak havoc behind enemy lines.

After hearing our story, the British lieutenant turned to us with greater respect. He said, "If you want to fight some more, you're welcome to tag along with us."

We agreed. That's what we'd come to do.

As we moved out, the British sergeant said, "If you'd said you was Yanks, I'd have believed you."

"I'd never have said that," I said. "I'm a Rebel from South Carolina. Before I'd call myself a Yank, you'd have to shoot me!"

Chasing the enemy was almost like a rabbit shoot. The soldiers were running, and we were behind them and firing. We chased them through vineyard after vineyard, down dirt road after dirt road. As the sun rose, the landscape was tinged with red.

We killed a lot of Italians and captured a lot more. This was what we had trained so long to do—to kill the enemy and win the war—so I felt good about it. After about two hours of this hot pursuit, a whistle blew, a hand went up, and everybody halted. I was puzzled. We weren't meeting any resistance. I walked over to the British lieutenant.

"Why are we stopping?" I asked.

"It's teatime," he said.

I couldn't believe my ears.

"You mean to tell me you're going to stop in the middle of a fire-fight, when you've got the enemy on the run, and brew up tea?"

"Oh, don't worry about the enemy," he said. "We'll catch up with them later."

"Paratroopers don't stop for tea," I said.

But we had no choice. The three of us couldn't go charging after a whole detachment of Italians. We sat down with the British, drank tea from our canteen cups, and ate a few crackers, which they called *biscuits*. This was the first of many teatimes while we fought alongside the British.

After tea, off we went after the Italians. We finally caught up with them, killed many more, and took additional prisoners. Everything we had heard about the Italian army turned out to be true. The Italians were extremely reluctant to fight.

We finally arrived at a town called Pachino, which we captured. It was a small farming village, a cluster of houses, a wine shop, a tiny restaurant, and one or two other small businesses. Obviously, this was a village full of vintners. After setting up a command post, we searched door to door for enemy soldiers, rousted a few, and found a building that would serve as a stockade for our growing contingent of captured Italians.

For us, the next few days became a mopping-up operation, though there was fierce fighting elsewhere in Sicily. We moved on with the British and joined up with a couple of men from our stick, as well as with men from another stick dropped in that area. Eventually, we constituted a small band of displaced Americans, ready to engage the enemy aggressively, anxious to rejoin our own units, and sick of British tea.

Only then did I learn what had happened to the three paratroopers who didn't make it out of the plane on the first pass. Eventually dropping 15 miles from us, they landed on a rocky beach. One broke his leg and was picked up by medics. The other two landed safely.

One day, we received bad news. The British were planning to send the Americans back to North Africa. The American officers, all of us lieutenants, went to see the British major in charge.

"Sir," we said, "we'd like to find our outfits and continue to fight. That's why we're here."

"Sorry, chaps," he said, "but we've already made arrangements. You'll be escorting a load of Italian prisoners back to our POW [prisoner of war] camp in Tripoli. Leaving immediately. Rum thing."

We argued with him but to no avail. I think he and the other British officers were tired of our gung ho attitude. They wanted to fight the war in their own leisurely way, and we were sending up too much flak.

After two or three days of mopping up, we moved to the beach area, along with the Italian prisoners, and were picked up by a British ship. We landed in Tripoli and dropped off the prisoners. Then our unit sent a plane for us, and we flew back to our base in Kairouan.

On our way back, we skimmed over the desert, which was littered with the charred remains of German tanks, trucks, and artillery. It was an awesome sight, and encouraging.

When I returned to Kairouan Air Base, I went looking for the chicken-hearted pilot who had dumped us out 50 miles away from our drop site. When I asked for him at his unit headquarters, the company clerk, an enlisted man, told me, "I'm sorry. He isn't here. He's gone on recuperative leave."

"Recuperation from what?" I asked. "He was only over enemy territory for a minute or two. He signaled for us to bail out 55 miles from the drop zone, and was back home in two or three hours—drinking beer and sleeping in a nice soft bed."

The clerk grinned and shook his head.

"That's not the way he tells it. He says he flew through heavy anti-aircraft fire for ten or fifteen minutes and continued to hold the plane on course until he was right over the drop zone." He paused. "Lieutenant, they've put him in for some sort of medal."

I was so mad that I couldn't see straight.

After talking with the men in our unit and other paratroopers who jumped with us, we were able to reconstruct what happened that night over Sicily. Apparently, ours wasn't the only C-47 pilot who panicked and dropped out. 1st Lt. Roy Hanna of Headquarters Company, who led a machine-gun platoon, relates a similar experience:

> Our first combat jump. . . . We all jumped in at 2300, the night before the main event, which was scheduled for 0700 the next morning.
>
> As we flew over Gela, German antiaircraft fire opened up on our slow-moving C-47s, prompting our inexperienced troop carrier pilots to scatter all over the sky. Our pilot just started to climb as fast as the plane would climb. I stood in the door and watched the tracers come toward the plane. At this time, I didn't realize that between each tracer there was a stream of invisible bullets.
>
> A few minutes later, the green light came on, and I took my eleven machine gunners out the door. It was the highest jump I ever made—well over 2,000 feet.

Paratroopers jumping from that height incurred a greater risk of enemy fire because they spent more time descending. On the other hand, the higher the better for the flight crew. Obviously, Hanna's pilot, like ours, was worrying about his own rear end more than the safety of the troops that he was transporting. Hanna continues:

> I watched as the 400-pound machine guns and ammunition bundle, with their 24-foot chutes, went directly down, while I—with my 200 pounds, including my equipment and my 28-foot chute—floated around in the night sky. I did watch the blue lights attached to our guns and ammo and got a general idea where they landed.
>
> I finally came down in an olive tree—my first tree landing. After cutting myself and my tommy gun loose (glad to have the switchblade in my jumpsuit), I dropped about two feet to the ground. The only sound on this beautiful moonlit night was a dog barking about a mile or two away.
>
> I started walking in the direction of the equipment and then heard a meek voice saying, "George," and I answered "Marshall." Our passwords for the mission.
>
> "Man, am I glad to see you," the soldier said. "I can't get this M-1 together."
>
> Riflemen jumped with their M-1s broken down into three parts. This man was challenging me with the barrel of an M-1 unattached

to the rest of the rifle. He turned out to be a new man who joined the 504th in Africa. He was not a member of my machine-gun platoon. Maybe I Company.

I put his rifle together and told him to head in the direction of the other men, while I hunted our equipment. About five minutes later, I heard one shot. After failing to find the equipment after a reasonable amount of time, I went in search of my men.

Shortly, I was halted by my runner, Private Salter. He immediately asked if I came through there a few minutes earlier. As it turned out, our stranger, when challenged, fired one shot and took off for the hills. We never heard from him again.

The eight men who were with Private Salter were not all from my machine-gun platoon, but they were from the 3d Battalion. After trying unsuccessfully to locate the rest of my original eleven men, I led my new combat team up a rather large hill. Because we had no idea where we were and heard no gunfire to direct us, we all just stretched out on the ground and took a nap. I must have forgotten my previous training, because I didn't establish an outpost or make any other security arrangements.

At dawn, we heard some shooting, and all nine of us grabbed our equipment and went to investigate. We came to a small olive grove and joined two paratroopers (I believe from H Company) who were flanking a German barracks. They told me a couple of their buddies were attacking the other side. As a German machine gunner began sweeping the area with fire, I ended up behind a tree about 10 inches in diameter, directly behind two men firing from a prone position. As the machine gun strafed the area, one of the prone men was shot in the side of the neck and the other through the thigh.

Before the machine gun again swept our way, I jumped over a hedge, ran opposite the machine gun, which I couldn't see, and lobbed a hand grenade in that direction. I was either lucky enough to make a direct hit or I scared the Germans into running. In any case, the machine gun quit firing. At this point, I looked through a broken-down section of a stone fence and saw many German soldiers running from the barracks.

Hanna ran back to the hedgerow, gathered up his nine men, and made a strategic withdrawal. Later, his platoon joined up with ten paratroopers from the 505th Regiment:

A first lieutenant (a mess officer, I believe) outranked me and so was in command. He decided we would cross a field about a mile wide and set up a defensive position in a large stone building located at the bottom of a hill. And, like trained soldiers, we started across the field in a skirmish line, with me on the extreme right flank.

We hadn't gone far before we started drawing machine-gun fire—my first experience with a "buzz" [the singing sound of passing bullets] and a "snap" [the sound when bullets hit an object]. Two other men and I jumped in a ditch that ran all the way to our proposed defensive position. One of these men was my platoon sergeant, Sgt. Yocuum, and the other a bazooka man from the 505th with a bazooka and three rounds of bazooka ammunition. The three of us stayed in the ditch all the way to the proposed defensive position. I lugged the bazooka ammo for the 505th man, but when we arrived at our destination, I found he'd left his bazooka behind. We waited for some time, but no one else showed up.

We investigated the stone building and found it to be a large Italian-style home, with many people gathered there. None spoke English. The three of us climbed the hill, and, from there, we could see Gela.

After wandering around for two and a half days from the time we landed, we got back to where Colonel Tucker was trying to reorganize the badly scattered 504th. I was the senior commander for a short time.

I wasn't a part of one interesting episode. Lieutenant [Willis] Ferrill had gathered up about twenty men, including some of my machine-gun platoon. Ferrill set up a defensive position (also, not knowing where he was) on a small knoll overlooking a highway that led from Gela. A German company was retreating back along this road; and, as fate would have it, the Germans took a break and sat along the road just in front of Ferril's defensive position.

During the ensuing battle, one of my machine-gun section leaders—Cpl. Dale Adams from Berwick, Pennsylvania—was firing his machine gun at the Germans when a bullet pierced the front of his helmet. He reached back and found that blood was running down his neck. He concluded from this that he was shot through the head and that—as he later stated—if he took off his helmet, his head would fall apart. As it turned out, the bullet just cut a groove across the top of his scalp. As the bullet came out the back of his helmet, a piece of metal flew down and cut the upper part of his neck, causing the bleeding.

Adams was later killed in Holland.

On 10 July, the night after we jumped, the second wave of para-troopers bailed out over Sicily just north of Gela—at least, those who reached the jump site. Many didn't make it that far. What happened to them was a tragedy—senseless, avoidable, and devastating to troop morale.

As soon as we had secured the beachhead on 9 July, the U.S. Army brought in antiaircraft weapons to protect its troops against air attacks. In addition, Navy ships were anchored along the coast; and they, too, had big guns with antiaircraft capabilities. Sure enough, on the night of 10 July, the Germans sent in a wave of bombers to attack our ships and ground forces. Our antiaircraft batteries opened fire immediately.

At this very moment, the C-47s arrived, bringing the second wave of the 504th. The night was dark, and no one on the ships or ground could see the planes droning above them and assumed that they were more German bombers. They opened fire. The deadly barrage soon began to take a heavy toll. C-47s burst into flames and fell out of the sky in trails of fire and smoke.

As soon as the sky lit up the first time, the paratroopers who had jumped the previous evening recognized the planes and started screaming at the antiaircraft batteries to cease fire. But they had their orders and kept blowing planes out of the sky. It was like shooting clay pigeons at the fair. Our C-47s were flying at an altitude of 600 feet, so they were difficult to miss. I heard later that, in less than five minutes, antiaircraft fire had demolished more than twenty American planes, six of them before the paratroopers could jump.

1st Lt. Edward J. Sims of H Company 504th tells what it was like to be standing at the open door of a C-47, poised to jump, while our own guns were firing at him:

> Suddenly, against the dark background of the sky, a buildup of red tracers from below engulfed our formation. I felt a shimmy go through our plane and then pandemonium reigned as antiaircraft guns of our own forces, at sea and on the beaches, were blasting away at our slow-flying aircraft.
>
> As my plane flew through the heavy flak, I could hear the hits as they penetrated. From my door position, I scanned the sky for other planes, but could see only those going down in flames. My plane developed a distinct shudder and banked away from the flak, with one engine starting to sputter. I ordered my men to stand up and

hook up. Then, before going forward to talk to the pilot, I instructed my platoon sergeant to get the men out fast if the plane started to go down before I returned.

From the pilot I learned he had lost the formation and had a damaged starboard engine. We decided, since there was land below, that he would stay our present course and allow me a few seconds to return to the door, then turn on the green light when the plane was in a jump attitude.

We both realized that with the heavy load he had, it would be difficult for him to fly back to North Africa. I rushed back to the door, yelling to my men to get ready to jump. As I arrived at the door, the red light came on, followed within seconds by the green light, just as I hooked up. I immediately released the equipment bundles from under the plane, then jumped into the darkness with my men following.

Landing was quick and rough. My parachute had opened just seconds before landing. The plane must have been less than 300 feet above the ground. When we assembled, I learned that one man had been injured when he hit a stone fence.

Lieutenant Sims and his men were among the lucky ones. The debacle resulted in a heavy loss and taught an expensive lesson. Scores of paratroopers lost their lives. The strategists at headquarters learned never to chart a flight of paratroopers over an active beachhead and friendly naval forces.

Like the rest of us who were dropped off course, Sims didn't know where he was or how to rejoin the main force. He continues his narrative:

I sent patrols in opposite directions along a nearby road to find signs and landmarks. One patrol located a road sign indicating that Augusta was 40 kilometers away. This was sufficient to allow me to locate our general position on the map. We were southwest of Augusta and about 25 miles from the vicinity of Gela, where we'd planned to land. Also, we were several miles behind the German forces opposing the beach landing of the U.S. 45th Division. I had fourteen men with me; so we moved in a southwesterly direction, on roads and cross country, toward Gela. At one point, we had a short firefight with a small German force, but they soon fled. Later we spotted a company-size German force moving north; but since they didn't see us, we held our fire and let them pass.

Our next contact was with advance elements of the 45th Division. They opened fire on us, and for a few minutes the situation was dangerous. We had a tough time convincing them that we were U.S. paratroopers.

Two days later, we joined with the remainder of the 504th near Gela and from there moved west through Agrigento to seize Sciacca. At one point during this move, enemy planes strafed our column. We took up dispersed positions and opened fire, but all of the planes continued to fly south. It was obvious we scored no serious hits.

As we approached Sciacca, I was leading my platoon when I noticed smoke rising from the road ahead; so I dispersed my platoon into firing positions and moved forward to check out the smoke. The road had been mined with antitank mines; and a two-wheeled cart, driven by an old man with a young child, had set off one mine, killing both of them, along with the mule pulling the cart. I looked to the left and saw, on the crest of the hill, a number of pillboxes flying white flags from the gun ports. We advanced cautiously and flushed out a group of about one hundred Italians, eager to surrender. We disarmed them and sent them under guard to our rear. As we moved on, I wondered why they had allowed that old man to drive his cart into the minefield.

We cleared Sciacca, then headed for Marsala. In an area called the Tuminello Pass, we were forced to make a frontal assault when a strong German force caught us by surprise and opened fire on our column. This turned into a long, hard firefight with a number of casualties on both sides. Eventually, we drove off the Germans.

We soon took Marsala and then seized and secured Trapani. Near Marsala a friend, Lieutenant Lutcavage, was accidentally shot in the elbow by one of his own men who was shooting at wine barrels. His elbow was shattered, and he was evacuated through medical channels to the U.S.

After we seized Trapani, the fighting in our area subsided, and we were placed on occupational duty. My platoon was assigned to police an area near the small town of Salaparuta, which was the milling center for a larger area. I established my command post in a house vacated by a Nazi collaborator and selected as my interpreter a local citizen who had been deported from the United States in the late twenties. He was a great help to me and served the community well. We immediately searched the surrounding area for holdouts and soon found a large building that had been used by the Germans for food storage. We confiscated the huge food supply, and I arranged with the local clergy to distribute groceries to the most needy in Salaparuta.

Pfc. Larry Dunlop of H Company tells a similar story. He landed in Sicily the same night that I did:

We loaded up some time before dark and headed for Sicily. Most everyone was gung ho. Maybe a few reservations or "ifs" mixed in. As we took off, I concentrated on recovering the small pilot chute when we landed.

Soon we were flying in a gale wind. The plane was flying very low, and the sea spray, I swear, was blowing in the open door. As we neared the coast of Sicily, the clouds gave way to moonlight, and the plane climbed much higher.

I don't remember any flak until I jumped out. Then I saw flashes, but off a ways. Coming down took a little longer than I expected. I looked below and saw what appeared to be a sand table area. I made a good landing and kept quiet a few seconds. Then I did pull in the chute and found the small camouflage pilot chute, which I folded up inside my jump jacket.

I was an LMG [light machine gun] operator and carried a Garand rifle. I crouched and started walking. Suddenly someone said, "George, George." I said, "Marshall." It was my squad leader, Sgt. [Robert] Tague.

The two of us went in search of the ammunition bundles. On the way, we bumped into a few more guys from that plane. They'd already found some bundles. All I wanted was my two MGs and some cans of ammo.

In a short time, we gathered up about twenty troopers from H Company. One of them was First Sergeant Sneddon. Sneddon was the ranking man in our group, so he was in command.

By now, explosions were going off all around us—though at a distance. It was like the 4th of July. We didn't know which way to go. So Sneddon made a decision and led us off in one direction. We finally ended up on a dark slope of olive trees. "We might as well dig in here," the sergeant said.

He put out pickets and ordered Ferrari, a South Boston guy who spoke Italian, to lead two other guys in search of a house—to find out where we were. An hour later they came back. With them were three Sicilians. They were carrying some big platters of egg-and-tomato omelet and a big straw-covered jug of Vino. Man, that was good.

When day came, we could hear shell fire and see a lot of black smoke. "OK, men," Sneddon said, "that's where the action is. Let's go!"

It was now 10 July, and we were about fifteen or twenty strong. After walking through another olive grove an hour later, we stopped. Someone said, "Quiet, men." We saw some strangers walking around in khaki shorts.

They were Germans. They were no more than 50 yards away, so we spread out and crept up on them. Then we lit into them, firing like hell, spraying shots into groups and into their tents.

Then we heard German machine guns—firing faster than our guns. We suddenly realized there were more of them than we could handle. We looked around and spotted a small German truck.

"Who can drive that truck?"

Sgt. Brady: "I can!"

We loaded our equipment on board and moved out, looking for our own troops.

Meanwhile, Lieutenant Sims was getting involved in local politics:

A number of local citizens came to me with information that the Mayor of Salaparuta had been obtaining money for his personal use through the milling operation by withholding grain from the input, then selling it on the black market. After investigating the allegations, I determined that he was guilty, so I removed him from office and ordered him to move out of the area for his own safety.

Then, I called for an election and managed to scare up three candidates who were willing to run. I set a time for the election, and on that day the entire adult population assembled in the town square. On the balcony of the town hall, I appeared with the three candidates. As I held my hand above the head of each candidate, citizens voted by raising their hands. A popular schoolteacher received the most votes, so I immediately swore him into office.

When word of the election reached the U.S. military government in Trapani, the officers were furious. I later heard the regimental commander was pressured to remove me and my platoon from Salaparuta and from further police action.

Soon after leaving Salaparuta, the entire 82d Airborne Division returned to North Africa to prepare for the next mission.

While the rest of us were chaperoning Italian prisoners back to North Africa, the 82d Airborne Division, along with Patton's 3d Armored Division and other ground forces, moved swiftly from Gela to Palermo. The British objective was to move up to the east coast and take the port city of Messina, the closest point to Italy. Had the strategy been exe-cuted quickly, Allied forces would have prevented the Germans and Italians from escaping and regrouping in Italy.

The British, commanded by Montgomery, were moving slowly through tough mountainous terrain, and Patton wasn't content to sit around waiting for them. He turned east from Palermo, captured Messina, and met the British on the outskirts of the city. Unfortunately, this maneuver allowed the enemy troops retreating in front of Patton to escape to the mainland.

These events demonstrated a radical difference in the fighting style of the British and the Americans. The British, particularly those com-manded by Montgomery, were very methodical. They fought by the book and its old military axioms: be sure you have superior forces before you move, establish an officers' club as soon as you take a town, stop for tea at every opportunity, and send the sergeants out to com-mand the troops under fire. Paratroopers preferred the element of sur-prise: strike hard and fast where least expected, keep the enemy off balance, take calculated risks when circumstances seem to justify them, and expect officers to set a good example by leading their men into combat.

Patton followed the same philosophy we did. The only things that ever stopped him were orders from above and running out of gas. As the war progressed, the difference between our style and the style of the British became more and more evident.

The invasion of Sicily was both a triumph and a lesson. Despite the fact that many of us landed many miles from the drop zone, the inva-sion proved the wisdom of our paratrooper training. From the begin-ning, we were taught to fight in small groups and behind enemy lines. Our purpose was to disrupt communication lines, divert the enemy's attention, and create general havoc in areas where we were least expected to be. When we were isolated from the main force, we didn't panic. We regrouped in twos and threes, then proceeded to seek out and attack the enemy. Avoiding superior forces that might have over-whelmed us, we nonetheless fought aggressively and killed many times our own numbers. We didn't fight by the book or wait to receive orders from headquarters. In an atypical situation, we improvised, as we had been taught to do.

Although, on paper, our separation from the main force was a tactical disaster, in reality, things turned out extremely well. We created the illusion of a much larger force behind the Italian lines and consequently diverted attention from the American and British beach landings. Despite the errors of some transport pilots, the performance of paratroopers during the Sicilian invasion proved to be a textbook operation—an illustration of just how well we had been trained and how effective we could be in battle.

We didn't have much time to relax and congratulate ourselves on our victory, however; we all knew where we were going next. We would be invading the Italian mainland. The Germans knew our intentions as well as we did and were mustering their defenses all along the coast. By the time we departed Italy for Belgium, Holland, and Germany and left thousands of our best men behind in newly landscaped cemeteries, we would remember Sicily as a midsummer frolic.

— 5 —

The Invasion of Italy

After the fighting ended in Sicily, the rest of the 504th Parachute Infantry Regiment returned to North Africa on 20 and 21 August for reorganization. We needed replacements and more equipment. We also needed to review our mistakes in preparation for the invasion of the Italian peninsula.

After the reorganization period, we moved back to Sicily in the Palermo area. At that point, as we were poised to move onto the mainland, Mussolini was deposed, a new government was formed, and Italy surrendered. It appeared as if no invasion would be necessary. Hitler, however, had other plans. Italy was a long peninsula full of mountains and valleys. If the Allies met with resistance there, they could be tied up in Italy for years or so Hitler reasoned. He believed one thing to be certain—as long as the Allies were fighting on Italian soil, they would not be fighting on German soil.

Hitler sent a commando force into Italy; rescued Mussolini, a political corpse; propped him up on the seat of power; and ordered the Italians, reinforced by German troops, to fight to the death.

With this sequence of events, it became obvious that we would have to invade Italy after all. At first, we were preparing to parachute into Rome itself, one of the most dramatic strategies ever proposed for paratroopers. That mission was quickly scrapped, however, when intelligence information revealed that Rome was well fortified with German troops and weaponry. There were political reasons, as well, though at the time we didn't know about them.

So the generals decided that, instead of helping to take Rome, the 504th would participate in a seaborne landing at Salerno on the western coast, and the 509th Parachute Infantry Regiment would jump seven miles inland.

At dawn on 9 September, the U.S. Fifth Army, consisting of the British X Corps and the U.S. VI Corps, made assault landings at Salerno. Those of us in the 504th had an easy time because the 3d Infantry Division had already landed and taken the brunt of enemy fire. When we hit the beach, it was already secured, and we poured out of our LSTs (U.S. landing ship, tank), seacraft especially designed for beach landings, and waded ashore in perfect safety.

Several days later, the men of the 509th weren't so lucky. They jumped east of Salerno in the mountainous region in an attempt to stop the German counterattack from breaking through to the beach. Tragically, they landed right on top of a German tank unit; many were dead before they hit the ground. Others were gunned down as soon as they landed. The rest fought for their lives as the Tiger tanks drove them back toward the beach and as we moved out to rescue them.

Tiger tanks were among the latest in a series of heavily armored German panzers. They were equipped with 88-millimeter guns, and their firepower was awesome. Infantrymen accompanying them advanced by using the tanks as shields.

Airpower or artillery can destroy a tank, and, when the moon is right, a bazooka, a rocket launcher operated by a two-man team, can knock it out. In the movies, one sees ground troops demolishing tanks right and left. In real war, it isn't that easy. Tanks shoot back, as do the infantrymen accompanying them. It was hard for our bazooka teams to move within range to set themselves up and launch rockets. In addition, the front of a Tiger tank was so heavily armored that bazooka rockets bounced off like tennis balls.

As soon as we moved forward to rescue the 509th, we engaged the Tiger tanks and began to sustain heavy casualties. We were forced to retreat, but we made the Germans pay heavily for every hundred yards they advanced. We knew that if they overran us, we would be pushed back into the sea and slaughtered. The beachhead would be lost and the invasion of Italy jeopardized. We had to hold our ground long enough for reinforcements to arrive.

And they arrived just in time—dive bombers, additional artillery, naval gunfire, more men, and even some of our tanks. When the noise of battle subsided for an instant, we could hear the waves beating against the shore. We were that close to annihilation.

Finally, after more than a week of hard combat, the Germans withdrew and our beachhead was secure. The Allies had arrived in Europe and were ready to move northward up the boot of Italy toward Austria and the Third Reich. We knew what this landing meant, and so did Hitler. As a result, we paid in blood for every mile we advanced.

As soon as Salerno was stabilized, the 504th was again loaded on LSTs and moved up the west coast of Italy to make another beach landing at Maiori. Again, Allied forces had preceded us ashore, this time the Rangers, and they also had met stiff German resistance.

After we arrived on 10 September, our numbers tipped the scales, and we began to drive the Germans back across the mountains toward Naples. By then, more reinforcements, including tanks, had arrived. We continued to advance, slowly climbing the mountains until we reached Chiunzi Pass as German tanks fired down on us with their 88s. The tanks wreaked such havoc on our forces that we renamed it "88 Pass." There, we dug foxholes and settled in. For a while, peace and quiet reigned. Then, the 88 shells whistled in. We hunched down in our foxholes as best as we could and began to reinforce them with sandbags. Unless a shell scored a direct hit on a foxhole, its occupants were reasonably safe. If one had dropped into our laps, we would have resembled Humpty Dumpty after his fall.

Lieutenant Sims gives the following account of the early Italian campaign:

On 10 September, we landed . . . on the narrow, stony coastal area near Maiori, which is about nine miles west of Salerno and part of the Sorrento Peninsula.

After landing, we moved inland and up into the mountains, where we seized some high ground near the Chiunzi Pass, including a vital tunnel. Two battalions of U.S. Rangers, after landing, moved north to positions that commanded the Pagni-Nocera Pass.

My platoon occupied positions at the tunnel on the right flank of the company. The company commander borrowed a truck from a local citizen to cover the wide area (about five miles) we had to defend.

This rugged mountain area was not difficult to defend because the heavy equipment of the Germans was, for the most part, restricted to road use. We had to consider two roads—one from Gragnano through the tunnel, and the other from Sorrento and Amalfi. It was our job to prevent the Germans from using these roads to get through to Salerno.

Certain local Italians in the area had friends in Castellammare di Stabia with whom they had phone contact. When a German unit passed through Castellammare, the locals were supposed to receive a phone call with information concerning the road the Germans were using. This information was to be relayed to the company commander, but I don't think the alliance worked.

During the ten days we defended this area, the Germans made a number of attempts to break through, but were repulsed. A few patrols did infiltrate our position, and on one occasion, the Germans took two of my men prisoner. For our action here, the company received the Presidential Unit Citation, among the first to be awarded to units of the 82d Airborne Division.

Sergeant Tallon writes his recollections of that bombardment:

I noticed that our battalion executive officer, Major [William R.] Beall, had his orderly construct the major's foxhole into the side of a terrace with about four feet of soil on top of it. This would prevent shrapnel from hitting him when we were attacked with aerial artillery.

During a quiet period, I crawled out of my foxhole. Then suddenly the 88s were firing on us. I made a dive for my foxhole as a shell hit a few yards away. As I settled in for cover, I noticed that my right leg was wet. I knew I was scared, but I could hardly believe I had wet my pants! After further investigation, I discovered that a piece of shrapnel about the size of my thumb had gone through my canteen as it was hanging around my waist, and that was where the water was coming from. It was a miracle that the shrapnel didn't hit me.

About 2230, a shell hit about 30 feet from me. Moments later a runner from one of the line companies, lost in the dark, fell into my foxhole, saying he had a message for Major Beall. I said, "He's just a few feet away" and then I called in a low voice, "Major Beall?" No answer. Then I called again. No answer. Suddenly my heart seemed to jump into my throat as I thought about the dirt on top of the major's foxhole.

As quickly as I could, I scrambled over to his foxhole. It had caved in and buried him under four feet of dirt. I called for help and medics. We dug as fast as we could with hands and helmets, but we were a little too late. When we reached his body, we didn't need the medic to tell us that he was dead.

Between my close call and the major's tragic death, I had a sleepless night. Two days later, I came down with yellow jaundice and was sent to a hospital in North Africa. It was nearly Thanksgiving before I was returned to the 3d Battalion.

I vividly remember what happened to Major Beall. I was one of those who started digging with his hands as I tried to reach the major in time. His death was a great loss to our unit. He was an outstanding soldier—a leader whom we had confidently followed into battle.

Within a few days, the Germans began to withdraw into Naples, and we were able to come out of our foxholes and enjoy the scenery. From the Chiunzi Pass, we could look down on the blue-green valley ahead of us and also see Mount Vesuvius, the unearthed ruins of Pompeii, and the city of Naples. If we could take Naples, it would be the first major European city to be reclaimed from Fascism and Nazism by the Allies.

During the period between 20 and 25 September, the rest of the 504th, which had been dropped at Paestum on 13 September, moved into the area we occupied. A few days later, the entire Fifth Army mounted an attack northward in order to seize Naples. The 504th encountered sporadic resistance. On 1 October 1943, the Allies took Naples. Afterward, we engaged in house-to-house combat with Germans who had been cut off and left behind. This mopping-up operation took about three days, and both sides sustained some casualties. The Germans left behind many booby-trapped buildings that killed both U.S. military personnel and Italian civilians. One of these booby traps exploded at the Naples post office during the busiest hour of the day.

On 1 October, ours was the first unit to enter Naples, even as the Germans were evacuating men and equipment. They were soon gone, and only the Neapolitans remained. To our surprise, the people rushed into the streets and cheered us as we moved from block to block in our search for German troops.

The Germans were in the mountainous area beyond Naples, where they were digging in to stop us, if possible, or, if not, to delay us indefinitely. We knew it would be tough going once we left Naples and started up the next mountain.

After arriving in Naples, the Army took over the city, moved its men into barracks, and established a military government. The city was relatively safe and its citizens in a holiday mood. A bunch of us went to a restaurant high on a hill and celebrated. It was an elegant place. When the sun had set, we could see the lights of the city reflected in the Bay of Naples.

After we finished eating the highest-priced items on the menu and drinking table wine, Col. Reuben H. Tucker, commanding officer of the 504th, ordered champagne and proposed a toast to our conquest of Naples. He drained his glass and smashed it on the table. The rest of us did likewise.

The restaurant owner, a short man with a receding hairline and curly black hair, started screaming in Italian. The waiters' eyes were flashing as they rushed about and scraped broken glass into paper sacks. Waving his hands, the owner rushed up to the colonel. The colonel's interpreter said, "He demands that you pay for the glasses."

"Tell him to go jump in the bay," Colonel Tucker said. "That's the price you pay for collaborating with the Germans."

We enjoyed a week of much needed rest in Naples. We had done a lot of fighting and had gotten little sleep over the previous several days. Mostly, we lay around on real beds, ate real food in nearby restaurants, and had conversations with real civilians. But, as we were forever being reminded, there was a war going on. After a week, the 82d Airborne Division was ordered to England to prepare for D-Day.

General Clark had asked for a regiment of paratroopers to stay in Italy, however, and help him flush out the Germans in the mountain area between the British Eighth Army to the east and the American Fifth Army on the western side of the peninsula. At the time, he was commanding general of the Fifth Army and the other fighting forces in Italy—and he got what he asked for. The 504th, by then composed of seasoned veterans, was ordered to remain in Italy with General Clark.

Our first mission was to clear the Germans from the mountain area just north of Naples and move on to the Volturno River. We moved out of Naples on 27 October 1943 and soon discovered that the Germans had left land mines all along the mountain paths. In addition, we had to face massive artillery fire almost every inch of the way. By then, the weather had turned on us. It rained and snowed every day as we fought our way to the top.

We hauled our supplies up the mountain either on the backs of mules or on our own backs. Every so often, one of the mules slipped off the slick, narrow trail; bounced down the mountainside; and plunged headlong, with our K rations and ammunition, into the canyon below. When we stopped for the night, we couldn't dig foxholes because we hit solid rock under a few inches of soil. With the rain or snow beating down on us, we wrapped ourselves in half-tents and lay behind rocks so we wouldn't turn over in our sleep and roll down the mountain like our lost mules. With the landscape and the elements against us, we also encountered stiff resistance from the Germans, who were firing down on us every step of the way.

When we were approaching Cassino, we climbed to the top of Ridge 1205 and saw the Monte Cassino Abbey perched on the mountaintop across the valley. It was an imposing site. Our mission was to capture the town of Cassino below the abbey; however, the Germans were shelling us from that direction. They were about to blow us off the ridge with their big guns, and it was impossible to move forward. We waited for our bombers to attack their position, but the weather was our chief enemy for several days. During that period, we crouched behind rocks on the mountainside and watched our lines bombarded by German shells.

I remember vividly the day when the clouds moved away and the sun broke through. Within the hour, we heard the sound of bombers—a drone that soon became a roar. The sky was literally dark with our planes. Then the bombs began to fall, as we watched, our fingers crossed. A few bombs struck the abbey.

We stood and cheered. The Germans, however, continued their artillery fire. As long as they did, an infantry attack on the town of Cassino would have been foolhardy. The 504th's attention was therefore focused elsewhere. Cassino would be fought over fiercely in February and March 1944, and the Allies would eventually capture the city.

Our chaplain, Capt. Delbert Kuehl, who was there every step of the way, tells how it was:

Mountain Ridge 1205 will ever remain in the memory of the 504th Combat Team. One night we crossed over the ridge in an attack on the Germans. Before dawn we withdrew to our side of the mountain. I overheard one trooper say, "We still have some wounded over on the German side." I talked with our medics. We said, "We can't leave our men over there to die." We found in the medics' supplies a tattered Red Cross flag, put it on a stick, took some folding litters, and started over the mountain to the German side.

We all knew that if the German troops were from the fanatical SS [Schutzstaffel, Hitler's protection echelon], or if they couldn't figure out our purpose, we wouldn't be coming back.

As we started down the open slope, a machine gun opened up, with bullets hitting beside us and spraying us with bits of rock. We thought, this is it. All they had to do was traverse that gun slightly and we would have been wiped out. Then the firing stopped.

We found a number of our wounded men. We put some on litters and draped the others across our shoulders, and struggled back over the rugged slope—back to our side of the mountain.

Around 20 December 1943, we were ordered to climb a particular mountain north of Naples. It was only about three miles to the top. We were hot from the climb, wet with sweat, and totally exhausted. As we cooled down, we found ourselves on top of a mountain where the temperature got very cold—about 20 degrees with a north wind of about 25 mph. We knew that if a person fell asleep under these conditions, he would freeze to death. Orders came down that we were to use the "buddy system." You choose a buddy; then you try to sleep or rest while he stays awake. Then you stay awake and he tries to rest.

I was wearing long johns, battle uniform, a heavy wool overcoat, raincoat, wool cap under my helmet, and gloves. I was freezing. In fact, everybody was miserable and morale was low. I just knew that if I wasn't killed by artillery, I would freeze to death. At this point, I did what I had done many times before—some serious praying. We made it through the night, and our prayers were answered: We were ordered back down the mountain to our reserve area.

I have never seen morale rise so quickly, troops gather their equipment so fast, or troops making ready to move out in so few minutes. A nice surprise awaited as we pulled into our rest area. Our kitchen had a good hot meal waiting for us. Never did so little mean so much to so many.

Lieutenant Sims continues his account of the mountain fighting:

The few mules we had were a big help, but progress was slow in those treacherous mountains. The numerous booby traps and destruction of trails made our movement more difficult. German resistance was sporadic, but, by 29 October, we had passed through Valle Agricola and seized Gallo.

From 30 October to 12 November, we moved higher into the Appenine Mountains toward Isernia. On our way, we cleared the villages of Macchia, Fornelli, Cerro, and Rochetta.

Near Colli, Company H was ordered to attack and seize what the Army called Hill 1017. We began by fording a raging stream, then climbing up the south slope of the hill. Resistance was moderate, but the entire area had been sown with antipersonnel mines. The first victim was the company commander, who had his heel blown off.

Within minutes, the officer who took command fell from a cliff while attempting to avoid incoming artillery and broke his leg. At that point, I assumed command of the company and continued to direct the attack.

Because of enemy fire and the antipersonnel mines, we had to proceed slowly and cautiously. Still, we activated many mines, which caused a number of casualties. The most dangerous were the Bouncing Bettys. Activated by tripping a wire, they would catapult up in the air and send shrapnel into your lower body.

I set off three Bouncing Bettys myself. The first angled up under a mule and demolished his rear end. The second failed to bounce and exploded on the ground while I was carrying a wounded man. The third bounced up but failed to explode.

By late afternoon, we were able to take the hill and set up a defense. I ordered everyone to stay in place until I could get our engineers up to clear the mines from the area.

On 23 November, the entire regiment was replaced by the 133d Infantry and went into two-weeks reserve near Ciorlano. During the period, we had an exceptional Thanksgiving dinner and received badly needed replacements. H Company had three new officers assigned: Lt. Jim ["Maggie"] Magellas, a Lt. [Peter] Gerle, and Lt. Richard G. ["Rivers"] La Riviere.

On 10 December, the 504th moved into the frontline position north of Venafro. My battalion, the 3d, replaced the U.S. Rangers on

Hill 950. A few days later in this position, Lieutenant Gerle was shot and killed by a sniper. We were unable to locate the sniper, but we did saturate the suspected location with artillery fire. On 15 December, the 2d Battalion attacked Hill 687, which was held by a strong German force. On the second day of hard fighting, they took the hill, but with heavy casualties.

Pvt. Francis W. McLane of I Company also remembers the Italian campaign, though, for awhile, he seemed to have an easier time of it than Chaplain Kuehl, Lieutenant Sims, and I did. Then things got rougher. McLane's account is particularly useful because it reveals the degree to which the American enlisted man was often on his own in the field with no officers to direct him and nothing to rely on but his training and native intelligence. Here he was, on unfamiliar foreign soil, hunting a well-armed quarry, being hunted himself, and picking his way through a minefield with all the confidence and purpose of a seasoned combat officer. There were hundreds of thousands more like him in World War II.

The following is part of McLane's recollection:

We sailed up the coast and landed at a town named Minori, then walked a short distance to its twin town, Maiori. We occupied Chiunzi Pass for more than a week. We had constant patrols because Germans were said to be infiltrating, dressed as civilians. My patrol was going up the road and a mortar shell slid down the roof tiles of a building, hit one of our men a glancing blow on the head, landed on the ground, and rolled into a gutter. It never exploded.

My patrol went up to an ancient castle right on the pass. Every-thing beyond that was exposed to direct artillery fire. A group of middle-aged officers were inspecting the valley with binoculars. They wore plain issue uniforms. I think Maj. Gen. John P. Lucas, Com-manding General, VI Corps, was one of the group. When we got close to them, we could see stars on their collars. We were so star-tled that we came up with some very peculiar salutes—hand salute, rifle salute, left hand salute, and "Hi y'all" type of hand wave. The generals laughed and complimented us on our military courtesy.

A few days later, we moved out over the side of the mountain. Then we moved on to Naples. The following week we patrolled the city, collected firearms, settled family disputes, broke up black mar-ket operations and drank Italian champagne (73 cents a bottle). The Rangers came to town, and I looked up my brother-in-law who was

a young second lieutenant in the 4th Rangers. It wasn't a very sen-
timental reunion. I was drunk and embarrassed him.

We were soon off on a new mission. We crossed the Volturno
River, a wet affair, as I remember it. We spent about a month travel-
ing in the high country, out of touch with our own army. We skirted
beautiful mountain towns, still occupied by the enemy, crossed
rivers and rain-swollen streams. Drenched either with sweat or with
water, my clothes literally rotted off my body. We came to an area
where we were using German communications wire. It was strung
in all directions. It was difficult trying to avoid the enemy as we
were approaching their main winter line of defense. We moved into
the mountain town of Colli with another antique castle on a hill
above a river.

Before daylight G Company moved out to lead the attack on Hill
1017. The donkey-cart trail was mined, and it was too dark for the
men to see where they were stepping. They lost a lot of men.

McLane continues his story of I Company:

My company was then sent in. It was light enough by then, and we
fared better. There was a nice spring on one side of the trail and a
brick wall on the other. Suddenly a machine gun started firing just
up the trail, and we couldn't advance. Rounds were ricocheting off
the wall and thudding into trees. We fired back. I became so involved
that I didn't stop firing until the machine gun stopped. I looked
around me. I was practically alone.

The rest of I Company was way out in a plowed field, circling
around the machine gun, which was mounted on an upthrust of
rock. This gun was not firing, so I decided to cut across to the
wooded hillside. Suddenly I found myself in a minefield. The morning sun made the trip wires shine, so I had little trouble getting
through.

By then, I Company was heavily involved with machine guns farther along the hillside, and I felt I could be more effective if I tried
to gain the top of the hill. I ran into Sergeant Engebritzen, who had
made the same decision. We stayed off the trail and kept to the
shadows as much as possible. We soon noticed a group of our people going up a boulder-crowded gully below and parallel to us.

When we got to the top of the mountain, we saw a pretty
meadow, a tent, and a large supply dump with stacks of boxes filled
with food and ammunition. Engebritzen covered me while I crossed
the meadow looking for a good spot for a defense position. I was

halfway across when I came face to face with a Jerry who was running toward me. I fired without a thought, just a reflex reaction. He called "Nicht schiessen!" ["Don't shoot!"] but it was too late. I didn't have to shoot him, but I couldn't think fast enough to avoid it. I think he had been manning the machine gun at the head of the gully and was coming for more ammunition.

The men from the gully came up and joined us—Lt. Henry B. Keep, Lt. Bob Blankenship, and Corporal Evenson. We had found a round depression edged by small trees—a perfect spot for defense. A column of Krauts came up to our position and then circled around it. They didn't see us, but we couldn't engage them because they held one of our boys prisoner. He had an Arkansas accent and talked very loudly all the time—obviously for our benefit. The Krauts headed down the hill and were taken care of there.

We waited until we collected ten more people. It was getting late in the day, so we headed for the peak at the end of the ridge. The fifteen of us got credit for the capture of Hill 1017, but the rest of I Company arrived after dark, and we had to fight a big part of the next day to keep it.

When Hill 1017 was secured, it was pouring rain. The river was too high to cross, so we had to make a wide detour to get back to Colli. We headed north across a plowed field. Every step we sank into mud halfway up to our knees. It was getting dark and we were exhausted from the effort.

When we found a big barn, we made the most of it. We covered the windows with blankets and built a fire in the middle of the floor. It was like heaven. We were in enemy territory, but it was worth the risk.

Next morning, we found a main road and traveled in the direction we wanted to go. As we moved along, we saw bottles and assorted trash along the road. The labels were in German. We came to a group of small buildings and could tell by the junk left behind that they had been recently occupied by Krauts.

Lieutenant Blankenship asked me to take a patrol northward to find out where the Krauts were now. He said, "Don't try to engage them. Just get as much information as you can. And above all, try to scrounge a meal for us somewhere."

We hadn't eaten in four days.

Our patrol skirted a hydroelectric plant and entered a small residential area. We contacted an Italian family, the mother of whom spoke excellent English. She gave us lots of detailed information about the area. The Krauts were as thick as fleas in the village. The family dug up a couple of bottles of wine and stuffed us with corn-bread and french fries.

Then I noticed the lady of the house was getting nervous. She wanted us to leave before the Kraut motor patrol came through. So we slipped out of town and got back to our company OK, but we hadn't brought any food—just the aroma of french fries and wine.

The engineers had rigged up a rope-and-pulley contraption to get us across a narrow section of the river. After some of us had crossed, the Jerries started to shell us with mortar fire. I fell flat where I was, and Lieutenant Blankenship dived down a grassy slope. When the shelling stopped, he came back up the hill, a disgusted look on his face.

"I just saw three piles of fresh crap that I slid through. "When we were relieved, we marched down the hill past Colli to the rest area—with tents, showers, and hot food. I was wearing a new German overcoat, which the intelligence officer took away from me. Disgusted, since it was warmer than anything I had, I sat down in the shadow of a tent and lit a cigarette. I heard some dictation going on inside. I heard a list of men recommended for medals with growing envy. Then I heard my own name. That boosted my spirits for weeks, until I realized the recommendation hadn't been approved.

After a short rest, we traveled by truck to Venafro. We were in a grove of trees listening to the din of distant artillery fire. Every once in a while, however, a round would come barreling into our area. In the midst of this bombardment, two Red Cross girls showed up with doughnuts and coffee. I appreciated what they were doing, but they seemed pretty out of place.

We moved along, walked through a narrow pass, and entered a moonscape—an inverted bowl of a stone mountain in front of us, covered with boulders and rocks. Not a speck of anything green and growing. On our left we saw another steep and desolate moun-tain, and on our right we saw a peak shaped like an upside-down ice cream cone. The ice cream cone was designated Hill 950, and we were ordered to capture it.

Artillery shells were screaming through the air and exploding on the mountainside. The magnified sound bounced off one mountain and then another. As the men started up the ice cream cone, orange flashes were followed by thunderclaps. The Germans were tossing grenades at close range. McLane describes the ascent:

We started up anyway. My old friend Engebritzen was waiting for me, but before we'd gone more than a few hundred feet, a grenade exploded near him. He fell and grabbed his thigh. I went over to help. I could see it was a nasty wound, so I called for medics. After they arrived, I moved on. The climb was so steep, I had to scramble up on all fours, like an animal. When I got to the top, my squad was digging in. But how do you dig in on a 45-degree slope of solid rock?

[Leo] Muri, [Bill] Leonard, Leolis, and Goodwin had found spots; but before I had started digging, Corporal Evenson found me.

"Lieutenant Blankenship wants you on top," he said.

"I thought we were on top," I said.

"There's a shelf on the other side," he said.

I followed him to the shelf and saw there was room for about 12–14 men. And the position was under fire. The Krauts were so close they were lobbing in "egg" grenades in such numbers that we were holding our rifles so we could bat them off the way you bunt a baseball.

Lieutenant Blankenship told me I was to protect the officers and get them out if we were overrun. The officers included Lieutenant Blankenship, Lieutenant Holmes, and a first lieutenant and captain I didn't know. As if the Krauts didn't pose enough trouble, Lieutenant Blankenship was suffering from an attack of malaria.

The enemy had a 170-mm gun in the valley below us, and when their troops weren't attacking us, the gun would shell us. Since the gun was so far below—and since the ice cream cone was so steep—the shells had a narrow area of impact, but they were inflicting some damage.

When it was dark, Evenson and I found a position behind a boulder. All night long, we took careful aim at the muzzle blast of the Krauts' automatic weapons, which were firing from 100 yards or less. And they, in turn, would fire at us. They sent a machine gun up the mountain in front of us, and Evenson knocked it out with a rifle grenade. Toward morning, he got hit in the face and had to leave. He'd been like a rock and I sorely missed him.

Near dawn there was a lull in the firing, and I must have dozed off. I opened my eyes when I heard several excited voices saying the Krauts were flanking us. It took a moment or two for my eyes to adjust to the light. I counted five helmet tops moving above a niche in the rocks. I had no way of knowing how many others had passed. The captain told me to get some help and stop them.

I ran along the 100-foot line, looking for men, but nobody was around. Then I came to a bare slope I knew the Jerries would have to cross. I fell to a prone position. Then I spotted them, stopped just below me in a jumble of boulders. I began firing. They got off one shot at me—and after that, not any.

Pinned behind the boulders, they tried tricks—the "Jumping Jack." From widely separated points, two would jump up to fire. Later the same thing with grenades. I never understood why they had to jump up and show themselves. Every time they did, I killed at least one. Finally, the three remaining made a run for it, but I fired at them and drove them back.

After this, the Jerries seemed to have lost heart. I could see helmet tops moving around aimlessly, and I tried to get a shot. Finally, one showed a couple of inches of his helmet and I blew it off. I yelled at him, "Hey, keep your head down. You want to get killed?" He turned back, looked at me, stupefied, then took my advice.

At this point, both sides were exhausted. The Krauts had quit firing, and some of them surrendered. Pfc. Schultz, the BAR man, had performed extremely well during the battle. His position had been about five yards below and to the left of me. He interrogated the prisoners who came in.

These men had served on the Russian front and had been sent to Italy as R&R [rest and recuperation]. They got more than they'd bargained for. They were terrified by our marksmanship. Many of their dead had been shot squarely between the eyes. Also, they said our firepower was too much for them, which seemed strange to me, because the German strategy was always based on superior firepower—more automatic weapons, higher rate of fire. Their weakness may have been that these fast-firing weapons climbed too much, thereby wasting a lot of rounds.

The estimated German dead after this battle—150. We lost around 45.

After the fighting had stopped and we were preparing to leave, the Krauts fired one last round from the 170. The shell landed in the middle of our position. I'd been on my knees, behind my boulder. I woke up about a body length away, facing the sky. Others were wounded, and I tried to help give first aid, but my eardrums had been damaged, and I had a very poor sense of balance and direction.

The trip back down the mountain took forever. I was sent to a hospital in Naples, where I enjoyed being pampered—clean sheets, clean body, and hot food. Before I had a chance to get used to it, I was hustled off to draw a new uniform, a new rifle, and a new bazooka. I hated to lose my old rifle, but I had no choice. We boarded an LCI at a port near Naples. The word was "Anzio." No one had heard of it, but we were soon to be acquainted with the place.

All of us were. After rugged mountain fighting, the 504th was relieved and moved back to Naples in preparation for the invasion of Anzio. During the briefing, we learned that we would jump, rather than ride in on an LCI (landing craft, infantry). Then, the strategists changed their minds and told us that we would make another seaborne landing. We were beginning to wonder if we ever would be paratroopers again.

— 6 —

Anzio

Back in Naples, Colonel Tucker called us together for a final briefing in the conference room of a Neapolitan office building. He began by outlining the overall strategy.

"Men," he said, "we've been ordered to land on a beach near the city of Anzio. We're expected to create a beachhead and then hold it at all costs. North of here, the Fifth Army is facing some of the best German troops in Europe. As soon as we land, the Krauts will have to redeploy some of their troops to defend against us. That'll take pressure off the Fifth Army.

"As soon as that happens, the Fifth Army will break out, join us, and we'll all take off for Rome."

The strategy sounded fine to us. We didn't know that our intelligence operations had failed to detect a major movement by German troops. Just prior to our landing, the Germans had reinforced their position on the Fifth Army front. Instead of bringing their troops from that front to attack our beachhead, they brought them down from Northern Italy and Rome, part of a panzer (armored) division, an artillery division, and some of their elite infantry troops. The panzer division was spearheaded by Tiger tanks—a terror we had already encountered. Though we didn't know it, we were heading into an oven.

After Colonel Tucker finished, our S3 (tactics officer), Lieutenant Keep, explained what the terrain looked like and how we would land and deploy our men:

"We'll be landing in LCIs," he said, "but we won't be the first wave ashore. The 509 PIR [Parachute Infantry Regiment] and Darby's Rangers will hit the beach first. They'll take the brunt of the defensive fire.

"Once they've established the beachhead, you'll come in behind them as reinforcements. We don't anticipate that you'll encounter much ground fire, though we may see a few Kraut aircraft.

"The Navy will take the LCIs close enough to the beach so you can wade ashore. Tell your men to keep their rifles high above their heads, because sometimes the breakers are high.

"The beaches will be sandy and about 20–30 feet wide. Beyond that, you'll see flat farmland and a few houses. About 12–15 miles across the flatlands are the foothills and then the mountains. The Germans have gun emplacements on the mountainside. So they'll be firing down on us—but from a distance. They'll be able to see you the moment you hit the beach, so you'll want to move out as soon as you land. The farm-houses and barns should provide you with some cover.

"The Mussolini Canal will be dead ahead on your right flank, and on the left flank you'll find the highway from Anzio to Rome. You'll know it when you find it because it will be the only paved highway. The rest of the roads are dirt. Eventually, we'll be moving up that highway toward Rome."

After listening to the briefing, we figured Anzio would be a little rougher than Sicily but nothing we couldn't handle. We were totally unprepared for the carnage that followed.

As promised, we arrived at Anzio after other troops, the 45th Division and a contingent of British troops, had landed on 22 January and taken the first defensive fire. As we approached the beach in LCIs, there was no ground fire at all. A Navy seaman stuck a pole in the water and called out to the LCI's captain, "Depth of three feet."

The captain said, "Lower the ramps."

The first man in my company to step off the end of the ramp was Lt. Rosie Rosenthal, who was 5 feet 2 inches tall. I watched him hit the water and disappear, still holding his rifle above him. He surfaced, grabbed the ramp, and hauled himself out of the water.

"Goddamn it, sailor," he sputtered, "how deep did you say this water was?"

The captain immediately backed up and made another approach. This time the depth was two feet and we started disembarking. At that very moment, however, two German Me-109 fighter-bombers came skimming over the sea, and one of them dropped a bomb right down the hatch of the LCI next to ours. When the bomb exploded with a fiery blast, it blew troops from G Company off the deck and into the water.

I was commanding Headquarters Company. We hit the beach an instant after the bomb exploded and immediately plunged back into the water to pull out the survivors from G Company, who were whirling and bobbing in the white breakers. Initially, I expected to be fishing corpses out of the shallow water, but I was surprised to find most of the men alive. When the bomb struck, they had already moved out of the hold and were on deck ready to disembark, so the concussion below simply blew them into the water.

On the other side of the bombed LCI was another one bringing in I Company. On its deck when the bomb hit were Lieutenant Blankenship, Lieutenant Ferrill, Sgt. ("Arky") White, Sgt. Leo Muri, Pfc. Francis Keefe, Pfc. Sam Cleckner, and other members of the 1st Platoon. Keefe dived overboard and started pulling injured men out of the water. Others rushed to assist. Keefe and three other troopers boarded the charred and smoking LCI to see if there was anyone trapped in the hold, but all of the men had either disembarked or had been blown overboard.

Private McLane gives an account of the same incident:

> I was sitting by the rail, watching the water, when Lieutenant Ferrill came up and sat down beside me. He had a glum look on his face.
>
> After a moment, he said, "How does the situation look to you?"
>
> "It looks like a yacht race to me, " I said. "Nice weather. Ships towing balloons. Peaceful shoreline."
>
> "I have a feeling I'm not going to make it," he said.
>
> "Sir," I said, "the whole company would appreciate it if you wouldn't stick your neck out too far, because we're used to having you around."

That seemed to embarrass him, and he left. I didn't get to talk to him again, though during a last-minute inspection, he did chew me out for not getting all the grease out of the bazooka. (My rifle was OK.)

Our LCI headed for shore, and suddenly we heard the whine of diving planes. A bomb hit G Company's craft and broke it in two. Other bombs landed in the water. I was lying flat on the deck, face down, when I felt a heavy blow on my back. It was a large chunk of wet sand.

Lieutenant Blankenship told me to lead the troops off the boat, since I was about average size and could test the depth of the water. The left ramp of our boat was jammed, so we all had to use the right ramp. The planes were still around, and we were in somewhat of a hurry.

The wounded from G Company were floating over toward our ramp. I told them to stay in the water until we could unload. Then I jumped in and found myself in water over my head.

I did an un-Christlike walk on the bottom until my head came to the surface. I saw someone on the shore whom I mistook for the beach master. I headed toward him and realized he was a news cameraman. I changed my facial expression and trudged on. If he got a picture, I never saw it.

Sergeant Tallon, who was on board the bombed LCI, gives this account:

I was standing on the top of the stairs leading from the main deck to the lower area of the LCI, when the bomb struck. I was hit on the head by flying debris. Dazed, staggering, bleeding heavily, I lay on the deck with troops running all over me. When I finally regained my senses and staggered out of their way, I discovered that while my wound was bloody, it wasn't too serious.

Tallon was taken to an aid station just in time to miss some intense fighting. Ahead, the German Tiger tanks were tearing up our ground troops, who were fighting them with bazookas, hand grenades, and rifles. The Krauts had also mounted a huge 240-mm gun on a railroad car on the side of the mountain, and it began blasting away at our positions. We called the gun "Anzio Annie," and she was lobbing shells onto the beach with devastating regularity. We named a second 240-mm gun "Anzio Express."

We ran across the sand and up a slight rise where sea grapes and other shrubbery grew. We saw the brown stubble of winter fields long ago harvested and a few stucco houses and barns with tile roofs. The farms were divided by dirt roads that ran straight toward the mountains.

Ahead, we heard the constant rattle and pounding of machine-gun and artillery fire. Huge rounds were exploding on the beach. We moved as quickly as possible to occupy the houses and barns. For a while, these abandoned buildings offered cover from the fire, which seemed to be growing more intense the farther inland we moved.

Some of our troopers ducked into a brick factory, and the building afforded them some protection until Anzio Annie zeroed in on their fortress. After three or four shells from Annie, the factory building, as well as many of the men who had been inside, no longer existed. Often, when men moved to occupy farmhouses, Annie blew them to pieces with one shell.

I know from reading military history that British soldiers distinguished themselves often during World War II and brought honor to their country. Unfortunately, at this particular time and place, they were routed. As soon as the Tiger tanks hit the British troops, they were thrown into a panic and came screaming back through our ranks like a dose of croton oil. One of them shouted as he ran by me, "It's another Dunkirk, laddies. We're done for."

They were so terror-stricken that many of them had abandoned their weapons and backpacks and were running wildly, like stampeding cattle. One couldn't call what they were doing a "retreat." It was a combination of a footrace and a riot. Had we broken ranks, as they did, we all might have died on Anzio Beach, quivering in fear. But, as they raced past—gasping for breath and wild-eyed—we were digging in, determined to hold the line.

When Private McLane reached the shore, he headed for a wooded area behind the sand dune in order to dry out:

> I dug a shallow slit trench and Keefe, who had joined up with me, went visiting. A Messerschmitt came screaming in on a strafing run. I jumped in my slit trench, and Keefe landed on top of me. I don't know how it helped Keefe, because the hole was only deep enough for me. I do know that 6 feet and 3 inches and 135 pounds made for a very bony bundle on top of me.
>
> After dark, I Company grouped and moved out on a macadam road. We passed two Kraut soldiers on a motorcycle. They were burned to a crisp. We went this way and that, trying to find the road we wanted. As we were marching down the road, we heard the

drone of engines and saw ahead blackout lights about five feet high. There was a whole column, and we figured they were too big to be anything but tanks. We scattered to the high side of the road. I didn't like the prospect of firing down on the top of a tank with my bazooka. The armor was too thick.

Before anything could happen, a jeep came down the road and skidded to a stop.

We heard, "Halt, who goes there?"

A very shaky voice answered in English. It was a bunch of our very large trucks headed for the Third Division. They'd been wandering up one road and down another and hadn't seen a sign of the enemy.

This was great! We started down the road again with renewed confidence. People were starting to chatter. Lieutenant Blankenship was in the middle of telling them to knock it off when a loud and clear voice shouted, "Halt or we fire!"—in German. We didn't need a translation.

Lieutenant Ferrill shouted, "This is it, men! Hit the ditch!"

The night lit up with tracer streaks—all fire directed toward Lieutenant Ferrill's voice. Only Ferrill and Schultz were killed, and one man wounded—a real miracle.

The tracers were going over in sheets of fire, hitting the middle of the road and glancing off. I was in the ditch on the left side of the road, and we were able to crawl out. On the other side, there was a culvert across the ditch, blocking the exit of everyone over there.

At Lieutenant Blankenship's direction, Sergeant Everson, two other men, and I gathered a light machine gun and two BARs and ran to a canal that paralleled our road. The canal had high banks, and that's where we set up our guns and directed our fire at the sources of the tracers. They immediately raised their fire to meet our threat, allowing the men to escape from the other ditch.

We withdrew back down the road and waited until dawn. That morning we attacked the crossroads of a farm community and cleared the area as far as the Mussolini Canal. In so doing, we lost one more man. It took trucks and a trailer stacked with bodies to carry off the enemy dead.

I Company dug in at the Mussolini Canal and occupied several nearby farmhouses. From then on, the unit was constantly bombarded by artillery fire. The men also fought off a German infantry attack and launched an attack of their own.

Because artillery shells were falling everywhere, a number of farm animals were killed as they ran about, frightened and disoriented. But the men didn't allow any of the meat to spoil. They feasted on pigs, chickens, cows, and maybe a horse or two.

Private McLane tells of conditions after the landing:

It rained steadily, and the holes we dug filled with water. Staying there became a miserable routine. When the higher-ups saw we were bored, they moved us to a woods east of Anzio. During the night, Thomas decided to brew some coffee. He ignored the fact that there was an air raid going on; and under the canvas cover of a truck, he overflowed the gasoline stove. We had a beautiful fire going in no time—visible from ten thousand feet. At that moment, we would gladly have traded off Thomas. Fortunately the bombers were concentrating on bigger game.

The next night, we moved to the front and dug in on the crest of a small hill astride the main highways at a place called Carraceto. The British were enjoying the full attention of the German army, and as we looked up the hill at their lines, we were shocked to see a jeep and trailer pull up with refreshments. There against the skyline the Brits were lining up for tea. Of course, the shells came in like rain and broke up their little tea party.

What followed was an intense shelling that lasted almost all night. I was sure I heard the distinct ring of the barrels of British 25-pound artillery pieces. No one seemed to get hit during this attack. The shell holes were very close to each other.

A tank that had been behind a small building spun out and came over to our side. It slowly climbed up the rise, and when it got just below Keefe's foxhole, it was hit by an 88. It burned all night, and when it got hot enough, its machine gun would fire from time to time. This in turn attracted enemy fire, and Keefe, hunched in his foxhole, wanted to return to the Bronx.

It snowed but melted fast. Very wet snow that brought up the water level of our slit trenches.

For a change of pace, we would sneak over to the area of a previous battle and pick up souvenirs. I was looking for a P-38 [German pistol]. I didn't have any luck, so I brought back seven burp guns. We didn't dare fire them because of their distinctive sound.

One night, the Jerries launched a major attack. It was directed toward the British on our right. It was very dark and Muri, Keefe, and I were running toward the area of fire, when we jumped into a convenient pit. It was half full of what we sincerely hoped was garbage, in spite of how it smelled. The air was full of machine-gun rounds that had slowed down to the point that they were making a strange chirping sound like a flock of canaries. Things were getting hot, and we withdrew to what was called the Factory.

The Factory was near the town of Aprilia. It had thick walls of concrete and an isolated tower that, from a distance, had the appearance of a smokestack. The men occupied a long sturdy building that looked safe enough, but the Germans soon started firing Anzio Annie at them. The barrage were so powerful that it penetrated not only the outer wall but all the inner walls as well.

McLane explains what happened next:

A mixed group of us (they were bringing in anyone who could stand on two feet) was assigned to a two-story section that projected out from the main building. It seemed to be a main entry and had floor-to-ceiling windows. Lieutenant Blankenship took me aside and told me that we had to hold, no matter what. We settled down for the night. At dawn, Anzio opened up again. Ju-87 Stuka dive-bombers were also making things jump. A hole was blown in the ceiling, and we could see second-story furniture hanging through the hole.

Except for Keefe and Muri, the whole group was falling to pieces. One of the fellows pulled a blanket down from a bed that was hanging above him and wrapped it around his head for protection.

Keefe and Muri had gone off on a project of their own when it happened: I didn't hear the shell. The archway in front of me suddenly dissolved in a huge explosion. I felt a blow to my right side that spun me around.

I knew I'd been hit, but not where. I felt my right side with my hand, but there was no blood. I checked here and there. Then I placed my hand over my heart. There was blood. By this time I was dribbling blood from my mouth and was feeling faint. I knew I didn't have time to look for the CP [command post], so I returned to the group and told them to get out as fast as they could.

I thought they'd make some effort to take care of me, but they thought I was too badly hit and cleared out. Later Keefe and Muri went looking for me and were told I had been hit. Muri brought medics to where they'd last seen me, and Keefe ran to the rear of the Factory and got an ambulance.

By then, I was unconscious most of the time, but, as they were carrying me out, I remember a shell hitting a wall above us knocking a stretcher bearer down and rolling me out of the stretcher.

They got me to a basement where the CP and aid station were located. I remember that Evenson came to see me off, as well as several others. On the way out, the ambulance was under severe fire until it went through an underpass. I arrived at the beachhead hospital, and, after the doctors worked on me, I sank into the bliss of morphine.

I awoke to the familiar sound of a diving plane. A Messerschmitt dropped six antipersonnel bombs on the hospital. I had clenched my eyes shut when I heard the bombs screeching down. When I opened them after the explosions, all I could see were bare poles, ropes, tatters of canvas, and blue sky.

I was about three beds from the end of the tent, where the bombs struck. There was a big rack of bedpans and urinals on my side of the door, which had protected me from the shrapnel. The Anzio beachhead hospital we immediately named Hell's Half Acre.

I was transferred to another large tent, which the heavy rain flooded. Except for "duck walks," the whole floor area was ankle-deep in mud. To add interest, the area was constantly being shelled. Word was that the hospital was conveniently near an ammunition dump.

I learned that after a week or so they'd planned to evacuate us to Naples, but our ships had been held up by a storm. Finally, they transported us to a docking area and loaded us onto landing barges, which took us out to a British hospital ship anchored offshore.

They were in the middle of loading us when "Anzio Annie" sent a round to the right of the hospital ship's bow. The next one was to the left. Then at the stern, and the ship was "bracketed." I was already aboard and felt the ship shudder as it got under way, leaving barges full of the wounded still sitting in the water. I don't know if there were any more shells, but things were very tense for a while.

We docked in Naples, and I was taken to a hospital. My first greeting was from a dizzy little nurse.

"My, you're so dirty and need a shave and you smell."

My reserve of strength was gone, and I just turned my head and cried. The silly girl didn't know what was the matter.

Eventually, I was transferred to the 17th General Hospital where I got special attention from the British actress Madeleine Carroll, who was a Red Cross worker. I was the first American paratrooper she had met. She and I carried on a pseudo-flirtation just to irritate my doctor, a major who had a serious case of the hots for her. The doctor was the surgeon who operated on my chest and put things back where they belonged. It was rotten of me to give him such a bad time when he had done so much for me.

After an uneventful trip back to the U.S., I was fattened up and sent to the Fitzsimmons Hospital in Denver, where I received my discharge papers.

Meanwhile, back at Anzio, I had a machine-gun platoon, and for awhile we were up on the front line. As the Tiger tanks approached, we were ordered to move back to our secondary position, a few hundred yards to the rear, and hold at all costs. One member of my platoon came running back to the secondary position without his machine gun. I was just driving up in a jeep when he sat down, out of breath.

"Where's your weapon?" I asked him.

"I had to leave it," he gasped. "The tanks were bearing down on me. I didn't have time."

"Soldier," I said, "we have to have that machine gun to defend this position. Get in this jeep. We're going back to get it."

His eyes widened, but he got in.

We covered only two or three hundred yards when a Tiger tank started firing at us, the big 88 breathing flame. One shell hit in the field close by, and the next one actually sizzled past between my face and the windshield, which I had left up because of the rain and snow. The canvas top of the jeep flapped like a rag in the wind.

To escape the barrage from the Tiger tank, I wheeled in behind a building, and we both bailed out into a ditch. But the tank continued to pump shells into the building, which began to come apart before our eyes. So we scuttled back to the jeep, hopped in, and took off toward our secondary position as the Tiger tank sniped at us all the way. At that point, zigzagging to avoid being hit, I shouted to the soldier, "I think we can probably get along without that machine gun after all."

After a relatively calm night, the attack resumed the next day; but we continued to hold our position. We called in fire from the artillery battalion that was supporting us, and we managed to stop the tanks, but at a heavy cost. My company was down from 8 officers and 119 men to 4 officers and 13 men. As ordered, many of these men had died to hold our position.

I set up my company command post in a farmhouse along our front-line position. I was on my way back to the barn, where three or four men were resting, when a mortar shell came crashing through the roof of the barn and exploded just before I entered. When I stepped inside, I saw a corporal holding the side of his face where a piece of shrapnel had completely removed his jawbone and a good portion of the flesh. I realized that he was holding his face together with his hand. I immediately called for medics, and they evacuated the corporal. He never returned to the company, and I don't know whether or not he survived. But I'll never forget the bloody mess that had once been his face.

After the corporal had been loaded into an ambulance, I went out behind the wreckage of the barn to a field bounded by a rock wall. I took my entrenching tool and toilet paper along to respond to nature's call. When I reached the wall, dropped my pants, and squatted down, an artillery shell landed in the field beside me and the earth trembled. I didn't think too much about it until the next one hit the rock wall right beside me. Startled, I looked up and saw the muzzle blast from a Tiger tank firing its 88 at me. Pulling up my pants and moving at the same time, I gave the "quick trots" a whole new meaning. As I hobbled toward the farmhouse, I saw my first sergeant, standing in the doorway, bent double with laughter.

"Look at that Tiger tank trying to keep you from taking a crap. I'll bet those Germans pointed at you and said, 'See that guy taking a crap? Let's see if we can pick him off.'"

At the time, I didn't think it was funny, but the sergeant never forgot it. After the war, when I was in the Army Reserve, I went to Fort Bragg for a training session and ran into him there. He started laughing as soon as he saw me, and he had to tell the story all over again.

Eventually, it became evident that we weren't going to be driven back into the sea, that this was not another Dunkirk. Our unit was moved back over to the right flank, where we rejoined the rest of the regiment and took up a defensive position along the Mussolini Canal. By then, we had been engaged in heavy fighting for weeks with extensive casualties, and there was no end in sight.

The canal itself was 75 to 100 feet wide, with a 20-foot–wide plateau and sloping banks on either side. While we were in position along the canal, we constantly sent out patrols at night to harass the enemy on the other side and try to take prisoners to determine their strength. One of our patrols captured a German soldier. When we searched his gear, we found a diary, in which he had written that he was facing American paratroopers who were "devils in baggy pants." He had continued, "The black hearted devils are everywhere. You never know when they are going to strike during the night and slit your throat." The word went around; thereafter our unit was known as Devils in Baggy Pants. Ross Carter later used the nickname as the title of his history of the 504th.

During the Anzio fighting, I discovered for the first time just how effective naval guns can be. A Navy spotter was assigned to our unit, and, while he was with us, we were getting considerable enemy fire from a nearby village.

I asked the spotter, "Do you suppose your ships could throw a barrage on that village."

"Sure," he said. "Let's look at a map and get the coordinates."

After he determined the exact position of the village, he called it in to one of the ships lying offshore.

"First, they'll fire a shot or two to zero in," he explained.

Sure enough, we heard a distant rumble and then the scream of a shell arching through the air. We kept our eyes on the village and saw an orange burst of flame right in the middle.

"You're on target," the spotter said over the telephone. "Fire for effect."

It was the most devastating artillery barrage I had ever seen. In two minutes, the village was completely removed from the face of the earth. Afterward, I had a greater respect for the Navy's role in the war.

Our casualties were so high during this lengthy siege that we were constantly receiving replacements, some of whom were hardly ready to fight in a battle like Anzio. I recall a sandy-haired, wide-eyed kid of eighteen reporting to me one night. In wonderment, he said, "Gee, sir,

I read about the Anzio beachhead six weeks ago as a civilian. The next day I was called into active service, given four weeks of basic training, and now I'm actually here—on the Anzio beachhead."

The following day, he was dead.

The irrepressible Chaplain Kuehl has his own Anzio story to tell. Chaplains are supposed to minister to the spiritual needs of the troops and leave the fighting to others. When you're being shot at, that's sometimes a difficult rule to follow. Chaplain Kuehl reports:

> For a part of the time on Anzio beachhead, I was with the 3d Battalion. The 3d Battalion was attached to the British forces so we could help hold the area where the main road from the east went down to the Anzio-Nettuno beach. The Scots Guards were on one side of the main road and the 3d Battalion on the other. Much of the area was made up of low-lying farmland, with stone houses where the farmers lived.
>
> It was getting toward spring; and on this particular day, it was sunny and quite warm. I was sitting behind one of these houses by a haystack with my feet in my foxhole, reading my Bible. On a blanket nearby, four men were playing cards, one of them Moffatt Burriss. Another man was daydreaming in the turret of a tank destroyer.
>
> All at once, we heard the roar of enemy fighters coming up the road from the beach at treetop level, with all their guns firing. One bullet clipped the hair from the head of the man in the turret, and he immediately dropped down into the tank destroyer. The four men on the blanket made a dive for their foxholes.
>
> I foolishly put down my Bible, grabbed a nearby M-1 rifle, and fired three rounds at the nearest fighter. The fire from the fighter clipped the haystack beside me and then ran holes up the side of the house. The plane was so low, I could see the pilot and the goggles over his eyes.
>
> As a chaplain, I didn't carry a weapon and shouldn't have been firing at the enemy, but I acted without thinking. Later someone said the plane had been hit and was smoking badly after it passed our lines. Evidently my aim was good.

2d Lt. Maggie Magellas, in a 1991 letter, gave his recollections of Anzio. Though he admitted his recall of names and details was not always reliable, he wrote, "My impressions of the nightmares we experienced during the period of February 1 to February 12, 1944, have been long-lasting and firmly embedded in my memory. They will accompany me to the grave."

The story that he told was remarkable for its focus on tough-minded infantry tactics. In the deployment of their dwindling force, Magellas and his superior officer, Lieutenant La Riviere, followed the book, more instinctively than self-consciously. When it came to sending out enlisted men to take risks, however, Magellas and La Riviere threw the book away and went themselves. Their actions were consistent with what I know of the officers of the 504th.

Initially, according to Magellas, the 3d Battalion was ordered to expand the beachhead to the west and secure the bridges over the Mussolini Canal. After accomplishing that mission, Magellas and the rest of the 3d were ordered to secure the right flank of the British 1st Division, which was under siege from the well-trained and highly motivated Hermann Göring Parachute Panzer Division. H Company moved in to occupy the right of the British and protect that flank.

While Magellas and H Company were taking their positions, the Germans unexpectedly brought in large numbers of men, tanks, and artillery. These reinforcements occupied the high ground north of the highway to Rome and were staring down the throats of both the Americans and the British. In fact, the Allied positions were well within range of Kraut artillery and mortar fire. For several days, American troops had led a groundhog's life and come out of their foxholes only at night when they couldn't see their shadows. Also, movement in the daylight was dangerous because the Germans could survey the entire beachhead and the flat farmland just beyond.

Magellas recalls the time that Lieutenant Sims called him on the field phone and asked him to report to the company command post. The command post, nothing more than a glorified foxhole, was 75 yards away, and Magellas was apprehensive about walking in broad daylight and exposing himself to enemy observation. But an order was an order.

So he leaped out of his foxhole and ran like a scared rabbit, his legs churning. About halfway to the command post, he stopped for a moment behind a haystack, took a deep breath, and made his final dash. A second later the haystack was hit by a 88-mm round and exploded like a piñata. Magellas's helmet flew off, and the concussion flattened him, but miraculously he wasn't hit by shell fragments.

He got up, ran the last few feet, and dived into Sims's foxhole. "What the hell are you trying to do?" he screamed. "Get me killed?"

The February rain poured down on Germans and Allies alike. Although foxholes were the safest places to be during a bombardment, they weren't the driest places during a steady downpour. On one particularly bad night, Magellas made a roof for his foxhole out of a rain parka. For awhile, he thought he had solved the problem of how to stay dry; however, the parka gathered rain, sagged, finally collapsed, and dumped about three gallons of water on him.

During the nights of 3 and 4 February, as a prelude to an attack in force, the Germans began to bombard the northern sector of the beachhead in order to soften up the 1st British Division and the 3d Battalion of the 504th, who were blocking their path to Anzio. The Krauts had also amassed considerable ground forces for a frontal attack. Among the units was the elite Hermann Göring Division, with whom the 504th had had numerous confrontations in Italy and elsewhere.

The Germans threw everything they had at the Allies—88-mm guns, artillery, flak wagons, tanks. American artillery on the beachhead responded with a concentrated counterbarrage. The noise was deafening. A shell of some caliber came screaming in every ten seconds throughout the night. In addition, the Germans brought up Anzio Annie on a railway car, and the gun's range now extended beyond the beachhead to the ships in the harbor. In terms of duration, this was, without a doubt, the most massive artillery barrage faced by any unit of the 82d Airborne Division during the course of the war.

During the day, planes of the German Luftwaffe came in low over the area and bombed and strafed the beachhead. All the Americans could do was fire back with rifles and other small arms.

On the night of 4 February, the Germans dispatched patrols to reconnoiter the Allied defensive positions. A German reconnaissance vehicle approached the H Company position from the north, and the men manning its forward outpost knocked out the vehicle, set it afire, and killed its crew. The husk burned and smoldered all night and lit the road that the Germans would probably use for a counterattack.

The Krauts put on a light show of their own when they sent up flares to brighten the sky in their search for artillery and mortar targets.

The flares were so abundant and frequent that we could have read newspapers in our foxholes.

But no one was interested in reading. The flares and the bombardment that followed were terrifying to anyone who lived through them—more terrifying, according to Magellas, than anything except the later crossing of the Waal in the Netherlands.

To no one's surprise, the Germans launched their counterattack the following day. They made a frontal assault across the entire northern front but concentrated on the British, who were perhaps the most vulnerable. The Germans overran the British Brigade Headquarters. In utter chaos, British soldiers broke and ran in hasty retreat and left their brigadier to the mercy of the enemy. At that point, it was up to H Company and the 3d Battalion to save the entire operation, including the beachhead.

On the evening of 6 February, H Company was pulled out of its position next to the Rome highway and told to stem the attacking German force. The northern segment of the beachhead was under heavy enemy fire. Machine guns and pistols echoed along the entire front. It was already dark, and the terrain was unfamiliar. No one knew how to find the Germans, much less how many there were.

At that time, H Company had only two officers, Lieutenants La Riviere and Magellas. The company had already sustained heavy losses, with only 25 men left. The normal strength of a parachute company was eight officers and 135 men. Lieutenant Sims, who had been acting company commander, had been wounded and already evacuated. All that the remaining members of the company could do was to push forward until they encountered resistance.

The first forces they encountered were units of the British 1st Division in wild retreat. Magellas reports an incident that illustrated the British panic and confusion:

> As we moved forward, I grabbed a British soldier running to the rear in hopes of getting information from him. He was of no help. He'd long since discarded his weapon so as not to impede the pace of his flight. He appeared panic-stricken as he struggled to break the grip I had on his arm. All he said was, "The bloody Jerries are everywhere!"

Magellas and La Riviere concluded that these particular British soldiers weren't going to be too much help in stopping the German counterattack. The Americans pushed down the slope of a hill until they reached a railroad embankment. La Riviere ordered his men to take up positions behind the embankment and to dig in, while he and Magellas went forward to reconnoiter the higher terrain immediately ahead. Magellas writes of this procedure:

> According to the *Infantry Manual on Tactics,* it was inappropriate for Rivers [La Riviere] and me to leave the Company in the hands of a sergeant, particularly in such a confused and fluid situation. In reality, this was typical of the officers of the 504th. We didn't send men out to do something dangerous that we wouldn't do ourselves. We led by example.

The two officers climbed the slope in front of them and took advantage of available cover as they moved forward. Suddenly, on both sides, they saw German soldiers moving toward the H Company position. They had just broken through the defenses of the British at this point and were attempting to exploit this initial advantage, though they were also regrouping their scattered units. The Germans were in high spirits and calling out to each other to determine who was where. It never occurred to them that American paratroopers were lying in wait.

La Riviere and Magellas now knew everything they needed to know: The Germans were everywhere. Heads down, they scuttled quietly back to H Company's position on the embankment. The men had already begun firing at the advancing Germans. It was obvious to both officers that the company was in a tough spot.

They still needed to know if there were friendly forces to the right and left. For the time being, however, they decided to make their stand behind that embankment. They probably couldn't do better, they reasoned, even if the enemy occupied their flanks.

La Riviere ordered Magellas to take a small patrol and reconnoiter the high ground to their left. Magellas took the entire 1st Platoon with him—just six men. (A full-strength platoon has two officers and thirty-five enlisted men.) He led the patrol up the high ground on his left, and Sgt. Thomas Radika, the platoon sergeant, brought up the rear. When they reached the crest of the hill, they encountered a very sharp drop on the other side, a cliff steep enough to protect their left flank from enemy attack.

At that moment, a German machine gun opened fire from the hillside across the road. The seven men were silhouettes at almost point blank range. They hit the dirt, and Magellas ordered them to withdraw down the hill to the company position behind the embankment. At that point, he was bringing up the rear. When he caught up with Sergeant Radika, he saw that the sergeant was motionless, his arms and legs still in a crawling position. Magellas said, "Radika, move out. That's machine-gun fire."

Radika didn't budge, so Magellas reached out to shake him and saw that his left side had been ripped open by machine-gun bullets. He probably had been instantly killed. They were under such heavy fire that they couldn't transport him, so they left him there on the hillside and crawled back to the company position. The patrol had determined that the left flank was secure, but at the cost of an important life.

They next turned their attention to the right flank. Magellas took another patrol of six men, followed the cover of the embankment to its farthest point, crossed over the road, and proceeded to reconnoiter on the right. After they had gone about 100 yards, they suddenly heard Germans talking behind a hill on their left. The Krauts were still regrouping after routing the British.

Magellas deployed his men at the foot of the hill to take advantage of available cover, and they waited for the Germans to move down— spiders waiting for flies. Just as they had settled into their positions, a platoon-sized force of Germans stormed over the top of the hill and headed toward the patrol, unaware that the Americans were positioned just below them. Magellas was armed with a Thompson submachine gun (tommy gun), one soldier had a BAR, and the other five carried M-1 rifles. They held their fire until the Germans came within close range and then began pumping bullets into them. A number of Germans fell with the first burst before they could take cover and attempt to return the fire. Confused and uncertain, the rest of them retreated over the hill.

The patrol reloaded and waited, fully expecting the Germans to come back at them. But nothing happened, probably because the Americans had killed and wounded so many Germans. For a while, the patrol crouched and listened to the anguished cries of the wounded as their German buddies attempted to retrieve them.

Of these German troops, Magellas writes:

> I might say here that the Germans we fought at Anzio were highly trained, combat-hardened, disciplined, and well-led, unlike the Wehr-macht forces we would encounter later in the war, particularly after the Battle of the Bulge, when the German cause was lost. They, like

the troopers of the 504th, would risk their lives if need be to retrieve their dead and wounded—a mark of good troops. The following morning, we scanned that area with field glasses, looking for dead bodies, but the Germans were careful to police the battlefield.

After the firefight, the Americans followed the contour at the bottom of the hill for another hundred yards. Again hearing Germans calling out to one another behind the hill, they stopped, took cover, and deployed at the bottom of the hill. Shortly, another platoon-sized German force—probably from the same company—moved over the hill. Apparently, the Germans were unaware that they would be running into a hail of small-arms fire.

Magellas and his men were in a position about which soldiers often dreamed—looking down the throats of their enemies. When the Germans moved into killing range, Magellas gave the order to fire and the men unloaded their weapons at everything that moved.

The firefight was a rerun of the earlier one. Magellas and his men inflicted heavy casualties on the enemy, and the survivors retreated behind the hill for cover. Attempting to locate the patrol's position, the Germans sent up flares and began firing mortars, but the mortars never found their range.

The Americans remained in place until the flares stopped and the nightscape was quiet. Then, they moved along for another quarter of a mile to see if friendly forces were positioned on their right. They encountered no one in that direction.

They crossed the road, headed west, and rejoined their company, which was still dug in behind the embankment. They had been gone for two hours, and it was well past midnight when they returned, only to learn that the rest of the company also had been engaged in successfully repelling German frontal assaults.

Magellas told La Riviere that he had found no friendly forces on the right, so that flank was vulnerable. Magellas also reported that he had "placed the BAR man, Cpl. John Grenado, on the high ground to our right, with orders to dig in and shoot anything that approached from that direction."

By then, the roadbed where H Company had dug in was the main line of resistance that kept the Germans from reaching the beachhead. The Germans continued in their attempt to dislodge the company from its position by employing mortars and automatic fire. A few of the enemy managed to reach the other side of the embankment and began lobbing grenades over the road and into the H Company position.

La Riviere and Magellas placed the machine gun in the draw to their left in the event that the Germans attempted to storm over the road and engage them in hand-to-hand combat. The situation was that grave, but the Americans didn't run. They kept lobbing grenades at the Germans on the other side of the embankment. The Germans must have thought that they were facing a full regiment because they had been repelled all along the line. Otherwise, they would have charged full force, overrun the fewer than twenty-five men, and pushed on to the beachhead. H Company was the cork that kept them bottled up.

At this point, Magellas suffered a flesh wound that immobilized his left arm. (Several days later, he would be evacuated to the hospital in Anzio and from there to the 45th General Hospital in Naples.)

What was left of H Company came through the night without casualties and, in the process, repelled every German effort to overrun the American position. At dawn, the two officers and their men were still entrenched behind the roadbed and determined to hold the position against any odds, whatever the cost. Magellas wrote later, "Surrender was never an option."

During the night, the Germans had managed to evacuate their wounded and most of their dead, but a few dead Germans still lay sprawled on the hillside in front of the American position. Magellas would later remember "zeroing in their weapons that morning by firing at the helmets of the dead Germans, who lay a few yards in front of our position."

On the high ground to their left, however, he and the other Americans could see the motionless body of Sergeant Radika. They couldn't risk an attempt to recover it during daylight hours, but the sight of his body on the side of that barren hill haunted them. They spent the day in the cover of their foxholes, while incoming and outgoing artillery continued to whistle overhead, as they waited for the enemy to make the next move.

Their situation grew worse by the minute. They were facing swarms of Germans and had made no contact with the British or the remainder of their battalion. Also, they were running low on ammunition with no prospect of resupply, at least during daylight hours. They knew that they probably couldn't repulse another concentrated attack with their remaining resources. They were also short of food and water—at the moment, the least of their worries.

Years later, Magellas remembered that he and La Riviere had promised each other to visit their respective mothers if either one survived and returned home. The chances seemed bleak at the time.

When darkness fell, they decided to bring back Sergeant Radika. Instead of assigning the task to two enlisted men, the officers crawled up the hillside to recover the body. With La Riviere lying on one side of the body and Magellas on the other, they dragged Radika by the harness straps, face down, foot by foot, until they regained the position behind the embankment. Magellas later explained why:

> The question might arise: Why risk the lives of the two remaining officers to recover the body of a fallen comrade? After all, the man was dead, and it made no difference to him. The answer: If he had been left to lie in enemy territory, his body would be disposed of by the enemy or left at the mercy of insects and the elements. In the absence of a body or a death certificate by a competent medical authority, the man would be listed as missing in action rather than killed in action. Any insurance benefits the next of kin might claim would be withheld until the status of the dead soldier was ultimately resolved. His remains would probably never be found or returned home for a decent burial. His kin would agonize over the uncertainty of his fate for the rest of their lives.
>
> Often—and particularly during night patrols behind enemy lines— it would be difficult to bring back our casualties. But we never thought it was impossible—at least, not in the 504th. The thought of being killed and left to the disposal of the enemy could have had a demoralizing effect on the men. So the paratroopers of the 504 would make superhuman efforts to ensure that this didn't happen.

While the men waited in the dark for the next German assault, which they expected momentarily, a runner from the 3d Battalion of the 504th came crawling up the embankment. It was their first contact with any friendly forces since their initial encounter with the Germans. The remainder of the 3d Battalion had taken up positions on their right flank, and H Company was ordered to fall back in line while the larger force provided overhead fire.

The officers passed the word: "Get ready to pull back." Magellas returned to the place where he had left Corporal Grenado, but the enlisted man was nowhere to be found. Although Magellas made a hurried search of the immediate area, Grenado had vanished.

The Germans had attempted to penetrate the right, and Magellas concluded that Grenado had been killed while defending that flank with his BAR. Because Magellas couldn't locate a body, Grenado was listed as missing in action. Magellas recommended him for the Distinguished Service Cross, and it was awarded to him. At the conclusion of the war, Magellas learned that Grenado had been taken prisoner by the Germans and had survived to return home.

As soon as Magellas returned, the company began to fall back. By then, Magellas's arm had gone numb and he was weak from loss of blood. In addition, like the others, he hadn't eaten for several days. La Riviere ordered the company medic, Corporal Flox, to take him back to the battalion aid station.

That night, light from a full moon highlighted the landscape, but the moon's face was frequently obscured by patches of heavy clouds. When the clouds hit the moon, Flox helped Magellas to move along, but they were unable to keep up with the rest of the company. The Germans had mounted another attack, and the two men could hear firing not far behind. The enemy also fired flares to light up the field. As soon as the flares went up, Flox and Magellas hit the muddy ground, face down, to keep from being seen. This happened about every 20 yards.

Artillery and mortar shells exploded all around them. Magellas barely had the strength to keep moving, and he later claimed that he probably wouldn't have made it without the medic. "The human body can endure much under duress," he said, "but I was reaching the limits of that endurance."

The two men eventually reached the battalion aid station, an abandoned house not far behind their defensive positions but still within easy range of German artillery and mortars. The Germans had advanced to the immediate area, and the possibility existed that the aid station would have to pull back to keep from being overrun.

The entrance was covered by two successive canvas flaps so the dim light wouldn't reveal the station's position. The room was full of paratroopers, many seriously wounded. Capt. William Kitchen and his staff were doing their best to provide assistance to the wounded, but they were overwhelmed by the sheer numbers of casualties. The aid station was short of medical supplies and beds to meet the sudden demand.

Kitchen took one look at Magellas's arm and said, "Maggie, there's nothing I can do for you here. I'm going to send you back to the evacuation hospital in Anzio."

An ambulance clearly marked with the symbol of the Red Cross roared up in front of the aid station to take on the wounded, then roared off toward the evacuation hospital. Driving at top speed as the Germans continued to lob artillery shells at the moving target (clearly a violation of international agreement), the ambulance driver somehow got the ambulance to the hospital in one piece.

Medics rushed Magellas into surgery. A doctor gave him an anesthetic and operated on the wounded arm. While Magellas stayed in the makeshift hospital for three or four days as he waited for evacuation to Naples, the Germans continually shelled the area, hit some of the hospital's field tents, and killed a doctor and two nurses.

While Magellas was coming out of the anesthetic that night, what was left of the 3d Battalion again repelled the German attack. At that time, the total strength of H Company was down to one officer, Lieutenant La Riviere, and fewer than twenty men.

Eventually, Magellas was transported to Naples in the hold of an LST. He did not return to action at the beachhead. On 24 March, he rejoined H Company for a trip to England and a rendezvous with the other two regiments of the 82d Airborne Division.

In summing up the terrible losses incurred during the Anzio operation, Magellas wrote:

> I was never certain how many casualties the 3d Battalion suffered during that period, though it's well-documented that the three Rifle Companies of the Battalion were down to about 20 men each or less from an authorized strength of 135 enlisted men and eight officers in a parachute company. Nor do I know the extent of the German casualties, except that we inflicted many more casualties on them than we suffered. Undoubtedly we dealt them a devastating blow. The battle at Anzio Beachhead has been recorded as one of the bloodiest battles of World War II. Other than Rivers [La Riviere] and Sims, I don't know of anyone else who was with us during that period who might still be with us, except for Moffatt Burriss, a 1st Lt. at that time—he commanded Hq. Company of the 3d Battalion—and Lt. Roy Hanna of G Company.

Maggie Magellas is writing his own wartime memoir. Because his contribution to the 504th's success at Anzio was substantial, it should be a good book.

Lieutenant Sims also gives an account of the Anzio beachhead and the fighting that followed:

On 27 December, the entire regiment was again replaced and moved to a rear area near Pignatoro, where we prepared for our next operation. Eight days later, we moved to the suburbs of Naples to continue preparation for a possible parachute drop near Anzio. Later, the plan called for a beach landing.

During this preparation period, a new officer, a captain whose name I forget, was assigned to command H Company. On 22 January 1944, the entire regiment landed on the beaches near Anzio. Initially, ground resistance was negligible, but our ship formations, while landing troops, were hit by German fighters and bombers.

After landing, we moved rapidly inland toward the Mussolini Canal, where we met stiffer resistance. On 24 January, H Company was ordered to seize no. 2 bridge over the canal. As soon as the attack started, we lost the new company commander, so I again took command and continued with the attack.

Here, for the first time, we were fighting German paratroopers, and they were a formidable fighting force but outnumbered. After several hours of hard fighting and heavy casualties, the Germans withdrew and the bridge was secured. During this action, I injured my back when, without looking, I stepped backwards into an open manhole. For a while, I had a difficult time standing and moving, but I made it through.

On the road from Nettuno to Carraceto, the British met strong resistance and were being forced back. Obviously, the German forces were attempting to cut the beachhead in half. The 3d Battalion was moved to the British sector and was initially attached to the U.S. 1st Armored Division to support them in an attack on Colli Laziali, a nearby mountain peak that dominated the beachhead area. The British were to attack through Campoleone, while the 1st Armored would be to their left (west). The attack started on 29 January, but because of mud and heavy enemy fire, the tanks were bogged down, so the attack was called off.

Within days, the Germans launched a major attack and forced the British from their advanced positions near Campoleone. On 4 February, my company was assigned the mission of straddling the Albano Road north of Carraceto to help support the withdrawal of the British troops.

Soon after I had positioned my company, British troops started passing through our lines, moving to the rear. They completed their withdrawal as darkness set in.

Within the hour, a strong German force attacked our position, but we responded with devastating fire, including heavy artillery bombardment, that disrupted their attack. They stopped and withdrew.

I was sure they would try again, so I told my platoon leaders to locate the British units on our flanks. I was disgusted to learn that they were several hundred yards behind us on an old railroad embankment. So I moved my company back to the same embankment in order to try to establish contact on the flanks with the British.

During this move, my company was subjected to enemy artillery fire, and I was hit in my lower right leg by a fragment. I decided the wound was not serious, so I had local treatment and continued to supervise the occupation of our new position, which was established before daylight on 5 February.

Shortly after daylight, the Germans intensified their shelling of our position. Numerous rounds landed in the area of my command post, and everyone dived for shelter. I dived into a large, open slit trench next to a building, and two men came in behind me, just as a shell exploded right above the trench. The fragments hurtled into the trench, killing the two men with me and hitting me in the right shoulder. The trench caved in on us, and men hurried to dig us out.

Medics took me to a hospital in Anzio, where I joined other wounded. That evening, the hospital was shelled by German artillery. So I located my clothes and gear, got dressed, and hitched a ride in an ambulance back to the front line and my company. During my absence, H Company had repulsed another German attempt to break through our position.

Here I must pay tribute to the medical personnel who were at Anzio. Medical installations were bombed and shelled frequently. On one occasion, early in February, a German fighter-bomber dropped a load of antipersonnel bombs on the 95th evacuation hospital, killing twenty-eight patients and hospital personnel, including three nurses. There were no safe areas at Anzio.

During the morning of 9 February, the Germans made another unsuccessful attempt to break through our position. They did, however, push through a British unit on our left, and came in behind H Company's position. I shifted a few men to face them and called for help. I Company was ordered to attack, and they soon routed this German force, then remained in line to reinforce my company.

During the next two days, the Germans made several attempts to penetrate our position, but failed. On February 13, a British unit replaced us, and the entire 3d Battalion returned to the control of the 504th on the Mussolini Canal. Two days later, the Germans pushed the British unit that replaced my company back several miles.

My company, after being deloused, occupied a defensive position on the Mussolini Canal and conducted mostly patrol action. One day we spotted a lone German fighter plane flying low toward our position. We took up an air defense position. As the plane started strafing our line, the men fired simultaneously and sent a barrage of bullets at the plane. We watched as it flew south, trailing smoke, and then suddenly plunged into the ground.

Late in March of 1944, the officer who broke his leg during the attack on Hill 1017 returned to take command of H Company. At that time, the wound in my right leg was badly infected, so I was evacuated through medical channels. At the Anzio evacuation hospital, they performed surgery to open the wound, then shipped me to the 118th Station Hospital in Naples for further treatment.

For its action in stopping the German breakthrough, the 3d Battalion was awarded a Presidential Unit Citation, one of three the 3d was to win during World War II. It's interesting to note the discrepancy between Lieutenant Sims's account of the events that prompted this citation and Lieutenant Magellas's account.

First, Lieutenant Sims:

A British brigadier on our left (west) with some of his staff had been cut off and surrounded during the attack by the Germans. H Company was ordered to break through to them and get them out if possible. This task went to Lieutenant Magellas, who took a small group of men and worked his way through German lines; and— after a short firefight—was able to extract the brigadier and his staff and bring them back to our position. We had one man killed during this rescue.

When asked about the rescue of the British brigadier, which is a part of the official record of the battle, Magellas had this to say:

> Specifically regarding the British division, after I was evacuated, I never saw nor heard of them again. I did not know the name of the British brigadier we were cited for rescuing, nor did I ever see him. I led the patrol that reportedly rescued him, but at the time I never knew that a British brigadier had been captured.
>
> On this account, I can only assume that the pressure my patrol put on the German forces, and the confusion we caused that night, might have created a situation where he was able to escape. We knew the Germans had broken through the British lines, but we were not aware they had overrun the division command post, which is normally very far to the rear.

I assume Magellas thought he knew what he was talking about when he wrote his account. He was unaware of a rescue mission and repeatedly said that he encountered no British forces during that particular patrol, the purpose of which was to reconnoiter our left flank. Yet, the patrol cited by Sims is clearly the one that Magellas led. Also, on the citation that accompanied Magellas's Bronze Star, the British brigadier is mentioned, though not by name.

I think it's more likely that we received our Presidential Unit Citation because we sustained one of the heaviest bombardments in the history of warfare and eventually helped to drive the enemy up the boot of Italy. From the beginning, we were repelling one German attack after another. The artillery bombardment continued day after day, night after night, without ceasing, as did the machine-gun fire. Some days, the men didn't leave their foxholes, and I took my life in my hands every time I made the rounds to check on them. Other units, as well, fought fiercely to save the beachhead.

No one who was there had ever experienced such a prolonged assault. It lasted for weeks and weeks, with few pauses during which you could stick your head up for a breath of fresh air, much less walk around comfortably. As we hunkered down and waited, we wondered when the Germans would run out of ammunition, but they never did. They pounded and pounded us until we finally got used to continuous bursts of flame and perpetual explosions. After a while, we could sleep as shells burst all around us. Yet, in the end, we prevailed.

One of the great questions arising from World War II will never be fully answered. How can Americans come out of civilian life, be trained as soldiers in a few short weeks, be sent into combat, and perform so well under the conditions that we faced at Anzio? I saw a number of magnificent officers and enlisted men who not only fought extremely well but also exhibited extraordinary courage under fire. I offer a final example to illustrate why we held that beachhead at Anzio and why our unit was decorated.

On 8 February 1944, near Carraceto, Italy, Lieutenant Hanna was transferred from G Company to I Company to take over as company commander. I Company had lost all eight of its officers and 40 percent of its enlisted men. Hanna quickly reorganized the company and took it back into battle. He was leading his men in an assault against well-entrenched forces with greatly superior firepower when a bullet tore through his rib cage and lung and exited from his lower back.

Nevertheless, he continued leading the attack until he lapsed into unconsciousness. When he came to his senses, he got up and continued the attack. He collapsed three more times and got up each time until his unit had driven the Germans from their seemingly impregnable position. Only then was he evacuated to a hospital and later sent back to the United States for thirty days. Afterward, he rejoined his unit for the remainder of the war. He received the Distinguished Service Cross for this action.

Lieutenant Hanna was simply one of thousands who displayed such loyalty and courage. Too many men never left Anzio. They still lie in the soil that they fought to win. That soil is now theirs for all time, a fitting legacy for men so brave in battle and so true to the faraway country in which they were born.

— 7 —

There'll Always Be an England

After two months on the Anzio beachhead, a trip to hell would have seemed like a vacation. We had been shot at for days on end, sometimes around the clock, and had seen most of our friends—the guys who had come over with us—either wounded or killed. Every waking hour, we had lived with the expectation of death. What little sleep we had been able to get was often interrupted by explosions and the rattle of machine-gun fire.

We left Anzio on 24 March 1944 to go to Naples and sailed from Naples on 11 April. The trip to England on the *Capetown Castle* was a luxury cruise—a dry place to sleep, good food, hot showers, and no one shooting at us. We played cards on our bunks, watched movies, or just stretched out on the deck and absorbed the sunshine. Under those conditions, we would have been happy to sail around the world a dozen times.

On 22 April, we docked at Liverpool, England, and were met by trucks that took us to Leicester, where we were housed in a tent city just outside of town. After living in foxholes for months, it seemed like the Waldorf to us.

Following Anzio, our ranks were severely depleted, and the first order of business was to bring our units up to full strength. New recruits, fresh off the boat from the United States, joined our battalion, and we had to teach them quickly what we knew about beach landings and firefights. We all knew why we were there—the Allies were preparing to invade France.

We also drew new uniforms. Most of our clothes were in rags and filthy beyond washing. More to the point, we received new equipment—new weapons, new mess gear, new tent halves.

One day, I was called into Battalion Headquarters, where Colonel Tucker was waiting.

"Burriss," he said, "you're being transferred to I Company. You'll be company commander. You've led your men well in combat. You're a good officer. I have no doubt that you'll do a good job."

"Thank you, sir," I said.

"And by the way," he said, "you've been promoted to captain."

I thanked him and saluted. I was pleased, but I knew I would now be in charge of four times the number of men, as well as seven officers. I thought about that additional responsibility and figured I could handle it.

After a year in combat, constantly fighting the enemy or preparing to fight, we were all relieved to be back in the civilian world, if only for awhile. It was pleasant to walk down the streets of London without considering whether or not we would be alive in thirty minutes. It was a good feeling to catch the city bus, ride downtown, go shopping, eat at a restaurant, go to a movie. For many months, we had done none of these things.

We soon learned that England wasn't like Italy, a land under siege, whose citizens hid from Allied and Axis forces alike. Although their city was under periodic attack from German buzz bombs, Londoners went about their daily lives without conceding much to the war. Of course, most of their activities were in support of the Allied cause. They were especially friendly toward soldiers, and I enjoyed being among them. I was struck by their cheerful faces and upbeat manner.

Sergeant Tallon also remembers the English in this account of his stay near Leicester:

The *Capetown Castle* docked at Liverpool, England, on 22 April 1944. Jolly Old England! What a wonderful place to be after leaving battle-scarred Anzio. It was wonderful to be back in an area of the world where we weren't constantly on the alert for an enemy attack. Our troops left Liverpool about 2300 that night for the city of Leicester.

Our training and routine were light there. We were allowed to move around and become acquainted with the country and the people—especially the girls. After what we'd been through, the girls seemed beautiful. They were nice to us and lots of fun to be with.

I was just a country boy from Dillon, South Carolina, who couldn't dance and had no opportunity to learn. However, I saw that troopers who could dance had a much better time than those of us who couldn't. So one evening I sailed out on the floor and danced. I still love to dance; and, fortunately, I'm a much better dancer now.

One afternoon a buddy and I were riding our bicycles, and we saw two girls playing tennis. So we wheeled in and started getting acquainted. The girl I met that afternoon has been a friend since 1944. My wife and I have been to England to see her, and she has visited the States to see us. Recently, she retired from a very exciting and demanding job with Exxon International.

In some ways, the troops were more fortunate than the English civilians. One day at camp, the mess hall served Salisbury steak. Since a number of the troops were away, there was a lot of food left over. I had made friends with an English family named Wright. They were Catholic and had eight children. When I saw all this uneaten food, I thought of this family and asked the mess sergeant for some of the leftovers. He immediately agreed and helped me pack the meals. Then, as I headed for their house, I wondered if the Wrights would be offended.

They were not!

Mrs. Wright told me that what I took to them that day was more meat than they were allowed to buy per month. She thanked me again each time we saw each other.

Shortly after we arrived, I began training with I Company. First, I had to learn the names of the men and begin to work with them. Then, I had to tell them what I expected of them and show them how I operated. Some of the replacements were returning veterans who had been wounded at Anzio, but about half were new recruits who had never been in combat. We had a limited amount of time to get them ready.

About two weeks before D-Day, the British Broadcasting Corporation (BBC) invited me to record an interview about my combat experiences. At that time, censorship was tight, and most of what I said was censored by the military. Later, I was asked to do the program again.

On D-Day, my regiment had been held in reserve because of the rough time that we had at Anzio, and the rest of the 82d left England without us. Shortly afterward, I was interviewed for the second time.

"When did you first realize the invasion was taking place? And how did you feel about missing it, since you had been involved in virtually every other major battle of the war?" the reporter asked.

"I realized the invasion had begun when I lay awake all night on June 5th and the early morning of June 6th, listening to hundreds and hundreds of planes roaring over my tent," I replied. "At first, I felt a bit of relief that I wouldn't be risking my life in the invasion. Then I felt disappointed that I was missing the 'big one,' when other members of my outfit would be participating."

Back in the States, Squee had been notified that my interview would be broadcast by shortwave radio at 1400 on 28 June. I had previously written her about the first interview, but she was unaware of the one after D-Day. On the 28th, she and some friends were vacationing in Myrtle Beach, South Carolina. The United Service Organizations (USO) there set up a shortwave radio so that Squee and her friends could hear the broadcast. Of course, they all thought the interview had occurred before D-Day. When the interviewer mentioned that I hadn't been involved in the invasion, they let out a cheer. Knowing that I was safe in England was a comfort to Squee, who had recently learned that her brother had died in a Japanese POW camp.

As it turned out, the 82d Airborne Division left the 504th Regiment in reserve because we were still pretty beat up from the winter campaign in Italy and from the battle on the Anzio beachhead. We were placed on standby to jump ahead of General Patton's armored forces as they broke out of the Normandy beachhead. Our mission was to capture key bridges and villages in front of Patton's advancing forces.

Three times, we were briefed on jump missions, only to be told that Patton had arrived ahead of us. Twice, we were at the airport, ready to take off, when we received cancellation orders because Patton had overrun the drop zone. One time, we were actually in flight over the English Channel when we received the order to turn back. We all came to believe that if Eisenhower and Montgomery would just turn Patton loose with all the tanks, ammunition, and gas he needed, he wouldn't stop short of Berlin. I'm still of that opinion.

After the Normandy beachhead was expanded and secured, the 82d and 101st Airborne Divisions returned to England to prepare for their next mission. The 504th, now up to full strength, was ready to go.

If I had any regrets about missing the Normandy invasion, they soon would be wiped away. We were about to become involved in one of the bloodiest and most destructive battles of World War II—the invasion of the Netherlands.

Lt. Moffatt Burriss and wife Louisa (Squee) pictured in April 1942, just before Moffatt's departure for North Africa.

All photographs are from Moffatt Burriss's personal collection unless otherwise noted.

Lt. Moffatt Burriss in his tent in North Africa, 1943.

The author using a camel trough as a bathtub in North Africa.

Burriss *(left)* and Joe Taylor *(right)* standing in the Sicilian vineyard where Burriss made a parachute landing just after midnight on July 10, 1943.

An Axis pillbox in Sicily.

American GIs buying apples from an Italian on the beach at Salerno, Italy, shortly after the Allied landings, September 1943.

A photo of the ruins of Pompeii taken by the author in September 1943. Mt. Vesuvius can be seen in the background.

Tanks and troops of the 3d Battalion, 504th Regiment, 82d Airborne Division, approaching the Chiunzi Pass near Naples, late September 1943.

A view of Ridge 1205 near Cassino, Italy. Burriss and his men climbed to the top of the mountain to see Monte Cassino Abbey across the valley. German artillery shelled the 504th, and it was impossible for them to move forward.

The LCIs *(three ships on the right)* that brought the 504th ashore near Nettuno during the Anzio landings. The smoking LCI on the right was hit by a bomb dropped from a German Me-109 fighter-bomber. The transport ships on the left are unloading equipment and vehicles onto the beachhead.

Chow time on the Anzio beachhead for Pvt. William Martin *(left)* and Lieutenant Burriss *(right)*. The dent on Burriss's helmet was caused by shrapnel.

Lt. Gen. Mark Clark *(right)* pins a Presidential Unit Citation on the Third Battalion Guidon for action at Anzio.

Lt. Roy Hanna *(left)*, Lt. Edward Sims *(center)*, and Lt. Edward T. Wisnieswski *(right)* recuperating from wounds received at Anzio.

Allied trucks cross the bridge at Grave, Netherlands, after its capture during Operation Market-Garden by I Company and E Company of the 504th Regiment on September 17, 1944.

The home of Herman Goering's aunt near Nijmegen, Netherlands. Burriss occupied the house for a few days during Operation Market-Garden.

American bombers dropping supplies to paratroopers in the Netherlands.

Moffatt Burriss *(right)* and son Francis *(left)* by the Nijmegen bridge for the fiftieth anniversary celebration in September 1994. The main objective of the 504th's daring Waal River crossing was to capture the bridge intact.

Moffatt and his son Moffatt Jr. fifty years later at the site of the 504th's Waal River crossing. The paratroopers had to paddle across the 300-yard wide river in flimsy boats and then charge across open ground on the other bank while under withering fire from German machine gunners and artillery.

The house across the river from Nijmegen where Captain Burriss killed a dozen Germans with a Gammon grenade. The author is pictured in front of the house in 1994.

Captain Burriss dispatched his men to ambush this German flak wagon during the
Battle of the Bulge. After they captured it, they quickly turned the 20mm gun
against the Germans to repel an attack.

Captain Burriss's "home" in the Ardennes on Christmas day, 1944, during the Battle of the Bulge.

Five of Burriss's rugged paratroopers at the Battle of the Bulge, January 1945. *Sitting (left to right):* 1st Sgt. Curtis Odom and T/5 Ray Moss. *Standing:* Lt. Ernest Murphy, Pfc. William Martin, and S.Sgt. Raymond Thornton.

Dragon's teeth defenses were an obstacle to Allied vehicles along the Siegfried Line near the German border.

Into the Reich. The author snapped this photo of the ruins of the town of Bergstein, Germany, as he passed through in February 1945.

Victims at the Wobbelin concentration camp in Germany, April 1945. Burriss's unit liberated the camp.

The remains of the Reichstag in Berlin, May 5, 1945. Captain Burriss and
three of his men, accompanied by a Soviet colonel, set off for the German
capital shortly after the fighting had stopped. Burriss was one of the first
American soldiers to set foot in conquered Berlin.

Lt. Harry Price *(left)* and Captain Burriss *(right)*, victors posing on a rubble-strewn street in Berlin.

Captain Burriss *(left)*, the Soviet colonel who accompanied them *(center)*,
and Lieutenant Karnap *(right)* in the German capital.

Capt. Henry Keep *(left)*, Lt. Bob "Booby-trap" Blankenship *(center)*, and Lt. Harry Busby *(right)*, May 1945.

Six of the original 504th Regiment's officers *(left to right):* Capt. James Goethe, Capt. Henry Keep, Capt. Carl Kappel, Maj. Julian A. Cook, Captain Burriss, Lt. V. F. Carmichael.

Home at last—Captain Burriss on the train that took the 504th Regiment from New York to Ft. Bragg after the war.

Moffatt standing by Major Beall's grave at Anzio.

The "old-timers" who jumped in the Netherlands for the fiftieth anniversary celebration of Operation Market-Garden, September 18, 1994 *(left to right):* Dutch Nagle, Burriss, Larry Reber, Elmo Jones, and Bob Murphy.

Burriss *(left)* and Dutch Nagle *(right)* preparing to jump.

Francis X. Keefe

Britain's Lord Carrington (Captain Carrington in 1944) on top of a tank *(right)* at the Nijmegen bridge for the reenactment of the Waal River crossing, September 1994.

I Company veterans John Gallagher *(left)* and Francis X. Keefe *(right)* are seen standing by the monument commemorating the Waal River crossing.

First Sgt. Joe Castellanos and Captain Burriss at the reenactment of the Waal crossing.

The highway bridge over the Waal River at Nijmegen filled with Dutch civilians celebrating the fiftieth anniversary of their country's liberation from the Germans.

— 8 —

Operation Market-Garden

Those of us who survived Anzio believed that we would never have to endure enemy fire more intense or more deadly. Had we known what lay in store, I'm not sure how many of us could have faced the future.

From the beginning, I had believed—as surely as I believed anything—that I would come back from the war. I thought I might be wounded, perhaps even lose an arm or a leg, but I was convinced that when VE-Day arrived, I would be going home. Therefore, in the middle of battle, when men were dropping all around me, I was never worried about getting killed.

Others were convinced they would never make it, and many of them didn't. Before we landed on Anzio Beach, Lieutenant Ferrill had been certain that his number was up, and he was killed that first night ashore. I don't know if his death was a self-fulfilling prophecy or whether he had a premonition, and I don't know if I willed my own survival or simply foresaw it. I suspect, however, that even with my unwavering optimism, I might have entertained doubts had I known what awaited me in Holland.

Initially, we liked the plan, which had been cooked up by British Field Marshal Montgomery and named Operation Market-Garden, *Market* representing the airborne forces and *Garden* representing the land forces. We heard the details during the second week in September.

"Men," we were told, "this mission will bring the war to a speedy end. If all goes well, you'll spend Christmas with your families."

That sounded good to us. Seated in a huge Quonset hut on hard-backed wooden chairs, we leaned forward and listened to the British-born strategy as outlined by Lt. Gen. Frederick M. ("Boy") Browning, General Officer Commanding British Airborne Forces.

Browning talked a good game. We were going to invade Holland and capture the towns, roads, and bridges along the Maas-Waal Canal. This quick strike would cut off all the western coast and trap a large portion of the German army. The loss of so great a force in such a short time would so demoralize the Germans that they would surrender in a matter of weeks, perhaps days. We cheered.

This would be a combined operation with British and Polish forces, and the field commander would be General Browning himself. He was called Boy because of his perennially boyish, rosy-cheeked face. He was still a good-looking man in his late forties who retained some of the swagger of youth; however, he lacked the military experience that his years suggested. Recognized as Britain's top authority on airborne operations, his knowledge was more theoretical than practical. He had less combat experience than either General Ridgway or Maj. Gen. Maxwell D. Taylor, and he had never commanded an airborne corps.

But he spoke eloquently and convincingly that day. He told us that the objective of the operation was to lay down a carpet of airborne troops over which our ground troops could pass. The 101st Airborne Division, commanded by General Taylor, would land at Eindhoven and link up with the ground forces moving to spring the trap. The 82d Airborne, commanded by Brig. Gen. James M. Gavin, would land near Grave and capture the bridges across the Maas and Waal Rivers. The British 1st Airborne Division, commanded by Maj. Gen. Robert ("Roy") Urquhart, was to land at Arnhem and secure the bridge there until armored tanks and ground troops arrived. The 1st Polish Independent Parachute Brigade, commanded by Maj. Gen. Stanislaw Sosabowski, was placed under General Urquhart's command. British Lt. Gen. Brian

Horrocks was in command of 30 Corps, which included two armored divisions.

With the use of maps, sand tables, and aerial photographs, my unit, I Company, was briefed in detail down to platoon and squad levels. Our initial mission was to land a few hundred yards north of the Grave Bridge, which spans the Maas-Waal Canal, and capture the north end of the bridge. E Company, 2d Battalion, 504th Regiment, was to land south of the bridge on the outskirts of Grave and capture that end.

Grave Bridge was huge—the longest bridge in Europe—and vital for the movement of our armored troops, so we didn't want the Germans to destroy it. By the time we finished the briefing, every man in the company knew the drop zone and assembly area and exactly what his role in the operation would be.

As a company commander, I had attended a larger-scale briefing that had the British 1st Airborne Division landing approximately seven miles west of the Arnhem Bridge, which spanned the Rhine River. This part of the plan puzzled us. Why drop troops so far away from their objective and make them march the extra miles? To say the least, these were unusual tactics, and we began to wonder about the capacity of the British to wage conventional warfare. The British strategists explained that the terrain near the Arnhem Bridge was too rough to use as a drop zone, but one look at the topographical maps indicated little difference between the two sites except that one was a lot closer to the bridge than the other.

Two or three days prior to the jump, intelligence reports and aerial photographs revealed the presence of German Tiger tanks in the vicinity of Arnhem. We knew about Tiger tanks from Anzio. They could be devastating to paratroopers. We carried only light weapons, so we had no effective way of knocking out those heavily armored tanks. Despite the protest of Maj. Brian Urquhart, chief intelligence officer at the British 1st Airborne Division Headquarters, Field Marshal Montgomery ignored this potential danger and ordered the mission to proceed.

Operation Market-Garden was to be the largest airborne operation in history. We began loading on the morning of 17 September 1944 at airbases all over England and took off, one plane after another, in a seemingly endless chain of aircraft. Countless Allied planes rendezvoused in the sky along the east coast of England and crossed the English Channel like a great swarm of migrant birds, the water below spangled with the myriad shadows of their wings.

Many of the planes were transports carrying paratroopers. Some were towing gliders loaded with infantrymen. Fighter planes were soaring above and below our formations to escort us into enemy territory.

It was nearly 1300 on a beautiful Sunday afternoon when we approached the Netherlands. Below were green, lush flatlands, but we also saw a lot of land underwater along the coast where the Germans had flooded the fields to prevent a landing. Moving inland, we saw only miles of aircraft on either side and heard only the steady drone of thousands and thousands of engines. It was a sound that, under different circumstances, would have lulled one to sleep.

Then all hell broke loose. Below, antiaircraft batteries opened fire, and we saw flaming tracer bullets streaking toward our planes. Immediately, several fighters broke formation and, spitting fire, hurtled toward the guns below. They were quick and effective. Suddenly, there were no more tracers, no more white puffs of smoke. Quiet reigned except for the steady hum of the motors.

As I stood at the door of my plane and watched the fireworks, I noticed smoke coming from one of H Company's planes to my left rear. The plane shivered and began to fall as seventeen paratroopers—an entire stick—streamed out the door. I watched as the plane eventually began tumbling out of control. No additional chutes opened. The pilot and copilot didn't make it. They held their course until all the troopers were out and then rode the plane down—another example of the courage and self-sacrifice so characteristic of Americans during the war.

As we continued our flight, an occasional antiaircraft gun opened fire with the same results—one of our fighters zoomed down and knocked it out.

As jump master of our plane, I continued to stand in the door and observe what was going on around and below us. At one o'clock, I saw the town of Grave and the massive Grave Bridge—one of our objectives. The red light flashed on. I gave the order to stand up and hook up.

This is it, I said to myself. In a minute, I would be bailing out for the second time in combat.

As we approached the bridge, a 20-mm antiaircraft gun mounted on the superstructure of the bridge started firing at us. Tracers streamed toward our plane as we flew directly over the bridge at a height of about 600 feet. Sergeant. Johnson, my communications sergeant, shook his fist at the German gun crew and shouted, "You dirty Krauts. You just wait a minute and we'll be down there to get you."

Chaplain Kuehl made the jump with us. This is his account from the time that we arrived in England until we jumped over the Netherlands:

Coming to England seemed like heaven after the bombardment at Anzio and the winter in the mountains of Italy. Once we were off the front lines, there was much speculation as to what would be our next mission.

During our training time in England I remember Captain Moffatt Burriss, I Company Commander, saying to me, "Chaplain, why don't you jump with I Company once in combat?"

In our jumps and on combat missions, I would rotate units, so I could be with as many men as possible over a period of time.

"You haven't asked me," I said.

He said, "Now you're asked."

It was an honor for me to be asked by this officer, because there was no braver man in the regiment. When we ran into strong enemy opposition, he didn't say, "You go there." He said, "Follow me." And his men did, because they respected him so highly.

When we took off for the jump in Holland, I was with Moffatt in his plane. As our plane crossed the Channel into Holland, we saw that the Germans had flooded great areas—evidently to avoid our seaborne invasion. We soon saw that there were many built-up areas with antiaircraft gun emplacements.

Soon they were firing furiously at us. We could see the tracers and knew that between each visible bullet there were many more rounds. We saw troopers jumping out of one of our wing planes and were shocked to look down and see only water below. Then we noticed the plane was on fire.

At that moment, we saw a stream of tracers coming right at us, as if we were going to swallow them. Moffatt and I were standing at the door. The instinct to survive made us both jump at the same time, away from the door and behind the paper-thin aluminum fuselage, which afforded us no more protection than the open door. The volley raked the back of the fuselage to the tail. Then Moffatt and I looked at each other and began to laugh.

Just how much protection that aluminum fuselage would have afforded us, I don't know. But we both jumped for cover at the same instant.

At that point, the green light flashed on. We bailed out just a few hundred yards north of the bridge. For a moment, I saw the landscape laid out before me—a giant semicircle of green grass, a dark river, an old Dutch town—then I hit the ground and rolled over.

If ever we had made a perfect jump, this was it. All of my company landed exactly on the drop zone. I touched down within a few feet of the assembly point. Within one hour, my entire company was assembled with all equipment and no injuries, and we had captured our objective. None of our practice jumps had ever gone so well.

If we could have pictured this event through the eyes of the enemy in one of the four-man antiaircraft crews manning the big gun in the superstructure of the Grave Bridge, we would have seen hundreds of paratroopers dropping on the south end of the bridge and hundreds more dropping on the north end just a few hundred yards from our position. Still more planes would be soaring over us in an endless stream. We would have been outnumbered at least 200 to 1 by crack American troops with a lethal reputation. We might imagine ourselves dead, blown to bits, within the next fifteen minutes. Clearly we would have been completely demoralized and ready to surrender.

And that's exactly what the Germans did. As soon as my men fired the first shot at them, one of them took off his white undershirt and waved it. It was a smart move. For them, the war was over, as it soon would be for the rest of the German army (but only after more fierce fighting and additional bloodshed). The four men in this German gun crew would be sent back through the lines and eventually end up in an Allied prison camp, where they would have a roof over their heads and three meals a day. In fact, they would soon be leading easier lives than we would, and no one would be shooting at them.

As for us, we were happy. We had captured our initial objective in a cakewalk. Meanwhile, E Company, which had dropped on the south side of the bridge, had captured its end. It took the men in E Company somewhat longer because enemy soldiers were entrenched in a concrete pillbox and refused to surrender without a fight. At its conclusion, however, our two companies had captured the Grave Bridge intact.

Once the bridge was secure, I ordered the men of I Company to expand our bridgehead and set up a perimeter defense around the north end. I got a call on the field telephone telling me that we had been designated as regimental reserves, which meant we would be held back from any fighting until needed.

"OK," I yelled. "Let's dig in. We're staying right here."

Shortly thereafter, one of my men ran up to me and said, "Captain, there's a big lead cable in the bottom of my foxhole. It looks like some kind of communications line. What should I do with it?"

I went over to look at what he had uncovered. It resembled the exposed torso of a giant black snake, but it was obviously a major telephone line. As part of our orders, we were to disrupt communications.

"Cut it," I said, and he did.

The next morning, an airborne MP (military police) showed up with two telephone linemen who spoke in a foreign tongue. The MP saluted and said, "Captain, we're here to repair the cable."

I led him over to the foxhole, and the two linemen slid in with their toolboxes and looked at the frazzled wires spilling out of their casing like multicolored spaghetti. The linemen began to babble at each other. About that time, my field phone rang. It was my regimental commander, Colonel Tucker.

"Burriss," he said, "what the hell's going on in your company area?"

"Nothing much, Colonel," I said. "It's pretty quiet."

"That's not what I meant," he said. "I'm talking about the fact that somebody cut the communications cable."

"Yes, sir," I said. "I told one of my men to cut it. Disrupting communications was part of our mission."

"Yes, said Colonel Tucker, "but I meant locally. You cut the international telephone cable. The 504th was planning to use it for our own communications."

Two days later, when I Company left that position, the linemen were still splicing wires and talking in what sounded like several languages.

Though our first objective was achieved with little or no effort, I should have known that the going would get rougher. On the night of 19 September, Major Cook, now commander of the 3d Battalion, 504th, called the four company commanders of the 3d Battalion to the tent that served as battalion command post and briefed us on a river crossing scheduled for the next day.

As I was about to step into Major Cook's tent, I handed my pistol to Private Gittman and told him to clean and oil it.

"Be careful, Gittman," I said. "It's loaded."

The major bent over a map on a metal table. An imposing figure, he was regular Army—a West Pointer.

"Men," he said, "the British paratroopers at Arnhem are being cut to pieces by Tiger tanks. They need immediate reinforcement and ammunition. If they don't get them, they'll lose the Arnhem Bridge and maybe their entire force."

This was the first indication that things weren't going according to plan. We shook our heads. We had encountered absolutely no trouble and had been counting the days until Christmas when we all would be back home.

"There's more," Major Cook said. "Germans also hold the south end of the Nijmegen Bridge, and they're defending it with armor. The 508th hasn't been able to dislodge them. General Gavin believes we can capture the Nijmegen Bridge if we attack both ends at the same time."

He paused.

"Our orders are to capture the north end of the Nijmegen Bridge. We'll be crossing the river tomorrow, using paddle boats."

It sounded so simple. Just paddle across and secure the bridge. At that moment, I didn't think too much about what might be involved.

In the middle of Major Cook's briefing, a shot rang out. A bullet whistled through the tent and barely missed our heads. We all fell flat on our faces. I knew immediately what had happened. I stuck my head out the tent door and saw Gittman with a hangdog look on his face.

"Sorry, Captain," he said. "You told me it was loaded, but you didn't tell me there was a bullet in the chamber."

His hand was dripping blood where the bullet had plowed a two-inch groove in his palm. All I could do was shake my head. When Major Cook finished the briefing, Gittman and I returned to I Company area to brief the men. They started kidding Gittman when they heard about our mission.

"Hey, Gittman, don't think we don't know why you shot yourself— so you wouldn't have to make that crossing tomorrow," one of the men taunted.

Gittman was so mad that he went to the doctor, had his hand bandaged, and came back to the company ready to make a one-armed assault on the river.

Early the next morning, the battalion commander, S3, and the four company commanders went by jeep to make a visual reconnaissance of the spot where we were going to make the crossing. We met at the power plant on the banks of the Waal to discuss the feasibility of the operation with the British high command.

The assembled officers included General Horrocks, commander, 30 Corps; General Browning, commander, Airborne Corps; Colonel Tucker, commander, 504th Parachute Infantry Regiment; Major Cook, commander, 3d Battalion, 504th Regiment; Capt. Henry Keep, Battalion S3; and the company commanders of Headquarters Company, 3d Battalion, G Company, H Company, and I Company. General Gavin, our division commander, was instrumental in planning the operation.

All of us climbed to the top floor of the tall building, where we had a panoramic view of the countryside. It was awesome!

The river at this point was about 300 yards wide, the length of three football fields, and we could tell by the swirling, foaming waters that the current was strong. This was no ancient, meandering river. It flowed straight and deep and swiftly.

On the opposite (north) side, we saw green, grassy flatlands that ran for about 900 yards, then rose to form a dike with a two-lane road on it. This was the route we would follow to the railroad and highway bridges.

As we viewed the area through binoculars, we could see enemy machine-gun positions along the dike and also on the flat terrain. We observed mortar and artillery units behind the dike and 20-mm guns on the railroad bridge. An old fort bound by a moat towered above the dike, a perfect observation post from which to direct artillery fire at our crossing site.

The railroad bridge was upstream to our right, 1 mile above our crossing, and the huge Nijmegen Bridge was 2 miles beyond it. The dike road between the railroad and highway bridges was lined with houses and buildings, which we assumed contained enemy troops.

What we saw that morning appeared to be an impregnable defense—a textbook example. The river itself was a dangerous obstacle. The terrain between the river and the dikes provided the Germans with a natural shooting gallery. They occupied the high ground and would be firing down on us all the way. Also, they commanded superior firepower. It looked like a suicide mission.

General Horrocks explained why we needed to run such risks. He told us that the British 2d Parachute Battalion, commanded by Lt. Col. John Frost, was holding the north end of the Arnhem Bridge. The situation was desperate. Frost's men were being pounded by Tiger tanks and superior German ground forces. Their casualties were extremely high, and they were almost out of ammunition. Unless they received reinforcements and resupply within hours, the whole outfit, as well as Operation Market-Garden, would be lost. (Their predicament was the direct result of dropping them too far from the bridge and ignoring intelligence reports placing German Tiger tanks in the Arnhem area.)

"We'll give you support," General Horrocks said. "British tanks will line up behind the dike on the south bank of the Waal and pound the enemy positions for thirty minutes prior to your crossing. Fighter-bombers will bomb the north side fifteen minutes prior to the crossing, and our tanks will fire smoke shells to engulf the river so the Jerries can't see the boats. At the same time, the 508 and our tanks—British tanks—will attack the south end of the bridge."

The ranking officers discussed the urgency of the mission. If we didn't capture the bridge across the Waal within hours, all the British paratroopers would be lost and our overall mission a failure.

We had looked across at the wide rushing river, at the green plain beyond, and the German gun emplacements along the dike. All of us knew, in an instant, the high risk involved and the casualties we would suffer, as did Horrocks and Browning.

That's why the British general asked, "What do you think? Can you do it?" In effect, he was asking us to lay down our lives for British soldiers. We felt a kinship with them, but we had been let down by the British at Anzio.

Colonel Tucker asked him, "If we take the bridge, what assurance do we have that your troops will get to Arnhem immediately?"

General Horrocks replied, "My tanks will be lined up in full force at the bridge, ready to go, hell-bent for Arnhem. Nothing will stop them."

All of us took that as a solemn pledge, one that made the whole operation meaningful. We knew (or thought we knew) that if we could put enough paratroopers across the river and take the bridge, his tanks would move to Arnhem, challenge the Tiger tanks, and give the British and Polish paratroopers the chance they needed to break out of the trap.

Then he looked at all of us expectantly and said again, "Can you do it?"

"Yes, if that's what it takes," we told him. I wasn't afraid, but all the while I was thinking of Anzio, where we had lost most of our officers and men to save another British unit.

We sympathized with the British more this time, however, because they were trapped in their position and bombarded by Tiger tanks. As paratroopers, we knew what it was like to fight tanks with rifles and grenades. They needed help. We would try it, though we knew that the casualties would be high and that we might not be able to make it to the bridge. As we rode back to our units in the jeep, we said little.

The British were to supply us with assault boats—paddleboats rather than motorboats—and they promised to deliver them by 1100. My men and I, along with the rest of the battalion, crouched behind the dike and waited for the boats to arrive. We watched 1100 come and go, then 1200, then 1300. The British paratroopers at Arnhem were running out of time, and so were we. We cursed the British high command. Finally at 1400, they arrived. They had been held up by a traffic jam along the single highway leading to Nijmegen.

When we saw the boats, we were stunned. They were flimsy, collapsible canvas boats that looked as if they wouldn't make it across a swimming pool. Each boat was supposed to hold sixteen men fully equipped, but the boats were much too small and frail. Instead of sixteen paddles, as promised, we typically found five or six in each boat.

"OK, men," Major Cook said, "use your rifle butts as paddles. And there'll be two engineers in each boat to show you how to steer and paddle. They'll cross with the first wave, then take the boats back to pick up the second wave."

It was like a Laurel and Hardy movie, only with real lives at stake—hundreds of lives. We would be crossing the swift river in clumsy flat-bottomed boats propelled by makeshift paddles while the Germans were firing at us with virtually every weapon at their disposal.

The platoon leaders and troops of the 3d Battalion had been crouching behind the dike for several hours as they awaited arrival of the boats. As soon as the truck stopped, the men of H and I Companies started unloading them. These were the two lead companies that would cross the river abreast.

The engineers began explaining how to assemble the boats. As the boats came off the truck, they looked like pieces of plywood with canvas wrapped around them and a few extra boards piled on top. The canvas sides were folded upward. The boards snapped into place to serve both as seats and as struts to hold the sides in place.

As the men assembled the boats, I could hear their mumbled comments.

"Don't tell me we're going to cross a river hundreds of yards wide in these damn things!"

"Where are the Boy Scouts to go with these toys?"

"You mean I'm trusting my life to that thing?"

"I can't even swim. Oh, shit, I'm in big trouble."

Meanwhile, we heard the drone of tanks and saw them swing into place right behind us. Then they opened fire on the enemy positions across the river. We could hear the boom-boom-boom of the shells landing across the river and see the puffs of smoke.

Then they switched to smoke shells and laid down a smoke screen to obscure our crossing. If the Germans hadn't already guessed, the smoke screen sent the message that we were coming across. We were poised near the top of the dike, ready to go as soon as the tanks stopped firing. I looked to the right and left. Everyone was prepared to move. I didn't see fear in anyone's eyes—only grim determination.

Then the tanks stopped firing.

Each crew grabbed a boat loaded with weapons, ammunition, and equipment and charged up the back of the dike, across the top, and down the front side. The wind had already blown away the smoke, and our position was completely exposed. This was the troops' first view of the river and what was on the other side, but nobody hesitated.

The air strike fifteen minutes earlier had hit few, if any, enemy gun positions. As we plunged into the dark, swirling water, we could see that the Kraut guns were intact and trained in our direction, but they were silent.

As soon as we launched the first boats, mine among them, chaos reigned. The water along the bank was much deeper than we had expected and the current much stronger. Several boats were swept downstream before everyone could scramble on board. As they spun out of control, the men already in them paddled frantically. Two or three boats capsized and dumped ammunition, equipment, and men into the river. Others became stuck in the muddy embankment. German shells began landing nearby. Finally, God only knows how, we got everybody on boats and started paddling across the river.

Behind us, the guns of the British tanks started booming, and we hoped that they had the range of the German guns. Moving slowly, we began to paddle a little better with each stroke. A few shells tore into the water around us, but so far no one had been hit.

When we were a third of the way across, the river suddenly exploded. As the Krauts unleashed their full firepower, the surface of the water looked like it was in the middle of a sudden rainstorm, the sky actually hailing bullets. They kicked up little spouts of water everywhere. Men began to slump forward in their boats. Some screamed, but most went silently. Paddles and rifles fell overboard and spun away in the dark water. One, two, and then three boats sustained direct hits from mortar shells and disintegrated in a burst of flame, with bodies cast in all directions. The men began to paddle desperately and zigzagged the boats across the water, not to avoid enemy fire but because their strokes were no longer coordinated.

I was sitting on the stern of our boat next to the engineer. Suddenly, I noticed his wrist turn red.

"Captain," he said, "take the rudder. I've been hit."

Just as I reached for the rudder, he leaned forward and caught a 20-mm high-explosive shell through his head, a round that was meant for me. As the shell exploded, I felt a stinging sensation in my side. I'd caught some of the shrapnel, though I felt no real pain. I grabbed the rudder and tried to steer the boat. At that moment, the upper part of the engineer's body fell overboard; and when the current hit his head and torso, the drag swung the boat upstream.

"Straighten out! Straighten out!" the men in the front of the boat shouted.

I couldn't. His feet were caught under the seat, and his body was acting as a second rudder. I was finally able to reach down, disengage his feet, and push him overboard. As I watched his body float downstream, I could see the red blood streaming from what was left of his head. We resumed our frantic paddling toward the opposite shore.

As we approached the north bank of the river, I looked across the 900-yard plain between us and the dike. The grass was bristling with machine guns, and the only way to reach our objective was to charge straight into them. Not a happy prospect, but we had no other choice. We landed and piled ashore, sheltered for the moment by an embankment. With the river still spouting water, three more boats arrived.

As I gathered my men, I was suddenly hit with a wave of nausea. I bent over and vomited. By the time I straightened up, I felt fine again.

"OK, men," I shouted. "Let's go. Straight ahead to the dike."

Without hesitation, every single man, including several who were wounded, jumped from the embankment and started running forward and firing furiously at the machine guns on the back side of the dike. At that point, the machine gunners shifted their fire from the boats to the charging ground troops—to us. Men began to drop on both sides of me, some grabbing their legs or shoulders and others falling like sacks of sand. But those who were miraculously unhit continued firing and running toward the dike. Two machine guns down on the plain opened up and started inflicting casualties.

I yelled, "Booby Trap!" and signaled to Lt. Robert ("Booby Trap") Blankenship to get one of the machine guns. Then I shouted to Sergeant Muri to get the other. They took a couple of men each and knocked out both machine guns. I wasn't surprised. Blankenship, short, stocky, and pleasant-faced, commanded the loyalty of all the men in his platoon; Muri, shorter and leaner, was a fierce fighter, and the men would follow him anywhere.

By this time, several of us had reached the front side of the dike and were now safe from the machine guns on the back side. The Germans could fire only over our heads.

"Use your grenades!" I yelled to the men on either side of me. They immediately took them, pulled the pins, and tossed them over the dike. The earth underneath us trembled with the almost simultaneous explosions. Then, there was a moment of silence in front, followed by the screams of wounded Krauts. All along the line, other German gunners stood up, ready to surrender. But it was too late.

Our men, in a frenzy over the wholesale slaughter of their buddies, continued to fire until every German on the dike lay dead or dying. Our wounded, strewn along the 900-yard plain, began to crawl back toward the riverbank, where the boats were waiting to return to the other side to pick up the second wave. The surviving engineers paddled the boats back across the river. They carried all the wounded they could and then brought back the rest of the 3d Battalion and also the 2d Battalion. Fewer than half of the boats that made the initial crossing were serviceable.

The medics and Chaplain Kuehl had a busy time as they took care of the wounded and the dying. Chaplain Kuehl, with a sharp face and black hair, was small of build but stout of heart. He was a true man of God and absolutely fearless. He faced enemy fire along with the rest of us, all the while carrying no weapon to defend himself. No officer in the regiment commanded greater respect than he did, and he went places where no other chaplain would go.

When the engineer in my boat was hit in the head, the explosion had spattered his blood and brains on my right shoulder, neck, and helmet. Also, my jacket was soaked with blood from the shrapnel wound in my side. Apparently, I looked a bloody mess. Throughout the next few days, fellow officers and soldiers kept asking, "Are you OK, Captain? You're covered with blood."

I said, "Yes," and kept on going. But, by the second night, an infection had set in and I couldn't use my right arm. I went to the aid station and saw Captain Kitchen, our battalion surgeon, who removed the shrapnel and bandaged the wounds.

"You better stay at the aid station overnight," he said, "just so I can check you in the morning."

"My men need me," I said. "A one-armed company commander is better than no company commander. I'll be OK."

Sure enough, in a few days I was operating at 100 percent. Many other officers and men also refused to stop fighting when they were wounded, even when their injuries were serious. They knew that if they dropped out of the fighting, their fellow soldiers would be put at greater risk. Even today, I'm moved by the memory of the river crossing and of the courage and self-sacrifice of these men.

Chaplain Kuehl also describes that crossing:

I happened to be with the 3d Battalion when I heard officers talking about a plan just down from higher headquarters to cross the river downstream and attack the bridges from the rear. I wondered what kind of boats would be used—certainly something with armored protection. And I assumed we would be crossing under the cover of darkness.

As I listened, I couldn't believe what I heard: We would be using canvas folding boats provided by British engineers and canoe paddles would be our means of locomotion. I was even more stunned to learn that we would be making a daylight crossing. All this against machine-gun positions, mortar, and artillery.

As I recall, H Company under Captain [Carl] Kappel and I Company under Captain Burriss were to spearhead the attack. As Regimental Chaplain, I would not ordinarily be going on such an operation; but I thought if my men would ever need me, it would be now. As we waited behind the riverbank for the boats to arrive, I doubt if there was one man who didn't consider this a suicide mission. But I heard not a word from any trooper that they weren't ready to go.

When the boats arrived, we couldn't believe how flimsy they were. . . . I was in the same boat as the Battalion Commander, Major Cook. When the order was given, we hoisted the boat over our heads and ran for the river.

We soon were slowed by thick mud on the river's edge. And when we climbed into the boat, it sank from the weight and stuck in the mud of the shallow water.

Finally, we were afloat. All who had paddles and some with rifle butts stroked furiously to get across the river. Soon tremendous fire came from the opposite riverbank, the railroad bridge, and the larger German guns.

I heard a thud, and a man sitting shoulder to shoulder by me must have been hit by an exploding 20-mm shell. His head was blown off.

As a battalion staff member, Lt. [Virgil] Carmichael, said later, "We lived and died by inches." Men were dropping in every boat. Some boats were blown out of the water and sank.

Major Cook, a Catholic, was loudly repeating, "Hail, Mary, Mother of God, pray for us. . . ." My words were, "Thy will be done." At that moment, I didn't think it was possible that any of us would make it across.

Finally, some boats hit the opposite shore. Of the twenty-six boats that left our side of the river, only eleven could return to bring a second wave of troopers.

I carried an aid kit and hurriedly began to tend to the wounded. I found dead and wounded men in every boat and many more lying on the riverbank. While I was on my knees helping a man with three bullet holes in his abdomen, what must have been a mortar shell exploded behind me; and a piece of shrapnel hit me in the back, knocking me prostrate over the man I was treating.

Even in his serious condition, he cried out, "Chaplain, did they get you too?"

I bled a lot, but I was able to continue to treat the other wounded and help them down to the boats so they could be taken back across the river to our aid station.

Over months of combat, I had observed many acts of valor, but I had never seen such a display of heroism as I saw in the crossing of the Waal River.

I was proud to be the chaplain of such courageous men.

Sergeant Tallon also crossed the river and survived to tell his story:

We approached the Waal River, about three football fields wide. Our Battalion Commander, Major Julian Cook, told us we would go in the first wave of troops across the river. . . . Several of the troopers in my boat were killed in the crossing. One very young replacement worried incessantly about what he was supposed to do if he were hit. Poor fellow—he was the victim of a direct hit.

After we finally scrambled ashore and were trying to fight our way up the high embankment under the German guns, I looked around, and there along the river's edge I saw Chaplain Kuehl busily tending to the wounded and dying. When he was urged to follow the troops fighting their way up the German side, he simply said, "No, my place is here with those who need me most." Even though he was hit by shrapnel, he continued to minister to the men and render first aid.

After securing the dike, which had a road running along the top of it, we hastily began to reorganize in order to move on our two main objectives—the railroad bridge and the main highway bridge. The men of H and I Companies were all mixed in together. We weren't organized into squads or platoons, and officers and noncoms took whatever men were available from among the survivors.

Lt. Sims and Lt. Rivers [La Riviere] took a group of men and headed toward the north end of the railroad bridge—the location of a 20-mm gun that had inflicted very heavy casualties as we crossed the river.

Another small group decided to attack an old Roman-style fort with a moat around it. The fort was being used as an observation post to direct mortar and artillery fire on our troops.

One of the men swam the moat, climbed the wall, and dropped grenades on the Krauts while others were making a frontal assault. It was an absolute impossibility for this small group to capture this fort—but they did it. Just one of many impossible acts of bravery during this operation.

The following is an excerpt from a letter written to me by Pfc. Larry Dunlop, a machine gunner from H Company:

You didn't know me, but I was an original H Company man, 1st Platoon. So I remember those days of 20 September 1944 very well.

The afternoon before at our command post area, when we learned about our mission, most of us figured this was it for us. And most of us had been wounded before at Anzio-Nettuno. Now, I took the MG [machine gun] belt out of one can and stretched it out, and replaced the tracers, getting ready for the crossing.

I remember sitting right next to the Sherman tank, behind the bank. While we were waiting, a battalion tanker man tossed down a bottle of booze. I didn't get a swig.

Then the boats came—another surprise. They were folded up like accordions. We swung into action, getting them assembled. Next the tanks were firing across the Waal River, and the word came—"Go!"

There was initial confusion, but we managed to launch the boats. I was holding my .30 cal. MG, and it was awful all around us. There was so much stuff coming at us, it looked like the river was boiling.

Our boat touched the other side. I scrambled up the bank along with my assistants [Sylvester J.] Larkin and Davis and said, "Let's set it up!"

We got down on our bellies and I let go some bursts at the Jerries. Then I said, "Let's go!"

I picked up the whole LMG. First, I threw the belt over my shoulders. "C'mon."

We were still close to the river—and then came the railroad. A tunnel ran through the railroad bank. We three went through.

Looking to my right, toward the river—cripes!—about thirty Germans on the railroad bank. They hadn't seen us. I set the MG down, almost drooling to get at them.

I fired about three bursts. The Jerries were sliding down the slope toward the river. I must have gotten some.

The MG jammed. I worked the bolt. No use.

"Let's get the hell out of here," I said.

"Where are we going?" Davis said.

"This MG is jammed," I said. "They'll soon be firing at us."

Then I got off another burst. I must have gotten some. How many, I don't know. I was no Audie Murphy [one of the most highly decorated soldiers in World War II]. If you wanted to live, you didn't stop to count bodies. . . .

So the three of us came to a fort with a plank across it. "Wonder if anyone's inside," I said, walking across the plank. "The hell with them. They don't dare come out."

I looked down. Holy smokers—wires!

The place was booby-trapped. I was scared. So I walked back just as I'd walked up. Nothing happened.

We were now wondering which way to go. Suddenly the dust kicked up at my feet. Some Jerry was shooting at us. The dust kicked up again. Where the hell was that SOB. Jeez, he was a lousy shot.

"C'mon," I said. "Let's get out of here. He's not going to miss again."

We started running.

Then a trooper sergeant ran into us. He was soaking wet. Apparently he swam the moat.

"Where the hell you guys been?" he said.

I yelled back, "Hey, man, we were here before you."

After that, I remember scrambling up a bank and over an iron railing. The shooting had continued, and you couldn't see too many of our guys. I remember that.

Then a noncom came up and told me and Legacie to stay near the left side of the bank, looking toward Nijmegen.

Just about dusk, the British tanks started coming over the bridge. We held our breath, hoping the bridge wasn't booby trapped, that it wouldn't blow sky high. Legacie and I waved at them, pointing north, shouting, "That way! That way!"

The damn tanks only went to the end of the bridge and stopped. We could hear Captain Kappel, Lieutenant Rivers [La Riviere], and Captain Burriss cussing at them.

Cripes! They were getting out their teacups! I know, because somehow I stole a cup from them.

After we had knocked out the machine guns on the dike, I took a group of about ten men and headed down the dike road toward the main highway bridge. The railroad bridge was about one mile to the east and the highway bridge about three miles. We passed Germans sprawled over their machine guns, shot and killed in that last, furious charge as they tried to surrender.

We knew there would be more Krauts between us and the bridges— live Krauts—and we were determined to get them. Our adrenaline was still flowing, and we were angry that our losses had been so heavy.

I told Sergeant Muri to take his men and head up the dike road. I would follow the hedgerow just north of the road and meet him where the railroad and the road intersected.

As Private Martin, my runner, and I were running forward behind the hedgerow, a 20-mm flak wagon started firing at us. The tracers lit up the sky like a 4th of July celebration. Suddenly, I heard a whack and I looked back to see Martin turning a flip.

I didn't expect a six-foot-two, freckle-faced country boy to engage in acrobatics, so I was concerned when he called out, "I'm hit, Captain. I'm hit."

Crawling back to him, I said, "Where, Martin?"

"I don't know, but I'm hit."

I checked him all over but found no blood. Then I noticed that his rifle stock was splintered. A 20-mm armor-piercing bullet had gone through the stock, and the force had knocked him over. Had he been holding the rifle in any other position, he would have been killed.

"You're OK, Martin," I said. "Let's go."

We continued running behind the hedgerow and dodging 20-mm bullets until we reached the railroad embankment. After picking up Muri and his men at the dike road, we proceeded to the railroad bridge over the river, a distance of 500 to 600 yards. As we approached the bridge, we noticed some of our own guys on the north end of it— Lieutenant Sims, Lieutenant La Riviere, and a handful of men. They had captured some machine guns, as well as the 20-mm gun that had given us so much hell as we were crossing the river.

"You guys are great," I shouted. "I'm taking my men and heading for the highway bridge."

La Riviere turned to Sims.

"You take care of the railroad bridge," he said. "I'm going with Burriss."

A few minutes after we left, the Krauts holding the south end of the railroad bridge broke and started retreating across the bridge. They were unaware that the north end was in the hands of the Americans. Lieutenant Sims allowed them to come three fourths of the way across the bridge, then opened fire. They broiled around like ants in a ruined ant bed. They could either die on the bridge or jump into the river. I guess they realized at that moment how we had felt when we were caught as sitting ducks in the middle of the river. Americans killed over two hundred Germans on the bridge, and many others surrendered. Sims and his men had done their jobs well.

As La Riviere and I proceeded up the dike road with about seventeen men, we approached houses on either side.

"OK, let's check each house to make sure no Krauts are inside," I said.

I stepped on the porch of the first house and opened the door. More than a dozen German soldiers were sleeping on the floor. One of them, a grizzled veteran, rolled over, opened one eye, saw me, and grabbed for his rifle. When he did, I tossed a Gammon grenade in the middle of the sleeping pile and dived off the porch. A Gammon grenade was a British grenade filled with plastic explosive that packed the wallop of a 75-mm howitzer. It was the most potent weapon carried by a paratrooper. The ensuing blast blew out the windows and the door. After the smoke had cleared, I peered inside. There were no survivors.

As we continued to move toward the bridge, I noticed an automobile headed in our direction at a high rate of speed.

"When it passes you, get it with a Gammon," I shouted to one of the men. He tossed the grenade at the hurtling automobile. The blast flipped over the car and killed the driver.

Then money began pouring out of the broken window on the passenger side—good, negotiable Dutch money. We had blown up a German payroll car. All of us grabbed handfuls of bills, stuffed them in our pockets and shirts, and continued toward the bridge. Other units following behind us did the same. (Some weeks later, when we moved to the rear for a rest, I saw some of the most incredibly high stakes in poker games that I had ever witnessed. The only money used was Dutch guilders.)

At sundown, we found ourselves under the shadow of the massive Nijmegen Bridge, which rose nearly twenty stories. The dike road ran under the north end of the bridge, which was supported by huge concrete columns. An eerie silence had fallen at the north end, and we didn't see any enemy troops. Could it be that the Germans posted no defense at this end of the bridge? Across the river, the city of Nijmegen was ablaze, and there was a great deal of firing around the bridge's south end.

As I stood beneath the north end, I saw a set of concrete steps that went from the lower road to the main highway at that end. I told Sergeant Muri to take some men and cut any wires that they saw around the supporting columns of the bridge. We didn't want the Germans to blow up the bridge because we needed it to be intact when the British tanks crossed the river.

Then I turned to La Riviere and pointed up the concrete stairway. "Let's go up!"

As I reached the top of the steps, I saw a lone Kraut standing at the end of the bridge. He was so surprised to see us that he dropped his rifle, held up his arms, and immediately surrendered.

La Riviere and an enlisted man were standing with me at the end of the bridge. I had just told La Riviere to take some men, start across the bridge, and cut wires, when a German hiding high in the girders shot and killed the enlisted man standing between us. La Riviere immediately wheeled around and shot the Kraut. As the man fell, one of his straps caught in the girders, and he was caught in the steel structure. When we left two days later, he was still hanging there.

It was beginning to get dark. As we looked at the south end of the bridge, we saw silhouettes of tanks heading across it in our direction. We couldn't tell if they were German or British, but I think most of us believed that they were Kraut reinforcements.

"Let's get off the bridge and over the embankment," I said, "until we can tell whose they are."

As we waited with Gammon grenades in our hands, two tanks passed within a few feet of us. They were British. When the third one arrived, we swarmed all over it and shouted, "Hey, we're Americans!"

The tank commander opened his turret and stuck out his head. I grabbed him around the neck.

"You guys are the most beautiful sight I've seen in months," I said. "Let's go on to Arnhem and save the paratroopers there."

As the next three tanks moved out, we could hear firing in the vicinity of the two lead tanks. We later learned that the tank commanded by British Sergeant Robinson encountered some troops in a ditch just ahead of him. Thinking they were Germans, he fired on them. One tossed a Gammon grenade back at him. Then they both realized their mistakes and, because no one had been hurt, they held a brief celebration.

Almost immediately, the lead British tank was knocked out by a German 88. The remaining four tanks backed up to the north end of the bridge. That's when the British tank crews brought out their teapots.

I was furious. I charged to the front of the tank line, where I found the British commander, Capt. Peter Carrington of the Grenadier Guards.

"Why are you stopping?" I asked him.

"I can't proceed," he said crisply. "That gun will knock out my tanks."

"We'll go with you. We can knock out that gun."

After crossing the river in those flimsy boats, taking out the machine guns, knocking out the German's 20-mm gun, and capturing the bridge, I had no doubt that we could handle the German 88.

"I can't go on without orders," he said.

"OK," I said. "I'm giving you orders."

He was a British captain. I was an American captain. He wasn't about to recognize my authority.

"No," he said, "I have to have orders from my British commander."

I couldn't believe what I was hearing.

"You mean to tell me you're going to sit here on your ass while your own British paratroopers are being cut to shreds—and all because of one gun?"

He shook his head.

"I can't go without orders."

I looked him straight in the eye.

"You yellow-bellied son of a bitch. I've just sacrificed half of my company in the face of dozens of guns, and you won't move because of *one* gun."

Then I cocked my tommy gun, put it up to his head, and said, "You get this tank moving, or I'll blow your damn head off."

With that, he ducked into his tank and locked the hatch. I couldn't get to him.

About a half hour later, Major Cook had a similar argument with him but to no avail. And hour or so after that, Colonel Tucker had the same argument. He told Carrington, "Your boys are hurting up there at Arnhem. You'd better go. It's only eleven miles." Still no movement. Twenty-four hours later, the tanks were still sitting there and the surviving British paratroopers at the Arnhem Bridge were forced to surrender.

In retrospect, we were probably too hard on Carrington. He had little option but to wait for orders; however, we took out our anger on him because the man responsible was nowhere in sight.

General Gavin's statement on the British failure to move is instructive: "I cannot tell you the anger and bitterness of my men. I found Tucker at dawn so irate that he was almost unable to speak. There is no soldier in the world that I admire more than the British, but British infantry leaders somehow did not understand the camaraderie of airborne troops. To our men there was only one objective: to save their brother paratroopers in Arnhem."

I saw no such camaraderie among the British. The tanks sat idle. The tank crews boiled water for tea. And most of the British and Polish paratroopers at the Arnhem Bridge, who had fought gallantly against overwhelming odds, were either killed or captured.

At that point, our mission was to widen our bridgehead to protect the north end of the bridge from a counterattack. During the early part of the night, several groups of Kraut soldiers, unaware that the bridge was in American hands, approached the north side. We heard them talking and saw them moving in the darkness, black figures walking carelessly into our hands. We waited until we could see their silhouettes, then fired a few rounds at them. When they called out and begged to be allowed to surrender, we obliged them. Other Germans, who had been trapped on the bridge during the daytime, began to filter back and surrender.

We discovered that the huge concrete columns supporting the bridge were hollow, so we used a room inside one of them to house the prisoners captured that night. By the time daylight arrived, we had more than two hundred POWs.

About 2300, I took the remnants of my company and started moving east along the dike road. As I was walking with my lead scout, a burst from an enemy machine gun 20 feet away virtually cut him in half. I wondered again—how many times can my life be spared?

I shouted to my company to deploy on each side of the road. Lt. Edward Kennedy and Sergeant White deployed their platoon on the north side of the road and were reinforced by a couple of machine guns from Lieutenant Collins's machine-gun platoon. Kennedy, with dark hair and a perpetual five o'clock shadow, was one of the most efficient officers in the battalion, and Arky White (from Arkansas) was the best fighting sergeant we had. They moved into position immediately.

G Company extended from my left flank to the main highway. Our two companies exchanged sporadic fire with the Germans throughout the night and into the morning. When we could see where the fire was coming from, we stepped up our attack. And so did the Germans.

About midmorning, Major Cook came to my company command post and asked Lieutenant Blankenship, "Where's Burriss?"

"He's with Lieutenant Kennedy's platoon behind that hedgerow in the field to the right," Blankenship said. "But you'd better be careful if you're going out there."

When I saw Major Cook coming, I was alarmed. A large man, he was crouching but not crawling.

"Keep it low, Major. That Kraut machine gunner can probably see you."

About that time, we heard a rat-a-tat-tat, and a barrage of machine-gun bullets followed him across the field and picked at his rear end. He dropped his butt fast.

When he reached my position, I asked, "Are you OK?"

"I think so," he replied.

Then, I noticed the hole in the seat of his pants and started laughing. He checked his pants, saw the hole, and tried not to laugh, but he finally broke into a grin.

After we discussed I Company's situation, he crawled away, this time keeping his butt as close to the ground as a snake's.

I called after him, "Major, you better look up Lieutenant Utterback [our supply officer] and get a pair of unventilated pants—and also send some artillery this way to take out that machine gun."

He called back to me, "You can rest assured I'll do both."

We spent the night of 20 September and all the next day in expanding our bridgehead, though the mission was already doomed. The fighting was heavy, and forward movement was slow. By nightfall, we had captured Fort Het Laauwik and eliminated the 20-mm guns and the machine guns that had caused us such grief. As darkness fell, we were told that the Irish Guards would relieve us during the night and, the next day, we would move to a new position south and east of the bridge.

Several men who made the Waal crossing have provided their accounts. To give additional perspective to the events, I quote them at length.

The first account is from a letter written by Capt. Henry B. Keep, 3d Battalion, S3, to his mother on 20 November, two months after the crossing. Keep gives a vivid account of what happened to us. In his opinion, at the time of writing the letter, this crossing was an event of historic importance. Keep began his letter as follows:

> To begin with, we are no longer at the front. We have been withdrawn and are now somewhere in France, getting rest and reorganized. I am fine and hope to put on some of the weight I lost during the last couple of months. We are living in old barracks and sleeping on hard wooden cots, and washing in cold water, but everyone is so thankful to be here, to have a roof over our heads, to be able to sleep in peace, and to have the leisure to wash, that this spot has taken on many of the aspects of Heaven in the eyes of the men and officers. The weather is foul, cold, raw, and constant rain—but perhaps it is a squall and not customary. . . .
>
> We took off on a certain Sunday to jump in Holland from airfields widely disbursed in this greatest of all airborne operations in history. It was a beautiful warm day, and it was hard to believe that in a few hours we would be in Hell. I am told the BBC broadcast on all stations gave blow by blow descriptions of this gigantic armada from

the moment it took off until the last jumper was on the ground and all planes back in safe territory. I fear none of America heard it for it was too early on a Sunday morning.

What a sight it was—this great herd of planes bearing men across the Channel, over the inundated lowlands, and on into the heart of enemy territory, so we were the group that was dropped in and secured the Nijmegen area. All around these clumsy, vulnerable troop carriers swooped the small, quick fighters, sweeping out of the sky from nowhere only to disappear a moment later, zooming around us like a bunch of wasps. What superlative protection they provided. A flak tower would open up from the incongruously peaceful looking Dutch country side and hardly before the first burst had died away, out of the sky would sweep one of the fighters, spitting fire as it rushed at the kraut gun.

This operation must have been a breathtaking experience to those privileged to watch it from the ground—hour after hour the constant drone of those thousands upon thousands of planes, a never-ending stream of fighting men. I wonder what the Germans thought when they saw it.

I was not bothered at all until after we crossed the Channel—until then it seemed just like any other routine jump. But when we hit Holland and began that long flight over enemy-occupied territory, expecting heavy flak, it was a little more uncomfortable. You feel so helpless in the lumbering, defenseless crates. Suddenly someone yelled, "Look!" and we all craned out the windows and the door. One of the planes in our flight was on fire and men were piling out of it, their chutes opening in the air. The pilot kept the plane level until all the jumpers had escaped, and then it plummeted to the flooded land below. (We learned later from two of our men in the plane, who returned to us a couple of months later through the aid of the underground, that the krauts captured the rest.)

Fortunately, our plane was not hit in spite of the fact that as we neared the DZ [drop zone], the flak became heavier. Luckily, at no time was it as severe as we expected.

I was glad to jump when we reached the DZ. Those planes were definitely too hot for comfort. The Air Corps dropped us perfectly on the DZ, at the exact spot we wished—and all together. Of course, it was daylight and naturally that helped immeasurably. (By the way, this was the first combat jump we had ever made in daytime. Sicily, Italy, Normandy—all had been at night.)

As I came down through the air, I could hear the flak bursting all around us. I did not know whether they were firing at the jumpers or the now-empty planes.

We hit the ground and assembled in record time. The men had been well-briefed, the Air Corps had dropped us perfectly, it was daylight, and the DZ was free of the enemy. The krauts had been taken by surprise and were totally unprepared for an airborne landing in this area. How different all these factors were from events of the past—Sicily where I wandered around alone all night in totally unfamiliar terrain, only to be hit by a tank and later captured at dawn.

As soon as we assembled, the regiment set off for its objective— a famous bridge within a couple of miles. We were to seize the bridge and hold it for the armor coming through in a couple of days. Of course, there were other missions of less importance, but the bridge was the all-important objective of the whole Division.

Speed was essential. We feared [the bridge] would be blown before we could reach it. As we learned later, charges had been placed in the structure when it was originally constructed. However, the bridge was not blown. I imagine the kraut army is very similar to ours. It would probably have taken a decree from Hitler himself to blow it. [Author's note: In this respect, Captain Keep was mistaken. The Germans had every intention of blowing up the bridge. They simply bungled the job.]

Our regiment moved up quickly; and after several hours of fighting, the bridge was ours, as were several other smaller bridges in the vicinity, as well as key road blocks and the surrounding terrain.

The 504 had accomplished its original mission, and now we were to sit tight and await either a counterattack or the armor rolling through us on our way to Arnhem. The majority of the krauts (except for those actually defending the bridge) had left as soon as we dropped. The first round was won....

The next undertaking lined up for us was a honey. All that was left to keep the armor and infantry from making a mad dash to relieve the beleaguered British parachutist at Arnhem was the famous Nijmegen bridge across the Waal—and the town of Nijmegen itself. Our regiment had accomplished all its objectives. The armor had passed through us, only to be stopped. Division gave the 504 the mission of taking the Nijmegen bridge, as well as seizing a railroad bridge nearby, which also spanned the Waal River.

Needless to say, [the mission] necessitated a river crossing. In our 18 months of almost steady combat, we have seen and done many things—from parachute jumps, to establishing bridgeheads, to acting as mountain troops, to say nothing of our frequent use as regular infantry. But a river crossing was something new.

As long as I live, I will never forget that operation and the couple of days that followed it. If you want to get a good picture of the actual river crossing, read *Time,* 2 October. Several clippings I have read from home compare it to Tarawa. However, I don't believe this operation got the publicity it ordinarily would have received, since no reports could be sent out of our sector at that time—for obvious reasons, even if a journalist had the opportunity to write the account of this great deed. Nevertheless, the crossing of the Waal River and the taking of the Nijmegen bridge on the part of the 3rd Battalion, 504th, have taken their rightful place in military archives. This action is ranked as one of the greatest military operations of all time. . . .

At 7:00 on that eventful morning, I went to the regimental command post with our Battalion Commander, Major Cook. We learned there that the regiment was to be given this job. The 2nd Battalion was to clear the sector approaching the Waal River so we could get up the bank and make the crossing. The 3rd Battalion was to be the assault wave. The 1st Battalion was to cross in later waves. H Hour was 3 o'clock in the afternoon.

As soon as we learned our battalion was the guinea pig, our battalion commander, the company commanders, and I went up to a large tower in a factory building overlooking the Waal near the place we were to cross. We wanted to see the terrain in order to formulate some kind of plan in the pathetically short time allotted to us. When we reached the top of this tower and had a glimpse of the scene below—which is indelibly imprinted on my mind forever—I had a strange feeling inside. I think everyone else did too, because no one said a word. We just looked.

The bank of the river on our side was a high plateau, absolutely open, with a flat top of between 200 and 300 yards. Suddenly, the cliff dropped off—a shear fall of about 200 feet along the beach. And there the Waal River itself—a seemingly placid 200-yard-wide waterway with a strong current sweeping everything away from the bridge.

Once across the river, the situation appeared little better. What greeted our eyes was a broad, flat plane void of all cover or concealment. The first terrain feature which would offer us assistance was a built-up highway approximately 800 yards from the shore against the bank of which we would have our first opportunity for protection and reorganization.

I knew then it would be every man for himself until we reached that embankment.

All along the kraut side of the river, we could see strong defensive positions—a formidable line of pillboxes, machine-gun emplacements, and two wicked-looking old Dutch forts between the plain where our boats would land and the two bridges.

One lone battalion was to overcome all that.

A 20-mm was firing at us as we stood in the tower, taking in this scene.

Standing in the tower, we formulated our plan: We were to cross the Waal and land at a point about two miles down the river from the bridge, fight our way across the broad expanse of field on the other side, and make for the road embankment, where we would momentarily reorganize before pushing on. After regrouping there, we would turn to the right and attack parallel to the river, overcoming all resistance and mopping up strong points in the two-mile area we had to take before reaching the bridge, which we would have to capture from the rear.

While all this was going on, another part of the Division would wrest from the kraut what remained in enemy hands at Nijmegen on the friendly side of the river. We were to shoot a flare as soon as both bridges were taken, and the British armor would cross; for, as you know from the papers, this was supposedly a British sector. That was the plan in a nutshell.

As we wound our way down the twisting stairs of the tower, no one said a word. But from ensuing conversation, I learned that all our thoughts were identical: How could this operation succeed? At least three-fourths of the battalion would be killed and the rest would drift downstream. It was an impossible undertaking.

However, it had to be done—and quickly. The bridge had to be taken. The road to Arnhem had to be opened up.

While we'd been making plans from our tower, the men had been brought to a defilade position behind the bank we had to cross to get to the river. We proceeded to organize them in boatloads, and then we waited until H Hour, all huddled together behind that bank.

Some of the men slept. Others talked in little groups. Fortunately, none of them had seen what we'd seen from the tower.

However, all of us officers told our boatloads the general picture.

"Don't be surprised," I told mine, "if you see a whole lot of fire as we start carrying the boat out on this bank. No matter what happens, we have to get across the river, and the boats must go back to pick up the next wave." (Three engineers had been assigned to each boat to help us paddle them over and then to paddle them back.)

The battalion was given 26 canvas boats. Flimsy, flat-bottomed things if I've ever seen any—smaller than Daddy's tin ducking boat, and, as I have said, made of canvas. There were to be 13 men per boat, and there were eight paddles to get us across. In such contraptions were we to cross the Waal River under withering fire from automatic weapons and small arms from the formidable defense line I have already described, so that we could attack two miles in order to seize the two largest bridges in Holland—our battalion. (I'm afraid I'm getting over dramatic, but I have kept this story to myself so long and I am trying so hard to make you realize what it was like that I fear I err too much in that direction. Please forgive me.)

A few dive bombers were to come over and try to put the krauts out of commission five minutes prior to H hour; this proved to be ineffective. A smoke screen was to be laid down as we came up over the banks; this was completely ineffective. Besides the supporting fires of our 2nd Battalion on our side of the bank (what a superb job these men did), their role was to lie there, take it, and continue to pour the lead over our heads back at the kraut. They took it, but certainly dished out a hell of a lot in return.

Besides these supporting fires, ten tanks were spotted on top of the bank, and they continually pounded away at all emplacements causing us trouble. They also deserve tremendous credit. They sat there in those exposed positions constantly. One that I know of was knocked out.

The trucks with the 26 flat-bottomed canvas boats arrived at ten minutes before 3:00. There was a rush to get them unloaded, and then we all stood around the boats to which we were assigned. The tanks were in position, the dive bombers came and went, the ineffective smoke screen was laid, we waited by our boats. Suddenly, a whistle was blown. It was H Hour. Each boatload hoisted their boat onto their shoulders and staggered out across the flat top of the bank. Our job had begun.

As we came out into the open, the weight of our boat seemed imponderable; our feet sank deep into the mud. We must have caught the krauts by surprise, because for the first 100 yards there wasn't a round fired from the enemy side of the river. Then suddenly all hell broke loose. We had run halfway across the flat-topped plateau prior to reaching the drop, when Jerry opened up with everything he had—LMG's, mortars, 20-mm guns, artillery, and rifles. As if in a rage at our trying anything so dangerous, he was throwing everything he owned at us.

And behind us, our 2nd Battalion and the 10 tanks were blasting away for all they were worth. I don't think I have ever been prouder of our men. Not one of them faltered. In spite of the withering, murderous fire, they lumbered forward, sinking ankle deep in the soft sand under their cumbersome boats. Here and there men would fall, but their places would only be taken by others. I felt as naked as the day I was born on that exposed spot.

At last we reached the drop. We let the boats slide down to the beach, and we ourselves slid alongside them. We pulled our boat quickly across the short beach, and everyone piled in. By this time, the situation was horrible. The automatic and flat-trajectory fire had increased, and the artillery was deadly. Men were falling to the right and left of me. Our ears were filled with the constant roar of bursting artillery shells, the dull wham of a 20-mm round, or the disconcerting ping of rifle bullets.

At first we got stuck in the mud, and several of us had perforce to get out and push off again. Finally we found ourselves floating, but in the wrong direction. The current was taking us away from the bridge.

Men grabbed paddles and started frantically to work. Most of the men had never paddled before; and had it not been for the gruesomeness of the situation, the sight might have been ludicrous. With all our strength, we would lunge forward, only to miss the water completely. Gradually we got our boat moving in the right direction; but several of us noticed that even though we paddled with all our might, we were not synchronizing our movements. We lunged forward at different times.

Suddenly, I had a vision of our coxswain at Princeton on Lake Carnegie, pounding rhythmically on the flimsy sides of the shell and of our rowing in unison, pulling to the time of his beats. So I started to count 1, 2, 3, 4 and then repeat. All at once—and for no apparent reason—I found myself yelling "nine" in a stentorian voice. Feeling silly, I stopped; anyway, I was out of breath.

Every movement in excess of the essential paddling was extremely dangerous since the bullets were flying so thick and fast that they gave a reasonable facsimile of a steel curtain. Occasionally I lifted my head to give directions to the engineer steering our boat and to cast a cursory glance at the other 25 boats. By now the broad surface of the Waal was covered with our small canvas craft, all crammed with frantically paddling men. It was a horrible picture, this river crossing. Set to the sound of a deafening roar of omnipresent firing, this scene of defenseless, frail canvas boats, jammed to overflowing with humanity, all striving desperately to cross the Waal as quickly as possible and get to a place where at least they could fight—this was fiendish and dreadful. We looked like a bunch of animals, void of dignity and normalcy in our frantic effort to get across the river.

Large numbers of men were being hit in all boats, and the bottoms of these crafts were littered with the wounded and the dead. Here and there on the surface of the water a paddle floated, dropped by some poor casualty before the man taking his place could retrieve it from the lifeless fingers.

The water all around the boats was churned up by the hail of bullets, and we were soaked to the skin. Out of the corner of my eye, I saw a boat to my right hit in the middle by a 20-mm shell and sink. Somewhere on my left, I caught a glimpse of a figure topple overboard, only to be grabbed and pulled back into the boat by some hardy soul.

I turned around as I heard a grunt behind me. I found someone taking the place of a man who had just received a 20-mm shell, which went in one shoulder and out the other.

1, 2, 3, 4, 5, 6, 7, 8, 9.

We were soaked, gasping for breath, dead tired, and constantly expecting to feel that searing sensation as the bullet tore through you. I wanted to vomit. Many did. Somehow or other we were three-fourths of the way across. Everyone was yelling to keep it up, but there was little strength left in anyone. It seemed as though the only thing one could do was to hang limply over the gunwale and drop the paddle into the water, letting it drift to the rear. But at last we reached the other side.

We climbed over the wounded and the dead in the bottom of the boat and—up to our knees in water—waded to shore, where behind a small embankment, we flopped down, gasping for breath, safe for the moment from the incessant firing. All along the beach, what was left of our flimsy boats were reaching shore and the men, more dead than alive, were stumbling up the beach to get momentary protection behind the unexpected but welcome embankment, before pushing across the broad, flat plain before us.

Out of 26 boats that made the initial crossing, I heard later that only 11 got back to pick up the second wave. The original plan had been for the engineers to paddle the boats back after disgorging us on the far shore. This they did with the 11 remaining boats. The rest had been sunk in the crossing, or the engineers had been killed, leaving the now deserted crafts to sink or float downstream, laden with their cargo of human dead and wounded. That, in some respects, was the most horrible aspect of all. But there was nothing to be done for the wounded. If the plan was to succeed, speed was essential. Five boats returned after depositing the second wave.

For about 30 seconds my men and I lay behind the little embankment just beyond the narrow beach, getting our breath. Then we got up and moved out across the open field into the fire. In many ways, this was the most remarkable scene of the whole operation. You have seen in movies pictures of infantry troops attacking across open terrain, employing fire and movement. Well, this made any Hollywood version pale into insignificance. The infantry school would have reveled in it.

All along the shoreline now our troops were appearing, deployed as skirmishers. They were running into murderous fire from the embankment 800 yards away; but they continued to move forward across the plains in a long, single line many hundreds of yards wide.

They cursed and yelled at each other as they advanced—noncoms and officers giving directions, men firing BAR's, machine guns, and rifles from the hip. And they moved steadily forward.

All this time, the 2nd Battalion and the tanks on the other side of the river were giving us marvelous support. Their constant overhead fire into the bank where the Germans were ensconced was heavy and effective. Somehow it gave you the feeling of security and warmth and pride in your buddies who were helping you out. Because of their efforts, you somehow didn't mind the dirt that was constantly being kicked up around you from the kraut bullets, or the continual whistle of rounds whizzing by you, or the men who grunted and dropped in their tracks on either side.

Many times, I have seen troops driven by a fever pitch, troops who for a brief interval of combat were lifted out of themselves, fanatics rendered crazy by rage and the lust for killing, men who temporarily forgot the meaning of fear. It is in such moments that the great military feats of history occur, those commemorated so gloriously in our textbooks. It is an awe-inspiring sight, but not a pretty one.

However, I have never witnessed this human metamorphosis so acutely displayed as on this day. The men were beside themselves.

Cursing savagely, their guns spitting fire, they continued to plow across that field in spite of all the kraut could throw at them.

Gradually the German resistance lessened until, as we approached the big embankment [the dike], it had almost ceased from that particular spot. The krauts had pulled back to the next defensive line between us and the bridge; and of these defensive positions, there were plenty—orchards, houses, embankments, a seemingly impregnable Dutch fort, to say nothing of the bridges themselves.

At this point, we were relatively safe. The river had been crossed. The beachhead had been established. The first phase was over. Keep described what happened next:

> For a moment, everyone lay on the rear slope of the bank, drawing deep, full breaths. A few of us stuck our heads up above the top to see what came next. One man had his head blown off. On the other side of the embankment was another field with an orchard at the end.
>
> There was little organization at this point. How could there be? Officers found themselves with heterogeneous groups from all platoons and companies. They mustered whatever men were near them (it made little difference who they were) and prepared to go over the top once more—to pursue the next objective. . . . The ensuing action was highly disorganized and of necessity the feats of small individual groups. The sector between us and the bridge had to be cleared of all enemy resistance. It was composed of many isolated strong points widely separated. To complete this phase successfully, many groups would be required, operating in a divergent area.
>
> So off the men pushed—this time in small bunches, each in a slightly different direction, each with a separate mission. But in the back of everyone's mind was one thought—to keep moving toward the two bridges, which had to be taken at all costs.
>
> I was with a group consisting of our battalion commander, Major Cook, another company commander, and about 30 men. By squad rushes, we crossed fields, worked our way through orchards and down ditches. From one house to the next we jumped. . . .
>
> In our own particular bunch, I witnessed countless acts of heroism—all of which deserve decorations, but which of course will remain unknown. I will recount only one incident in our movement toward the bridges—humorous rather than heroic.
>
> In one particular hot rush across an open field, the bullets were whizzing around us so persistently that I was forced to dive into a

nearby hole until things quieted down a bit. Evidently I was not the only one who spotted that hole; for just as I made a lunge for it, two forms slid underneath me, and I found myself the third layer of humanity in a foxhole for one. My rear end was sticking up what seemed yards above the top of the hole. On the bottom was some poor GI who was practically smothered and kept working to get up—something that wild horses couldn't get me to do. The middle man in this human sandwich was the Major, then I. The Major and I couldn't help but laugh at the situation. When the bullets stopped whizzing past my fanny with such regularity, I thought it was safe to continue our rush. I passed the word down to the two below me, and the three of us—the GI, the Major, and I—squeezed ourselves out of this tight fit and continued on our way. . . .

Now, by late afternoon, the north end of the railroad bridge was in our hands. Keep portrayed the completion of the paratroopers' mission:

We organized [the bridge's] defense, knowing the krauts would counterattack to get it back. We heard rumors that German tanks were coming from one direction, infantry from another.

However we did face fanatics who constantly crept toward us from the middle of the great bridge, coming as close as they dared, then throwing potato mashers. It was suicide, but such individuals are ever prevalent among the present-day representatives of the Herrenvolk [master race].

Then at dusk, a strange thing happened. Out of the darkness loomed a tremendous mass of German soldiers walking from the middle of the bridge and approaching our end. There must have been 200–300 of them. We all thought our goose was cooked and were prepared to open up with what small fire power we had left when one of the krauts called in German that they wanted to surrender.

Fortunately, we had a man among us who spoke German. He told them to go to the other end and surrender—the Nijmegen end, where by now we assumed the rest of the Division would be approaching, after having cleared the town of Nijmegen. Lucky for us, they understood and complied. Had they realized what a paltry group we were, I fear all thoughts of surrender would have vanished and they would have turned bellicose.

About this time, we learned that another group from the Battalion had seized the north end of the large highway bridge, a little further on from where we were. The fighting had been bloody, but our men had done the job and established a thin close-in defense of the bridge.

The railroad bridge was taken over by the 1st Battalion, and we moved on to reinforce the protection of the all-important highway bridge—the lifeline to Arnhem. It was dark now; and everything seemed grotesque and unreal in the eerie light of the flames from burning buildings, set afire by artillery. As we ran quickly in the shadows of houses and trees, moving towards our men at the highway bridge, I thought of the day that had just ended.

The 3rd Battalion, 504, had accomplished the impossible. We had crossed the Waal. We had attacked across two miles of heavily defended open terrain. We had seized the two vital Nijmegen bridges. We had opened up the lifeline to Arnhem. And it had cost the krauts plenty.

I have seen a lot of gruesome sights since this war began, but I have never witnessed such absolute carnage as I did that day. Everywhere the bodies of krauts were sprawled grotesquely. In places, they were piled high. (For censorship reasons, I can say nothing of our own losses.)

The town of Nijmegen had been taken, and both ends of the bridge were in the hands of the Division. Major Cook radioed the regimental commander that the north end of the highway bridge was now in our hands and that the British tanks could cross. What a welcome sight that was when those tanks rumbled to our side of the river and on up the highway.

There was one more thing that was causing us trouble. Countless krauts who had been trapped in the middle of the bridge when both ends had been secured had sought temporary refuge high up in the steel girders of the great bridge. From these vantage points, they had continued to fire at us and also at the vehicles passing beneath them. In spite of the darkness, we constantly sprayed them with our automatic fire.

At dawn, a gruesome sight greeted our eyes. Intertwined grotesquely throughout the massive steel girders were the bodies of some 200 dead krauts, looking for all the world like a group of gargoyles leering hideously at the passersby hundreds of feet below.

We hoped that now we had taken the bridge, someone else would push on and secure the bridgehead more advantageously. But it was not to be. The British took over the close-in defense of the bridge itself, and we attacked 1,000 yards to the north to establish an outer defense ring.

And at 9:00 that night, our dead-tired men moved out, knowing damn well what they would run into—stiff, bitter opposition on the part of fanatical crack Nazi troops who were furious at the loss of the vital bridge. Sure enough, our greatly depleted companies met determined resistance as they pushed forward in the darkness. The fighting was bitter. But by 2:00 a.m. in the morning, we were in position, holding the line assigned to us.

The next morning, with the aid of a couple of British SP's [self-propelled armored vehicles] and British artillery, we pushed forward another 1,000 yards. Every inch of this advance was hotly contested. The krauts had all the advantages. They controlled the orchards, ditches, the farmhouses, and other strategic positions; and it was necessary to wrest every square foot from them. By late afternoon, once again we had reached our prescribed line, and here we held on, with determination fighting off numerous counterattacks. We continually ran out of ammo and had to replenish it every hour or so.

About 10:00 that night, the Regimental commander called Major Cook over to his command post. I went with him, and we were told we would be relieved at 0600 the next morning. The word "relieved" is a strange term to use in conjunction with this operation. We were to pull out of our present positions, but no one was to take them over. It had been decided that a close-in defense of the bridge was sufficient and that we were no longer needed.

It was going to be a ticklish situation. We were to withdraw from our present position, with the Nazis hot on our tails as soon as they realized what was going on. Could our companies get back to the security of the bridge without being cut off by the krauts? We were to receive no assistance or cover from anyone.

That night, our company commanders started to move their wounded back, as well as other non-combatants; and at dawn the rest of the men started to infiltrate to the rear. It was a skillfully directed maneuver. One platoon would cover the withdrawal of the other, and then the unit that had just pulled back would stop and perform the same service for its former covering forces.

Just what we expected occurred. As soon as the Nazis realized what was taking place, they were breathing hard down our backs. To make a long story short, our troops eventually reached the security of the British close-in defense of the bridge; and we moved across this huge structure, still littered with the dead we had killed what seemed like aeons ago (in reality, barely two days).

We turned the bridge completely over to the British. We had captured it. Now our job was finished. We were needed for other things.

Albert Tarbel was a sergeant in H Company who kept a diary. In diary form, he gives his version of Operation Market-Garden:

17 September 1944

Light drizzle early in the morning. Went to church services. Received general absolution and Communion from Father Kozack. Combination breakfast and dinner of hotcakes and syrup, fried chicken with all the trimmings, hot coffee with apple pie. Take-off time—Spanhoe Airfield, England, at 1040, Sunday, 17 September 1944, for Market-Garden Operation, Holland.

Plane ride across the English Channel was really something to see. It seemed like you could walk from plane to plane there were so many aircraft in the air. C-47s, gliders, fighter planes, and in the water you could see the rescue ships here and there, ready to pick up anyone in case there were problems—that is, any planes or gliders going into the channel. Until we hit the coast of Holland, we were awestruck by the sight of our air armada. Then we started to get antiaircraft fire, and one of the fighter planes went right to work on the area, immediately taking care of that gun position.

A while later, someone wanted to know if we had reached our drop zone. There were chutes from one of our company planes next to us. I was seated next to Captain Kappel by the door of our C-47. We looked out and could see the flames and smoke under the plane. We started to count the number of chutes from the plane, but in a few seconds the plane was down and out of sight....

As we went farther inland, I was carrying on a conversation with 1st Sgt. Mike Kogut, who was seated directly across from me. We were talking about the possibility of the plane being hit, when, in the next instant, he was thrown from his seat and landed on his back in the middle of the aisle. He had a funny look on his face, as if to say, "What the heck is going on?"

Then the guy next to him noticed a bullet hole where he had been sitting. The bullet had missed him but had gone into his chute and the impact had thrown him out of his seat onto the floor.

A few seconds later, we came onto our drop zone. As we prepared to jump, Captain Kappel told Mike Kogut he didn't have to jump with that chute. Kogut said there was no way he was staying on that plane. By that time we were getting antiaircraft fire from one of the flak towers near the Grave Bridge. Captain Kappel led the stick, followed by Sergeant Kogut and me and the operations sergeant, Gonzales.

Right after my chute opened, as I was descending, I heard Mike Kogut yell to me to be careful of someone behind the barn below us. We landed on either side of the building. I came in backwards and landed in an apple tree, but the weight of my equipment, ammunition, and gear brought me onto the ground easily.

I got out of my parachute harness and with my tommy gun confronted a young lad standing near the barn doorway. He had seen us jumping from the planes and was just observing this historic incident. There was a wheelbarrow next to the building, and, using sign language, I motioned him to bring it over to us. He loaded our equipment onto it and wheeled it to the road where our company was gathering.

One of the first persons I saw on the road was a priest, and I asked him to bless my Rosary beads. There were quite a few civilians with their children. I suppose they were there to show their support for us.

20 September

We arrived at the dike next to the powerhouse and waited for the British trucks to arrive with the boats we would be using to cross to the north side of the bridge the Germans still controlled. We realized we were in for a rough time because there was a rumor that a tank had blown a hole in the wire mesh fence that a lieutenant had crossed while on reconnaissance. He had been shot and killed.

When the trucks finally arrived, we couldn't believe what they considered "assault boats." They were made of canvas. . . .

I was assigned to the same boat as the company commander, Captain Kappel, and was walking behind him. We each took hold of a side of the boat. . . . When we got the word to go, we ran down to the river bank, and all hell broke loose!

I saw Captain Kappel remove his webbing with pistol, canteen, and other gear and throw them in the boat. Without thinking, I did the same thing. Why? I don't know. At that moment he dived into the river and pulled out one of our men, who was drowning. The water was very deep there, so we reached to help them out.

Right after that incident, I got into the first boat I could, and everything seemed so crazy. We were the target of machine-gun fire and small-arms fire so thick it looked like rain hitting the water. Our boats were going in every direction because the current was a lot stronger than everyone had figured, and most of the men had never paddled before.

Several men in our boat were hit, and I tried to count casualties so that we could straighten our boat. We started receiving artillery and mortar fire. The boat to my right took a direct hit, spinning the boat around. To this day I can still see the look on Lt. Louis Holt's face as our eyes met. The boat went down and out of sight. We finally did make the other side—after having lost all but 11 of the 26 boats we started out with.

As I was making my way up the road, I met Pfc. [John] Rigapoulas. He showed me the nub of his left thumb, which had been shot off.

"Well," he said, "Here's another Purple Heart." John Rigapoulas and I came from jump school to join the battalion in Anzio as replacements. He was also one of the volunteers for the Pathfinders for Normandy. He was killed that afternoon, shortly after we spoke.

After fighting with different groups from our H Company, I was trying to rejoin Captain Kappel. I finally met with him at the railroad bridge. We also had quite a fight there. At one point, we were passing Gammon grenades to Captain Kappel, who was throwing them at the German soldiers through an opening in the north bridge tower entrance. Needless to say, we neither offered nor gave any quarter to the Germans on the railroad bridge.

From there, we started for the next bridge. There were so many things going on in that short period—from the moment of our launching to making it to the main bridge—that it's impossible to put it in words.

The following day, 21 September, we had set up our H Company command post in a building northeast of the Nijmegen Bridge. The CP was in the cellar of the building. I was directly above with my SCR 300 radio set; and the company clerk, Pfc. Harold K. Shelden, was sitting next to me, and three mortar men—Reith, Rosser, and Zimmerman—were standing at the far end of the room, opposite the window.

Shelden and I were making a list of our casualties. I was contacting the different platoons, and Shelden was writing down the names as I was receiving them. We started getting artillery or mortar fire and shells were hitting closer to our CP with every round. Sergeant Kogut yelled for me to get down to the cellar with the radio. He said it looked like they were zeroing in on us.

The radio was on the floor between Shelden and me. To my left was a large window looking out onto a courtyard. As I leaned over to pick up the radio from the floor, Shelden's head was next to mine, helping me to pick up the radio, when another shell whistled down and landed in the courtyard behind me. The shrapnel blew in from the window, catching Shelden in the head and nicking Reith, Rosser, and Zimmerman. Shelden died instantly, and the other men were only slightly wounded. I was nearest to the opening where the shrapnel came through, and I wasn't hit at all. The worst part of the incident was adding Shelden's name to the casualty list he'd been transcribing only seconds before the shell hit.

How I ever made it through that day I'll never know. When I went down to the cellar, the captain had the medic give me some kind of shot. I went to sleep under the stairway.

Lieutenant Sims was also in Holland. Again, he gives a detailed account of the action as he saw it:

My second combat parachute jump took place during daylight hours on 17 September 1944 in Holland, some 50 miles behind enemy lines. Though my right leg continued to bother me, I had no desire to remain in England while my unit went into combat.

Over the Scheldt Estuary in Holland, German antiaircraft weapons opened fire on our formation, but this time our own fighter planes were on them immediately and were able to neutralize most of them. One plane in my formation was hit, and the men were forced to make an emergency jump from the crippled aircraft. All but two of the men who jumped were taken prisoner. The pilot and copilot went down with the plane.

The remainder of Company H jumped at about 1305 hours on the designated area near Grave. Initially, we supported other units in securing the Grave Bridge over the Maas River and other bridges over the Maas-Waal Canal. Intelligence reports placed some four thousand SS troops and a German tank park in the Grave/Nijmegen area, but resistance near Grave was light, and all our initial objectives were secured by 1800 hours the first day.

When landing, I reinjured my back, but I didn't go in for treatment because I felt nothing could be done. For the next several weeks, I carried on in less than top physical condition.

We set up a company command post near a small cluster of homes, and it was there that I met the first Dutch family and their 15 children. The mother made room for me to stay with them, and that evening she prepared a delicious stew, using beef she had previously preserved. They wanted to celebrate our arrival and their liberation from the Nazis.

On 19 September, we moved to an area west of Nijmegen and received a briefing on a new mission that included crossing the Waal River in assault boats and seizing the north ends of the railroad and road bridges spanning the river at Nijmegen. The south end of each bridge had not yet been taken, and the Germans were fiercely defending them.

We learned that the British parachute units (Red Devils) who had the mission to seize the bridge over the Neder Rijn River at Arnhem were unable to accomplish this. Elements of the German IX and X SS Panzer Divisions were mauling them. Because of this tense situation, it was imperative that we take at least one of the bridges over the Waal River before the Germans destroyed them. This would allow the British Armor coming up from the south to cross and go to the rescue of what was left of the Red Devils.

For our crossing, the British provided twenty-six assault boats. My company was on the right, nearest to the railroad bridge. I Company was to our left. The remainder of the 3d Battalion would cross in subsequent waves.

Our first objective was the north end of the railroad bridge. The plan included support from artillery and a smoke screen, neither of which helped. We did get good supporting overhead fire from our own 2d Battalion and a few British tanks that had arrived earlier from positions along the south bank of the river.

The time for crossing had to be moved up to 1500 hours on 20 September because the boats were late arriving. We were all amazed at the flimsy assault boats. . . .

It took us a few minutes to adjust and secure the canvas sides and then move to the river's edge for launching. Within minutes, we were receiving incoming enemy fire from the north side and the railroad bridge; and as we progressed, enemy fire became more intense.

Many boats received direct hits and sank. A number of boats had trouble navigating. But the men with me . . . were calm and rowed in unison. (Only eleven of twenty-six boats made it back to the south bank.)

It seemed an eternity before my boat landed on the north bank, but it was only ten minutes. My group landed some distance west of the railroad bridge and disembarked rapidly into a skirmish line.

Another boat landed with many casualties, so I ordered those who had not been wounded to join with my men and then led this combined group of eighteen men in a frontal assault of the dike, which was several hundred yards further north.

I carried an M-1 rifle and directed the assault forward by bounds, with rapid fire from all, including me. Enemy fire from the dike was heavy, but the men with me didn't falter. I admired their obvious courage and determination. Because of these few men, the dike was seized within a short time; and those German defenders still alive were routed or taken prisoner. I learned later that there were numerous enemy dead on the part of the dike we'd taken.

After seizing the dike, I was joined by other members of H Company. Lieutenant Magellas took his platoon and moved out to seize an old fort that was nearby, and I took my eighteen men and headed for the north end of the railroad bridge. Lieutenant La Riviere, with a few men, moved east to flush out a sniper who had shot and killed one of his men.

Resistance at the north end of the railroad bridge was light, and it soon fell into our hands. Next I ordered a few men to look for explosives and to cut all wires. Then I set up a defense around our end of the railroad bridge. Two hours later, Burriss was giving the same orders to his men at the highway bridge.

During a hasty search of the supporting abutments, a holdout sniper shot one of my sergeants. He was wounded badly, but he received fast medical treatment and eventually recovered.

Lieutenant La Riviere and the few men with him joined us—and not a moment too soon. German troops en masse were suddenly coming across the bridge toward our position. We let them come in range, then opened fire and continued to blast away until all enemy movement stopped. After we stopped firing, we allowed those still alive either to withdraw or surrender.

The advantage here was ours, because the Germans on the bridge had nowhere to deploy. As a consequence, they suffered a large number of casualties. Several weeks later, I learned that the bodies of 267 Germans had been removed from the railroad bridge. The number who jumped or fell from the bridge will never be determined.

At the time of this action, my men and I were tense and angry because of the strenuous fighting and the loss of so many of our own men during the crossing. . . .

Often in my mind I relive this particular action and always conclude that this terrible slaughter of humans is not something to be proud of or brag about. It continues to bother me that I had to make the hasty decision that led to the death of so many young men, our own and those opposing us. When will nations stop wasting their young?

I remained at the railroad bridge while the rest of H Company moved out, along with I Company, to help seize the road bridge. After a brief firefight, the north end of the road bridge was taken, but the Germans continued to hold positions in the center of the bridge, and this took some time to eliminate. Lieutenant La Riviere and his men did their share in eliminating these holdouts.

Later, during darkness, I joined my company at the road bridge, and, with the few men we had left, we occupied a defensive position east of the road leading to Arnhem. Earlier, a British tank unit came across the road bridge and lined up their tanks on the side of the road facing north. There they remained until the following day, when they moved north. By then, the British Red Devils at Arnhem had many more dead and wounded.

I will never understand why the British did not immediately push north in order to take advantage of the turmoil we had just created among the German defenders in this area.

During this period, H Company had fifteen men killed in action and thirty-eight wounded. In my opinion, this specific operation was poorly planned and lacked adequate support. Its success was accomplished only because of the courage and determination of the junior officers and the fine men they led. For my part in this action, I was awarded my first Silver Star.

Back at I Company, we established a new position along the highway running east from Nijmegen to the German border. My company command post was in a large house owned by the aunt of German Reichsmarschall Hermann Göring. The house was sitting on the side of a hill overlooking the highway, and Wilder Meer, a wide flat area between the highway and the south bank of the Waal River. This area was occupied by the Krauts. Our mission was to contain them and prevent them from moving toward Nijmegen and the bridge.

Because my company was depleted, I received replacements. It was bad enough to take inexperienced troops and try to teach them to survive in heavy combat. It was worse to be sent men who had proved to be misfits in other outfits. This time, one of them was Eightball, whom I had already encountered briefly in North Africa.

Eightball was a good-looking soldier with a military bearing. He could throw the best salute in the division, but he was also the no. 1 jerk in our regiment. No company commander could stand him for more than a month or two, so he was constantly being transferred. Now, it was my turn.

I sent him to the platoon commanded by Lieutenant Kennedy, with Sergeant White as the ranking NCO, and told them to put him on the front line. They assigned him a position and told him to dig a foxhole. It was pitch dark at the time. About an hour later, I heard a conversation on the sound-power telephone between Sergeant White and one of his men—something about a soldier digging a foxhole out in front of our line. When White went to investigate, he found Eightball.

"What the hell are you doing out there?" White yelled.

"I just thought I'd get a better line of fire from this position," Eightball replied.

After giving Eightball a severe chewing out, White took Eightball to his original position and told him to dig in. About an hour later, a flash of light illuminated Eightball's foxhole. He had struck a match to light a cigarette—strictly forbidden on the front lines because it usually brought a volley of enemy artillery.

At this point, Sergeant White brought Eightball to the company's command post and said, "Captain, we can't have this guy in our platoon. He's going to get us all killed."

I said, "OK, let him walk guard around the command post for the rest of the night."

Two minutes later, there was another flash of light. I was livid. I called them both over.

"Sergeant," I said, "if he lights another cigarette, shoot the son of a bitch on the spot—and that's an order."

Things were quiet for the rest of the night, but it wasn't over yet.

About 0900 the next morning, I looked out the window of my command post and saw a vehicle approaching from the same direction the enemy would be coming during an attack. I blinked my eyes in disbelief. Someone was driving a Lincoln automobile down the road that constituted our main line of resistance (MLR).

I said to Sergeant White, "Get that car out of there and bring it up to me before it attracts a barrage of artillery."

When the car arrived, I saw the grinning face of Eightball behind the wheel.

"How did you get this car?" I demanded.

Shrugging his shoulders, he said, "After finishing guard duty this morning, I knew you wouldn't be needing me for a few hours, so I hitched a ride into town [Nijmegen], went to see the mayor, and talked him into lending me his car so I could take a sight-seeing tour of the city. While driving around, I thought I'd cruise by our company area to be sure everything was OK."

He smiled. "It looks like all's quiet," he said, "so I guess I'll return the mayor's car."

I won't repeat what I said to him—and that wasn't the last time I had occasion to scream at him.

After two or three days in our position along the highway, we relieved a unit of the 508th PIR defending the east flank of the division near the Den Heuvel Woods, right on the German-Dutch border. (The 508th was an independent parachute infantry regiment frequently assigned to the 82d Airborne Division for combat missions.) By then—24 September, one week into the Netherlands campaign—I had already lost half of my company, which, at full strength, consisted of eight officers and 119 enlisted men. We spent the next several days defending our position and sending out patrols to capture enemy soldiers and to determine the enemy's strength. The Germans were doing the same thing, and it soon became evident that they were building up for a major attack. We had to be prepared.

Den Heuvel Woods consisted of a finger of trees projecting into an open field in front of our MLR. If the Krauts held these woods, they would be able to observe our every move, so Major Cook decided we should seize and hold it. We knew from previous patrol reports that Krauts were in the woods, but we didn't know how many.

On the night of 26 September, 2d Lt. Bernard Karnap took his I Company platoon, supported by British tanks, into the woods and wiped out a Kraut patrol. He had only one casualty. We called Karnap "Babyface," not only because of his cherubic look but because, like the gangster Babyface Nelson, he loved to kill, even if it meant exposing himself to danger. At that time, he must have already received four or five Purple Hearts.

The next night, Major Cook ordered me to take the rest of my company to the woods and set up a defensive position. Apparently, the shellacking that Karnap had given the Krauts alerted and angered them, so they were laying for us.

As soon as we had made our way into the woods, carefully and quietly, we heard the boom of the artillery and the whistle of shells. Then, the treetops burst into flames all around us and the ground shook like an earthquake.

From midnight until 0500, the Germans poured in the damnedest artillery barrage I had ever witnessed. An artillery barrage in the woods is deadly. As the shells hit the treetops and burst, they scatter a shower of shrapnel in every direction. Anyone without a cover over his foxhole became an endangered species. We hadn't had time to build covers, so our casualties were extremely high.

Just at daylight, the barrage was lifted as the Krauts jumped down our throats with three Tiger tanks and a battalion of SS troops. I saw my bazooka man fire at a Tiger tank and watched the shell bounce off the armor like a tennis ball. The tank continued forward and ran over him.

The three tanks continued to spit machine-gun and 20-mm fire into our position. During the artillery barrage, Sgt. Robert Dew, who was in the trench with me, had received a shrapnel wound in the chest, and Lieutenant Blankenship suffered a concussion. Dew, a huge, quiet man, lay gasping beside me. He was in a bad way. Two medics, one carrying a stretcher, came running toward us.

"Put the sergeant on your stretcher and get him out of here!" I yelled, knowing he couldn't last much longer without medical care.

They nodded, slid into the trench, and expertly rolled the sergeant onto the stretcher. Just as they had lifted him out and had started to move between the trees, a burst of 20-mm fire from one of the tanks ripped through the middle of the stretcher and killed Sergeant Dew instantly.

By this time, the tanks had overrun my frontline position, and the SS troops were moving along behind them. I could see the ground troops, their droopy helmets, and their weapons. They were so close we could have exchanged recipes. I radioed the situation to Major Cook, and he ordered us to withdraw to the battalion's MLR. No man moved from his position until I gave the order. By this time, the Krauts had overrun our position; as we withdrew, they were running side by side with my men, both sides shooting at each other.

As I was running across the open field just outside the woods, I tripped and fell. Just as I did, one of the Tiger tanks fired an 88 at me, and the shell whistled through the very spot where my head had been just a second earlier. It passed over me and blew apart the fellow running in front of me. I scrambled to my feet and continued running.

When we got back to the MLR and regrouped, twenty-three of my men were missing. I had lost half of my company while crossing the river, and now I had lost almost half of those remaining—after only eleven days of combat.

On the evening of 27 September, an Army Air Corps captain and lieutenant had dropped by battalion headquarters and spoken with Major Cook.

"We're on leave for a few days and just thought we'd like to see what frontline life was all about," the captain told him.

"And we'd like to pick up some souvenirs," the lieutenant said. "I'd like to get a Luger off a dead German."

Major Cook thought the pilots were crazy, but we were shorthanded, so he agreed. "OK," he said, "you can go with Burriss and I Company into the Den Heuvel Woods when darkness falls. There are plenty of dead Germans still in there."

As we entered the edge of the woods, we saw corpses of Krauts lying all over the place. Our men were ripping off their insignia, digging into their pockets, or just walking over them. But the flyboys seemed to be awed by the scene and walked around the bodies as if they were booby-trapped.

"When did all these Germans get killed?" the captain asked.

"Lieutenant Karnap brought his platoon down last night and wiped them out."

At about 2200 that night, one pilot strolled by my foxhole.

"What should we be doing?" he asked.

"Digging a foxhole," I told him.

"Why?" he asked.

At that moment, one of our nearby machine guns let out a burst of fire. A sergeant strolled over and said, "Captain, we just got four Krauts trying to sneak through."

The lieutenant shook his head in wonder.

"You mean you just killed four Germans?"

"Yep," the sergeant said and strolled back to his foxhole. The lieutenant took off to find the captain. They came back with two borrowed shovels and started digging in a frenzy.

The next morning during the withdrawal, I bumped into the captain and lieutenant about halfway back to the MLR. The lieutenant had caught a piece of shrapnel during the night, and the glassy-eyed captain was helping him hobble along.

I stopped them a few yards from one of our 37-mm antitank guns. As I was about to say something, the gun boomed, sending several rounds at a Tiger tank coming out of Den Heuvel Woods. The shells missed. The Tiger tank spouted flame, and it didn't miss. The 37-mm gun was turned into a steel pretzel, and the four-man crew was killed instantly. The body of one man sailed through the air and landed with a thud about three yards in front of us. His vacant eyes returned our stare.

I turned to the lieutenant.

"You need to get that wound dressed. The aid station's just ahead. Follow me."

As we approached the aid station, a mortar shell went through the roof and exploded. I rushed inside and found Lt. Charles ("Charlie") Snyder, one of my platoon leaders, lying unconscious on the floor. I knelt down, lifted his head into my lap, and said, "You're going to be OK, Charlie."

He let out a groan and that was his last breath. He was killed not by shrapnel but by the concussion. That was a hard one for me to take. Charlie was one of my best friends.

But I got up and led the lieutenant and the captain into the next room to see a medic. As the lieutenant was being treated, I turned to the captain and said, "Well, what do you think of the front line?"

He said, "I never had any idea of the kind of hell you guys go through. When we come off a bombing mission, an hour later we're at a bar having a drink, wearing clean clothes, eating three hot meals a day, sleeping in a bed. Sometimes we make snide remarks about the 'dog faces' down on the ground. If I ever hear one of my fellow pilots call you dog faces again, I'll knock his teeth out."

The lieutenant was evacuated, and he received a Purple Heart for his one day on the front line. The captain was diagnosed as suffering from shock, and I heard that his leave was extended during his stay in the hospital.

I wish I had their names and addresses so I could hear their versions of this nightmare fifty-four years later. They probably think it was a typical night on the front lines. I'd like to tell them that it wasn't. That night of 27 September was one of the worst nights I experienced in 2½ years overseas.

Pvt. Alfred ("Al") Essig was a member of I Company—a pathfinder (forward scout). He was captured at Den Heuvel Woods by the Germans and spent the last months of the war in a POW camp. This is his account:

> Although I was a pathfinder, I was also a member of I Company and was used as an infantryman, or regular soldier, when I wasn't being used as a pathfinder.
>
> After a pathfinding mission, several of us were ordered down to Devil's Den Woods. I still don't know why we were sent there, and no one ever told us. I'd still like to know, but Major Cook, who might have had the answer, is no longer around, and I think Colonel Tucker may be gone as well. I do know we had no withdrawal route except an open field and an open road, and we were approximately 2,000 yards ahead of the main fighting force.
>
> As we started down a slope, we heard an officer talking on a field telephone, screaming at someone at the other end of the line.
>
> "If you order I Company down into that wooded area with no withdrawal route and they get massacred there, I'll see to it you're court martialed."
>
> Apparently what he said made no impression, because we moved down the slope and entered Devil's Den Woods, where we were ordered to take up positions. Some of us positioned ourselves along the front edge of the woods, facing the Germans. Others were covering our rear. And a command post was set up about 200 yards behind me. To the rear, there was also a .30-caliber machine-gun nest about the same distance but to one side of the command post.

I don't remember who was manning the machine gun, but it was one of the original 82d Airborne men.

I moved up to the front line. We didn't dig foxholes, but we found some foxholes already there. I just lay down on the ground right at the front edge of the woods, approximately two feet back from the open field.

Things remained quiet all day, except for the occasional crack of a German sniper's rifle. I heard someone shout out that one of our I Company men had been killed. I crawled over to see who it was and discovered it was a guy I knew. Suddenly I was angry. I didn't have a sniper's rifle or sights, but I started firing my Thompson sub-machine gun across the field where I thought the sniper was lying, and another guy started blasting away with his M-1.

I lay at the edge of the woods for about two hours. It was still daylight when I saw a small figure—I'd say about 1,000 yards out—walking across the field from my left to my right. I took my M-1 and aimed about one inch above the figure as he was walking. Then I squeezed off a round. I knew that, at that distance, the bullet might fall a little short. But the figure dropped to his knees. I wondered if I'd hit him. I lowered the rifle another quarter inch and fired another round. The figure fell flat on the ground and never moved again. Without a sniper scope or an Enfield rifle, it was just luck. I was a sharpshooter, but I wasn't that good.

Later I got my Thompson submachine gun. If you've carried this weapon, you know that we taped two clips of ammunition together in reverse. When we fired off all the rounds in one 30-round clip, we could quickly eject it, flip it over, snap in the other 20-round clip, and have a total firing capacity of 50 rounds. I lay there cradling the gun as the sun set and darkness settled over the field and woods. I felt gratified that I'd probably killed a German soldier.

There was no moon that night; and as I lay in my position, I heard sounds in the black field ahead—the rustling of underbrush and hoarse whispers. From that direction it had to be an enemy patrol. Suddenly they passed within five feet of me—just at the edge of the woods.

I estimated the patrol consisted of six to eight men. When half had passed by, I came up on one knee and fired my Thompson sub-machine gun from right to left in one continuous burst. When I'd exhausted my 30 rounds, I hit the ground and reversed the ammunition clips, expecting return fire. None came.

Then, out of the darkness, I heard moaning, and a voice cried out in pain, "Mama, Mama." It was the voice of a young boy. At this point, with the Allies closing in on them, the Germans were sending untrained kids out on patrol rather than their elite troops. The kids were expendable.

I listened to these cries for about fifteen minutes. If he'd been vindictive, he could have tossed a grenade into the woods and I'd have been blown to bits. But he was in too much pain to care. He just wanted help.

I had three options. One was to fire another burst in his direction, hoping to hit a vital spot and put him out of his misery. The second was to go out and use my trench knife. The third was to try get him back to the command post, where I knew there was a medic—a low-ranking officer.

I took up my issue blanket, crawled out to where the German soldier lay, and spread out the blanket beside him. Then I rolled him onto the blanket. Every time I tried to touch him, my fingers went into his body and he screamed louder. I must have hit him six to eight times with those .45-caliber slugs, which make a pretty good-sized hole.

His German buddies should have been doing this job, but they were too afraid of my Thompson, so they let me drag him back to the command post on the blanket, screaming in pain all the way.

When I got there, the medic, a Second Lieutenant, was furious.

"What are you bringing him here for?" he yelled.

"I hoped someone would give the man some morphine to stop his pain."

"You get back to your position," he barked.

I did. But I could still hear the hollering. It lasted for about ten minutes. Then I heard a shot, followed by silence. The German soldier would feel no more pain.

As the field began to lighten with the dawn, Essig and his fellow troopers braced themselves, knowing that the Germans liked to attack at sunrise. They also knew that if it was a major force, the Germans would roll right over them. Their line was thin—the men were fifty to a hundred feet apart—but they had been ordered to hold their positions.

Essig continues:

Expecting the artillery barrage to come first, I spread my blanket out and lay my Thompson submachine gun on it, then I lay on top of the gun, knowing that if artillery shells started kicking up the ground, I would protect my gun from dirt or anything that might foul the mechanism.

Sure enough—at daybreak the barrage started. We weren't sure whether it was the Germans or our own fire falling short. Whichever it was, it literally tore those woods to pieces. In the middle of shells exploding and tree trunks splitting, I felt a sharp pain in my right leg. I was lying spread-eagled on the ground, and branches and clumps of dirt were falling everywhere. I was almost covered by both. I thought a piece of shrapnel had lodged in my right calf, but—buried under the rubble—I couldn't turn my head to look.

When the artillery barrage stopped, I started to brush off the leaves and debris in preparation for the German attack. But when I looked up, I saw three German soldiers, all pointing their machine pistols at me.

Right in front, about 20 feet away, rumbled a German tank, its 88-mm gun pointed right at me.

I weighed my options. I could try to get to my forty-five, but that would have been suicidal. Before I had moved my hand more than an inch, I would have had twenty rounds of ammunition in my body. Besides, I expected them to start firing at any instant. It was light enough, and they were close enough to put a bullet between my eyes.

A sudden calm came over me. Never—either in Sicily or on Anzio Beachhead—had I thought I would become a prisoner of war. And at that moment, I didn't think so either. I thought I was going to die, and I wasn't afraid. I just wondered what my mother would think when she heard about this.

Then two German soldiers bent over and pulled a huge branch off my leg. That was the pain I felt and not shrapnel.

Why they took me prisoner, God only knows. Right in front of me were the bodies of three German soldiers I had killed the night before. Yet they dragged me back towards their own lines and hauled me into a building. I don't remember much about the building, but there were six or seven other Americans already there. A German officer interrogated us one by one. He spoke perfect English, and I suspected he'd studied at one of the Ivy League universities.

Finally he got around to me. Every question he asked I would answer with my name, rank, and serial number—as we'd all been instructed to do. It was a little unnerving because, standing behind me, two German soldiers were pointing their rifles at my head.

Finally, the officer said to me, "I don't want to hear your name, rank, and serial number any more."

He asked the next question.

"Can you read a map?"

"No," I said.

"Do you know where you were captured?"

"No."

"Have you seen any British tanks?"

"No."

At this point, the officer lost his temper.

"Do you know I could have these two soldiers take you out into the courtyard and shoot you?"

Paratroopers have a certain swagger to them. We never quite lost that, even in the worst of situations.

"I don't know your rank," I said, "but I would guess you're a Lieutenant or a Captain. If I took you prisoner and interrogated you, would you answer my questions?"

He stiffened.

"Absolutely not."

"Well," I said, "I'm not going to answer yours either."

He turned to the two soldiers and said in German, "Take this schweinhund outside."

My grandparents were German, so I understood everything he said. But somehow I didn't believe they were going to kill me. I thought he was signaling that he'd finished with me.

Sure enough, the other prisoners and I boarded boxcars and rumbled off into Germany, where we were shuttled from one POW camp to another. Sometimes we'd stop for a week, then move on further and further down the track—always in the direction of Switzerland.

Essig lost about 50 pounds before he and other POWs were liberated by American troops.

After the Den Heuvel fiasco, the battalion, along with what was left of my company, moved to a new location, with the 1st and 2d Battalions on our right, in the vicinity of Inthal and Vossendaal.

The first day, I set up my command post in a small Dutch farmhouse. It was great to have a roof over my head for a change, but even greater to have a bathroom with a shower. Water for the shower was heated by a gas heater, which we lit, then waited until we had a full tank of hot water. I could hardly wait to get into the shower, and I vowed to stay in it until every drop of hot water was gone.

After about fifteen minutes, I started feeling a little light-headed and decided to step out of the shower. I staggered to the bathroom door, opened it, and fell semiconscious into the adjoining room. Lieutenant Blankenship, with the help of Pvt. Al Hermanson, an artillery forward observer, and another guy in the room, dragged me into the fresh air and revived me.

I had been almost asphyxiated by the unvented heater.

Still groggy, I put my bedroll on the floor and decided to take a nap. While I was asleep, Lieutenant Karnap came in and put his musette bag on the floor near my head.

"How're you doing?" he asked.

"OK," I said. "I just need a little sleep."

"In which case," he said, "I'll leave you alone."

He picked up his bag and went out the door. As he did, I heard something heavy hit the floor and then roll.

"Grenade!" someone yelled.

It *was* a grenade, and the pin had come out, activating the thing, which was about a foot from my head. I automatically rolled over, fortunately away from the grenade. At that moment, Booby Trap Blankenship grabbed a wadded blanket off the table and threw it on the grenade, then hit the floor. The explosion was deafening inside that room, but the blanket absorbed the shrapnel and saved my life.

I jumped up and chewed Karnap's ass. For about a week after that, he avoided me.

Hermanson, who was with the 376th Field Artillery Battalion, was attached to I Company at that time. This is his version of the hand grenade episode:

Besides me, there were two other men in the room on the floor in sleeping bags. Captain Burriss was one and Lieutenant Blankenship was the other. I was manning a sound-power telephone to our out-post positions. It was early morning, and another lieutenant came into the room, stirring, moving his gear around. He suddenly stopped and uttered an oath.

His voice rang with panic, so I turned to see. There on the floor was a GI fragmentation grenade, its fuse smoking. The ring had been caught in the netting of his helmet; and when he moved the helmet, out came the pin. The captain was still in his sleeping bag, one eye glaring at the device, not six feet from his head.

I instinctively hit the floor when the detonation came. The next thing I recall was a burning sensation in my eyes and the strong, acrid smell of spent powder.

I felt a hand probing me and a voice calling, "This one's OK. How's that one?"

It's hard to believe, but no one was hit. I've seen the same kind of grenade go off and give a man fifty yards away a chunk of iron in the butt.

And the day had just begun. Now it was the Krauts' turn to try and kill us. Late in the afternoon, they started firing Nebelwerfer rockets—we called them "screaming meemies"—into our position. As the rockets left the guns, they made a loud screaming noise that increased in intensity as they approached our position. When the noise suddenly stopped, that meant the rockets were starting to descend.

About dark, we heard a barrage of screaming meemies coming our way. One suddenly turned silent right in front of our position, and we waited for it to hit. It landed on the concrete walkway with a clang-clang-clang and then skidded toward the house and slammed into the front door. Expecting the house to disintegrate any second, we held our breaths. Nothing happened.

"It may be time delayed!" I yelled. "Get the hell out the back door!"

After a few minutes, we crawled around to the front of the house and there was the rocket—leaning against the front door.

We called for a bomb disposal squad, and three men arrived about an hour later. They approached the rocket slowly, the way one would approach a coiled rattlesnake. All three knelt down and looked it over without touching it. Then, with two of the men standing back, the third man began to disarm it with the care and precision of a brain surgeon. After what seemed ages, he stood up.

"It's a dud," he finally said, with a twisted grin.

At that moment, I said to myself, "This is the third time today lady luck has snatched me from the jaws of death."

After checking the frontline positions of my men, I returned to my little farmhouse to get a few hours of much needed sleep. Just before I dropped off, I said, "Thank you, Lord, for another day."

We stayed there for approximately three weeks. By then it was the middle of October. For the next month, our battalion remained in another defensive position in the vicinity of Vossendaal, Lagewald, Wyler, Inthal, and Zuffich. Virtually every night, we went on patrol with orders to make contact with enemy troops, harass them, and try to take prisoners. The Krauts did the same thing. Every day and night, the two sides exchanged mortar, artillery, and machine-gun fire. Casualties mounted daily. And also every day, because we were so close to the German border, we heard buzz bombs (unguided jet-propelled missiles) roar into the air and head westward toward London.

On 30 October, Lieutenant Kennedy and Sergeant White took a night patrol into enemy territory and ran into a minefield. Kennedy's foot was blown off. The men brought him back to the company command post, where they lay him down on a bed and ran for medics. I looked down and saw a bloody stump where his foot once had been.

He looked up at me with glazed eyes.

"Captain, my foot feels numb. Is it OK?"

I said, "It's banged up a bit, but you'll be fine. In a couple of hours, you'll be in a nice hospital, surrounded by pretty nurses, sleeping in a nice bed. You're a lucky guy."

He grinned and nodded.

On the way to the hospital, he went into shock and died. I couldn't believe it.

It was only after the medics had carried off Lieutenant Kennedy that one of the men came up to me and said, "Captain, we lost Sergeant White, too. Stepped on a mine."

I was stunned.

"Where is his body?"

"We had to get out in a hurry. We left him there."

I called the patrol together.

"Go find him, and bring him back. Now."

They searched all night and couldn't find his body, so I had to report him missing in action. Both Kennedy and White were fine soldiers—a great loss for I Company. But our company wasn't the only one that sustained such losses. Two days later, Lieutenant Wright of H Company was killed in a minefield.

About the middle of October, I received a call from Lt. Col. Warren Williams, Commanding Officer, 1st Battalion.

"You remember that fellow in your outfit who's always screwing up?"

"Eightball," I said.

"Yeah, well, we've got another one just like him here at battalion. I'm going to send him over to you. I want you to send this guy and Eightball on a two-man patrol into that village you're facing."

"That's a hot bed of Krauts," I told Colonel Williams.

"Precisely," the colonel said.

"Sounds good to me," I said. "Send your man over."

When the two men arrived, I briefed them on the importance of their mission.

"We need intelligence on the German outfit we're facing. So you've got to take at least one prisoner. Don't come back without a Kraut in tow."

"You can count on us, Captain," Eightball said, and the other man agreed. "We won't let you down."

About an hour later, Eightball came back to my command post, face blackened, wearing a camouflage helmet, two or three grenades, and a tommy gun. He had a wicked-looking knife in his hand.

"What do you want, Eightball?" I asked.

"I'd like you to take my picture, sir," he said. I had a camera handy, so I agreed. He put the knife between his teeth and posed for me.

The two of them set out shortly after dark. We listened all night but heard no gunfire in front of us. The next day and night, we had no news. I reported their absence to Colonel Williams.

"Sounds good," he said. "It looks like they got themselves captured. They'll drive the Germans crazy."

Then I checked with the 1st Battalion on our right flank and received a disturbing report. During the previous night, the two men had been seen moving back through our lines and toward the rear. They had disobeyed orders.

I called up the MPs and reported them AWOL (absent without leave). The MPs conducted a massive search in the townships behind us. Sure enough, they found the two men holed up in a Dutch civilian's home. They were put under arrest.

On 15 November, we were relieved by Canadian troops and moved in British trucks to Camp Sissonne in the town of Sissonne, France. We spent the next months in training replacements, getting new equipment, retrieving our wounded from the hospital, and going to Paris for a few days of R&R.

After we had moved back to Camp Sissonne, the MPs delivered Eightball to me to hold for trial. I put him under house arrest, which meant that he was confined to his quarters. He answered roll call the first morning; the second morning—no Eightball. We searched the camp but no Eightball.

I asked the men in the company if they knew where he might have gone. One raised his hand. "Sir, I did hear him say he'd like to see his girlfriend."

"Do you know where she lives?" I asked.

"In Leicester, England."

A search of his belongings turned up a letter with her name and address on it. I wired the MPs in Leicester. They wired back that he had been there the previous night but had already departed. They also reported that he had left a parachute with his girl so she could make a wedding dress. They planned to be married as soon as she got a divorce from her husband, who was a British soldier.

The next morning at roll call, Eightball answered, "Here!" The first sergeant sent him to my office for questioning.

I glared at him.

"Eightball, where the hell have you been?"

"Been?" he said, wide-eyed. "I haven't been anywhere."

"That's not what the MPs in Leicester told me yesterday."

"Oh, yes," he said, suddenly remembering. "I did drop over there a couple of days ago. And I planned to be back the next morning, but my plane was fogged in."

"Your plane? What plane? Tell me exactly what happened."

"Well, sir," he said, " I put on my major's oak leaf, went down to the airport, and hitched a ride to Leicester. I knew no training was scheduled for yesterday, so I didn't think you'd need me. Sorry about that extra day, but the fog prevented my plane from taking off."

"What about the parachute you left with your girl? Where did you get it?"

"That's the one I used when we jumped at Nijmegen. I've been saving it. I didn't think we'd be making any more jumps, so I gave it to her to make a wedding dress. Did you know that it's impossible to buy a silk dress in England?"

As I listened, I was saying to myself, "We've got him cold. AWOL. Impersonating an officer. Stealing a government parachute. Plus the charges in Holland."

I had him arrested and put in the regimental stockade. I told the police and prison sergeant to put him in a pup tent, keep an eye on him, and give him nothing but C rations and water.

At inspection the next morning, Eightball was discovered in his tent with a battery-powered radio, candy, cigarettes, and comic books. I told the prison sergeant to confiscate everything and not to let this happen again. The following morning, Eightball had cigarettes and comic books.

I chewed out the prison sergeant and concluded by saying, "If this happens again, you'll be in the tent with him."

The next morning—no candy, no cigarettes, no comic books, and no Eightball. He wasn't anywhere in the stockade. He had escaped.

An investigation revealed that when the guard changed at midnight, Eightball walked up to the new man and said that he was the prison sergeant. He pointed at his tent. "I want you to watch the guy in there. He's a slippery son of a bitch."

Then he walked out of the stockade, through the main gate of the camp, borrowed $5 from the gate guard, and disappeared.

The next day, we had every MP in France looking for him. He didn't surface. Then, a few days later, he showed up at the stockade.

"Let me in," he said. "My conscience has been bothering me."

On 17 December 1944, the Battle of the Bulge started, and our unit was moved to the front again. Eightball was left behind in the stockade. What happened to him after we left, I don't know. I never saw him again. But of one thing I'm certain—he was never tried because all the witnesses were gone. He probably ended up as prison sergeant. Maybe he came home and ran for Congress. He would have prospered in Washington.

After all these years, I can laugh at the antics of Eightball, though they weren't funny at the time. When I think of Operation Market-Garden, however, I still feel anger and frustration over the loss of so many men in a failed effort that could have been successful.

Who was to blame? Fifty years later, the argument still rages.

Carrington maintains his position that he acted properly. Carrington told me that he didn't have orders to move forward after his lead tank was knocked out. He was the senior British officer at the battle site, but the man in command of British tanks was General Horrocks. I'm convinced that Horrocks told Carrington to stay exactly where he was, thereby dooming not only the rescue mission but also the entire operation to end the war.

Some have asserted that the British tanks were held back by a shortage of gasoline and ammunition. If so, why did Horrocks boast earlier that day that his tanks would be out "in full force?" Was that just an empty boast? Hadn't he checked his own supplies? Besides, if he couldn't have committed all his tanks, he could have sent at least a scaled-down force, which, with the fuel and ammunition available, might have turned the tide. Given the stakes, it was certainly worth a try.

Others have claimed that the supporting infantry was tied up in a traffic jam south of Nijmegen and was not available to support a tank attack. That's baloney. Despite our heavy losses, I told Carrington that we were prepared to back them up, to knock out the single gun that had disabled their lead tank, and to move with them to Arnhem. German documents reveal that had we removed the gun, we would have encountered no more heavy fire between that site and Arnhem.

Still others have maintained that the difficulty lay in the terrain—the road from Nijmegen to Arnhem was elevated and not suitable to support a tank attack. That observation is certainly true, but this was also true of many other roads along the attack route. The elevation of the road was known in the planning stage of Operation Market-Garden, and it was certainly understood by the decision makers just hours before the bridge was taken.

Perhaps the road was not favorable for an armored attack. Maybe Captain Carrington would have lost several of his tanks. But would that have been as bad as losing the lives of all those British and Polish paratroopers at Arnhem?

In this soldier's opinion, had General Patton been in command with his tank corps, without question, he would have been in Arnhem in an hour. Colonel Tucker said as much in a later statement, quoted in Cornelius Ryan's *A Bridge Too Far:*

> We had killed ourselves crossing the Waal to grab the north end of the bridge. We just stood there, seething, as the British settled in for the night, failing to take advantage of the situation. We couldn't understand it. It simply wasn't the way we did things in the American army—especially if it had been our guys hanging by their fingernails eleven miles away. We'd have been going, rolling without stop. That's what Georgie Patton would have done, whether it was daylight or dark.

In fact, Tucker had considered sending the 82d paratroopers to Arnhem on their own, but he finally concluded that General Gavin would never have approved such a decision.

No, Arnhem was not a "bridge too far." It was a British general unwilling to go far enough—a general who broke his word.

I know. I was there and heard him with my own ears: "My tanks will be lined up in full force at the bridge, ready to go, hell-bent for Arnhem. Nothing will stop them."

We crossed the river, captured the bridge, and suffered some of the greatest number of casualties during the European war, but General Horrocks refused to follow up with his tank attack. He failed us and failed his own troops. And General Browning apparently went along with Horrocks.

As a result, our battalion lost some of the finest men ever to wear the American uniform. Not one of them hesitated to plunge into the water, cross the Waal in a canvas boat as bullets rained all around him, run across 900 yards of flat land into the teeth of machine guns, and help to capture the bridge at Nijmegen in order to save the lives of British troops they had never seen. Had Horrocks and his tankers shown the same kind of bravery, I'm convinced that together we could have rescued the surviving remnant of paratroopers at Arnhem and turned Operation Market-Garden into an Allied victory. All of our bloodshed was in vain, however, because of a lack of will at the crucial moment.

Upon returning to the battle scenes of World War II after fifty years, I felt a profound sadness as I stood in the American cemetery at Anzio and touched the white crosses marking the graves of my dead comrades. I felt the same way in Belgium, at the place where we had fought the Battle of the Bulge. But when I was standing in the Liberation Museum in Groesbeek near Nijmegen and looking at the bronze plaques that listed the names of all the men killed during Operation Market-Garden, my sadness and my admiration for the courage of those who died there was mixed with a bitterness and anger undiminished after half a century.

— 9 —

The Battle of the Bulge

W e came late to the party, after the Germans had launched a last-ditch major attack directed at a weak spot in our line along the Ardennes region of Belgium and northern Luxembourg. They had massed all their forces—some 500,000 men—at that particular point to launch the attack.

We were still at Sissonne when we received our orders. At about 2230 on the night of 17 December 1944, all company commanders were called to Battalion Headquarters. A grim-faced Colonel Tucker was waiting for us.

"Gentlemen," he said. "The Krauts have scored a major breakthrough in Belgium. The situation is desperate. As best we know, here's what happened.

"The First Army and Third Army of the 12th Army Group were defending the line between the Huertgen Forest and the Luxembourg border. They'd taken a beating, and since nothing seemed to be happening at that position, General [Omar N.] Bradley sent the 106th [Infantry] Division and the 9th Armored Division—units just off the boat—to relieve the 4th and 28th. The 106th and the 9th Armored are composed almost entirely of men who've never been under fire.

"As soon as they moved up to take over, the Krauts hit with everything they had—artillery, Panther and Tiger tanks, the best troops they've got left—several hundred thousand of them, as best we can tell. They overran our new guys in a matter of hours. What's more, they captured men, ammunition, and equipment.

"At this moment our lines are weak and wavering. We've been ordered to move in, reinforce the green troops, and drive the Krauts back. Tonight, I want you to issue battle equipment, ammunition, and K rations and be ready to move out at 0900 tomorrow morning."

Then, an officer from S3 took over to talk about tactics.

"OK, men," he said, "here's what you'll be facing. Rolling hills, woods, and valleys. Lots of rivers and streams. This is farm country, so mostly you'll see houses, barns, and not much else. The fields are covered with snow, and S2 tells us that the Krauts are dressed in white parkas, so they'll be more difficult to see than we will."

We groaned. We knew we would be wearing our camouflage fatigues and hence easy targets as we moved against a backdrop of steadily falling snow. The S3 officer held up his hand.

"There's a positive side to the situation. This is not good tank country. In the first place, you'll be able to spot Panther and Tiger tanks more easily in the snow—and that helps to even things up. Also, there are too many deep creeks and rivers for the tanks to move forward easily. If we blow a few key bridges, we can keep them off our backs.

"Our orders are to make contact with the enemy and hold our position for a few days—until General Patton can move up with the Third Army. At that point, we'll have artillery, tanks, and maybe some help from the First Army. With that kind of support, we should be able to drive the Krauts out of Belgium.

"Until then, we'll be fighting them with rifles, Gammon grenades, mortars, and bazookas."

We nodded. We'd been there before—at Anzio.

"One more thing. We have to be doubly careful. We've already heard that Germans, dressed in U.S. Army uniforms and driving jeeps, have been slipping back through our lines. So we'll be changing passwords frequently. Question everybody you come across. If they don't know the password, kill them on the spot. We can't take any chances."

Such an order didn't surprise us. We knew the Krauts were desperate, and we were prepared to confront them with desperate measures of our own.

After the S3 officer sat down, I raised my hand.

"Colonel Tucker, some of my men are still in Paris on leave. They won't know about this."

"Yes, they will," the Colonel said. "As we speak, all military personnel in Paris are being rounded up. Your men should be back by daylight."

He was right. Swearing and complaining, they came piling in toward morning, but they immediately began to pack their gear. When the time came to move out, they were all ready.

We climbed on board Air Corps semitrucks and moved out of Camp Sissonne about 1030 the next morning and arrived at Werbomont, Belgium, about 0130 after passing near the city of Bastogne, Belgium.

The 101st Airborne Division being trucked behind us wasn't so lucky. As we moved beyond Bastogne, a German force crossed to our rear and cut off the 101st.

The situation was critical. The Krauts had gained confidence from their success with our inexperienced replacements, and they were poised to cut another "green" unit to pieces. Maj. Gen. Maxwell Taylor was divisional commander of the 101st, but he had flown to Washington for a few days. Brig. Gen. Anthony McAuliffe, assistant divisional commander, was in charge.

At that point, the Germans sent General McAuliffe a note demanding that he surrender his entire division. Obviously, they didn't know they were facing veteran paratroopers. McAuliffe gave his now famous reply—"Nuts."

The men of the 101st were subsequently besieged for a week and their casualties were heavy, but they held the line, killed large numbers of German troops, and helped to stall the German offensive. It was a heroic, epic defense, but, in some ways, we liked to think that the 101st didn't have it as tough as we did. In reality, both of our units were getting shot to pieces. They were getting pounded in and around Bastogne, while we were living in the country, crouching in snow-banked foxholes, and fighting tanks with hand weapons.

As we moved into position, we saw the devastation caused by the German attack—charred shells of U.S. vehicles, some of them still smoking; the evacuation of wounded Americans; and the snowscape scattered with mess gear, remnants of half-tents, masses of twisted steel, and other debris.

The first day, the company commanders sent out patrols to probe the Kraut positions. The men from I Company fanned out to the right and left to determine who was on our flanks and eventually linked up with our own troops. We encountered no resistance straight ahead, only a white snow scene that could have been painted by Grandma Moses. Yet we knew that, at any second, a snow bank could transform itself into a platoon of Krauts wearing white parkas.

Elsewhere, other patrols engaged the enemy almost immediately and dug in, with orders to hold their positions against any further attack. Clearly, the line was ragged, marked by salients where the Germans had penetrated more deeply.

Having determined that the Krauts weren't directly in front of us, Colonel Tucker ordered us to move forward the next day until we made contact with the enemy. The 82d was located in the vicinity of the towns of Stoumont, La Gleize, and Cheneux. I Company was positioned near Cheneux. As we approached the town, we heard the simultaneous popping of gun and rifle fire ahead and the soft kerplunk of bullets striking the drifted snow around us. We immediately returned the fire and dug in, as ordered.

Then, we heard a more ominous sound—Kraut tanks rumbling in the distance. The dreaded Tigers began zeroing in on our position, along with a highly visible flak wagon, a lightly armored half-track with automatic 20-mm and 9-mm machine guns. I realized we might be pinned down and blown to bits. With only hand weapons to combat the German tanks and artillery, we were sitting ducks.

The flak wagon was located close to our lines. From that range, its firepower was withering, but, in its advanced position, the unit was also relatively unprotected and therefore vulnerable. So I dispatched a squad to ambush the wagon. As always, the men moved out without hesitation—dark silhouettes against the white backdrop. Ignoring the heavy bombardment, they flanked the flak wagon and then rushed in, killed the crew, and captured the equipment intact.

We immediately turned the flak wagon's 20-mm gun on the Krauts, along with our own machine-gun and mortar fire, and repelled the attack.

I sent out a patrol to explore our right flank, and the men encountered the American 119th Infantry Regiment. We immediately closed the gap and presented a solid front, from which we continued to exchange small-arms, mortar, and artillery fire with the Germans. As long as they didn't launch a major attack, we could afford to sit tight and wait for General Patton. If the Third Army was on its way, we knew we wouldn't be pinned down for long. Soon enough, we would break out and go on the offensive.

A heavy fog had hung over the entire area for more than a week. For a while, we thought that nature was conspiring against us. The Germans had a major armored force and more artillery, so, under present circumstances, we were outgunned. Because our fighter-bombers—the best equalizers we had—couldn't fly in that fog, the Germans were able to bombard us almost at will, but we held our position.

On the evening of 23 December, the fog finally broke. At dawn on Christmas Eve, the sky was a clear blue—an early Christmas present to the beleaguered Americans. We awoke to the sound of motors droning above us. These weren't the Piper Cubs that had been flying below the fog to reconnoiter the German troops. They were our fighter-bombers. Then, we heard the rumble of explosions all along the German lines.

On Christmas Day, some of the Allied forces were on the move, but we were still holding our position against superior numbers. The ground was covered with two inches of snow. My command post was my foxhole, and my Christmas dinner was a can of C rations.

As I made my rounds to visit my men, I said two things: "Merry Christmas" and "I've arranged for a fireworks display later in the day." They grinned wryly. They knew that the German guns, silent for the moment, would begin to pound us again before the day was over. And Kraut ground forces might also make one more attempt to break through our lines.

Sure enough, at about 1700, our position was attacked by a company of Krauts supported by tanks. The flashes and booms beat any 4th of July celebration we had ever seen. Perhaps it was even the biggest Christmas display of the century. We called in artillery and mortar fire and turned our captured 20-mm gun on them, which inflicted heavy casualties and sent them into frantic retreat.

Then we received word that the Krauts had converged on a section in the middle of our lines. They were bunched together as they attempted to find a place to cross the Meuse River. All bridges had been blown. Suddenly, an attack that appeared to be successful had stalled and left the Krauts stranded and vulnerable. We moved out immediately.

In the days immediately following Christmas, we continued to exchange fire and move forward, now in the vicinity of Manhay, Beneau, Bra, Floret, and Lierneux. The first week in January, Second Lieutenant Amos and his platoon, along with tank support, attacked Mont and Petit-Halleux and cleared out the villages. Although both of his feet were injured by a mine, Amos kept on going. Lieutenant Reese returned to the company area with thirty-four Kraut prisoners.

It was evident that the Kraut offensive was losing its punch. The bridges across the many canals and streams were blown, which halted the German tanks. Our artillery and armor strength was increasing daily, and we were unmercifully pounding the Krauts. By then, the snow, which had continued to fall, was waist deep.

We began to inch our way toward the town of Herresbach. Because of the snow, progress was slow—about 100 yards an hour when there was no opposition. The point men, who were breaking a trail in the drifts, had to be relieved every thirty minutes.

As I walked along behind the scouts, I noticed an unfamiliar officer coming up behind me. When he came closer, in helmet and fatigues, I saw that he had a baby face and thought he couldn't be more than 18—just a kid slogging through the snow in a faraway country. But I knew that he wasn't one of my men. Then, I saw the two stars on his helmet. It was General Gavin, who was thirty-four years old but still looked like a high school senior.

"General," I said, "you shouldn't be up here with the scouts. There's too much danger of your being picked off by a sniper."

"Don't worry, Captain," he said, "I'll be OK."

He stayed with us until dark, then rolled out his blanket and slept for a couple of hours until we moved out again. He wanted to see what was happening on the front lines, and, like the best field officers, he wasn't afraid.

On the other hand, the danger was very real. During one of the breaks on this trek, I was standing behind Cpl. Ed Hahn when a sniper took a shot at him when he was bending over. The bullet went between his helmet and his head and cut a groove across his scalp. When he removed his helmet and put his hand on his scalp, it was quickly covered with blood. I could see the panic in his eyes.

I knew from experience that scalp wounds often bleed a lot, so I quickly examined his head and reassured him, "Just a scrape. They can fix you up in no time."

He brightened up and said, "That's great. It will get me out of this damn snow."

I agreed. He was lucky. A warm bed, pretty nurses, three good meals, and a Purple Heart.

After our company had taken the point for awhile, we switched and H Company went ahead. The next day, as Lieutenant Magellas and his platoon reached the edge of the woods, he spotted a Kraut company moving across an open field right in front of him. He immediately got on the phone and called for three tanks to support his attack. The Krauts kept moving, still unaware that they were about to be ambushed.

When Magellas and his men opened fire, the Germans were caught by surprise and could find no place to take cover. It was a massacre. The white landscape turned red with German blood. Magellas and his men killed almost one hundred Krauts and captured many more.

Lieutenant Sims was also in the Battle of the Bulge. This is his account of the action:

On 16 December 1944, the Germans, in a major offensive, penetrated Allied defense positions in Belgium. The 504th Parachute Infantry Regiment was immediately alerted, then ordered into Belgium on 18 December. The lead element of the regiment—on semi-trucks—departed from Camp Sissonne at 0900 hours and arrived at Werbomont, Belgium, about 1730 hours the same day.

There we went into a hasty defense northeast of the town. On route to Werbomont, we could see a number of U.S. artillery pieces that had been abandoned in place.

On 19 December, the 3d Battalion, my unit, moved to the east on what became a most fluid combat action. Near the town of Rahier, we contacted and relieved an element of the U.S. 119th Infantry, and a few moments later, we had our first contact with German troops, whom we quickly routed.

On 20 December, the 1st Battalion was ordered to take the town of Cheneux. G Company of the 3d Battalion was attached to them because A Company was not available. The attack started at 1400 hours but hit stiff resistance from elements of the German 1st SS Panzer Division. Probing action continued through the night without progress.

The next day, my company helped to seize the village of Monceau, north of Cheneux, then turned to attack the northern part of Cheneux. As the 1st Battalion consolidated their position in the town, my unit drove the Cheneux defenders back across the L'Ambleve River, then set up a defense along the river bank.

At this point, I felt a wetness on my left hip, and when I reached back, I discovered that my canteen had been penetrated by a slug that left a jagged hole where it came out.

The after action report for Cheneux lists, in addition to many German casualties, the following items captured: fourteen flak wagons, six half-tracks, four trucks, four howitzers, and a Mark VI tank. Other units of the 82d Airborne Division were also engaged with elements of the 1st SS Panzer Division near Trois Points, Ottre, and Regne.

On 24 December, my unit moved to a new position southwest of Lurneux and there repulsed a strong enemy attack. The next day, the 3d Battalion occupied a defensive position on the right flank of the regiment's defense line, which extended along the line of Bergifax-Bra-Vaux-Chavanne. On the 82d Airborne Division's right was the 7th U.S. Armored Division and on the left was the U.S. 30th Infantry Division.

On 27 December, while checking company positions with two platoon leaders (Lieutenants Magellas and La Riviere), we ran into a German patrol. The three of us became involved in a firefight with the Germans. Magellas tossed a fragmentation grenade, which exploded in their midst as they scattered. At the same time, La Riviere was able to get the attention of a few of his men about 100 yards away and ordered them to fire on the patrol. Later, we moved into the area the patrol had occupied and took one prisoner. A number of dead bodies lay on the ground, and the rest of the patrol had withdrawn. After this action, we shifted our right flank to cover the hidden road the patrol had used.

On 28 December, our company positions were subjected to a major attack by a large force from the German 9th SS Panzer Division. For several hours, we engaged in stiff fighting and sustained heavy artillery fire. Then suddenly the Germans withdrew and left many casualties in front of us which, in time, we had to deal with. This same day other units on line were attacked by the German 62d Volks Grenadier Division. On our left, a battalion's position was overrun, but they remained in place long enough for a reserve unit to move in. At this point, the Germans withdrew. These German failures ended their offensive efforts in our area. From this time on, they resorted to defensive and delaying strategies.

On 4 January 1945, the 3d Battalion assumed responsibility for part of the 517th sector and conducted an attack to take the high ground south of Fosse. During this attack the company commander was wounded and evacuated, so I again assumed command of Company H and continued to direct our attack on Grand Halleux on the east side of the Salm River. Later we cleared pockets of resistance in Petit Halleux on our side of the river. On 11 January, we were replaced by units of the U.S. 75th Division and moved to a reserve position near Remouchamps.

As the Battle of the Bulge progressed, we continued to hear stories about Krauts going to battalion and regimental headquarters, posing as American troops from an adjacent unit, looking over our battle plans, and then slipping back across their lines.

In addition to changing our password frequently, we also challenged unfamiliar troops with such questions as "Who won the World Series last year?" or "What's your shoe size?" If we didn't get the right answers, we shot them. We didn't run across any infiltrators, but H Company did. Lieutenant Sims reports on the incident:

On 27 January, the regiment moved to an area near Hunnage, north of St. Vith, and the following day moved northeast through the 7th Armored Division in pursuit of the withdrawing Germans.

The snow was deep. And over our clothing we wore white mattress covers that had been altered by women at Remouchamps.

Approaching the town of Herresbach, we spotted a U.S. jeep coming toward our lead element. Suddenly we realized there were German soldiers in it. The platoon leader at the head of the unit lifted his rifle to his shoulder and shot the driver. The other three, including an officer, were taken prisoner.

The first week in February, we hit our last formidable barrier—the Siegfried Line, named after the epic hero of Germanic folklore. The fabled defense perimeter consisted of concrete "teeth" four feet high, spaced three or four feet apart. Inside the concrete barriers were bunkers in which troops could eat, sleep, and live for long periods of time. Also called "the dragon teeth," the Siegfried Line was laced with land mines and covered by artillery fire.

As we prepared to breach the line, we were reinforced by tanks, tank destroyers, and artillery. The fire from both sides was extremely heavy, and so were the casualties. Fortunately, we had the greater firepower, inflicted more casualties, and accomplished our mission, but not before we had rushed the bunkers with bazookas and grenades. We directed our machine-gun and rifle fire at the die-hard German soldiers blasting away at us through slits in the concrete.

Lieutenant Sims gives additional details about the tactics that we used to breach the Siegfried Line and to penetrate into Germany:

On 30 January, H Company attacked to seize the high ground west of Holzheim, Belgium. On 2 February, we moved east through the 505th to attack the Siegfried Line in the Mertesrott Heights/Forest Gerolstein area south of Neuhof in Germany. This defensive line was composed of rows of concrete pillboxes, trenches, and elaborate concrete forts (bunkers) with walls many feet thick and numerous firing ports placed to cover the most likely approaches.

The Germans who occupied the bunkers slept and ate inside and were able to communicate with troops in other bunkers using an underground phone system.

It was difficult to seize these bunkers. The German troops inside at first refused to surrender and would even call for their own artillery to fire on the bunker while we were outside. We used rocket launchers and Composition C to blast our way through the heavy steel doors below ground level. Once we were inside, the occupants surrendered. Fortunately for us, the fortifications that composed the Siegfried Line were not fully manned.

On 4 February, we were replaced on line by units of the U.S. 99th Infantry Division and moved to an area near Schidthof, Germany. And, during the period of 10–13 February, we attacked eastward with other units of the 82d Airborne Division to help seize the high ground dominating the west bank of the Roer River. Elements of the 504th Parachute Infantry Regiment then occupied an area on the river, extending north from Zerkall, Germany. My unit prepared to cross the river to seize Nideggen; but on 19 February, the U.S. 9th Infantry Division replaced the entire 82d Airborne Division, which returned to France. My unit went to a new location near Laon.

The U.S. Army's casualty report for the entire European Theater during December exceeded seventy-eight thousand. In addition, non-combat losses numbered fifty-six thousand. Most of these men were either disabled or had died as the result of disease and exposure. The price was heavy, but the Battle of the Bulge sealed the fate of Nazi Germany.

Hitler's last-gasp effort to regain momentum and prevent the Allies from entering the Fatherland had failed. The Krauts had been stopped. When we broke through the Siegfried Line, we were trespassers on German soil, the hallowed ground of the Third Reich. The 3d Battalion had again accomplished its mission against strong odds. We had fought through two months of freezing hell; confronted tanks with rifles, mortars, and grenades; and never backed up.

There are no words in my vocabulary to describe properly the bravery and determination of the men in my company. They gave everything they had, including, in some cases, their lives.

With the Siegfried Line behind us, its teeth pulled forever, we moved back to Schmidthol, then Aachen, and on to Camp Sissonne, where we arrived on 21 February to await word on our next mission. But we all knew the end was in sight. The Krauts were retreating now at a more rapid rate, and they were running out of real estate. Both sides could feel the shift in momentum. When troops are being pounded by a well-trained, well-equipped enemy, their self-esteem can suffer and they often take a gloomy view of life and of the future. But when they know that they have the upper hand, the adrenaline starts flowing and they engage the enemy with enthusiasm and confidence.

I'm sure the German troops were driven by adrenaline during the first stages of the war when they were running over France, Belgium,

Holland, Poland, and the rest of Eastern Europe, including huge chunks of Russia. Now, they were demoralized and stripped of hope.

On the other hand, our troops, even the hard-bitten veterans of the 82d Airborne, were ready to cross the Rhine and race the Russians to Berlin. Somehow, we knew we had fought our last desperate battle. Never again would we be decimated by superior firepower, as we were at Anzio, Normandy, Nijmegen, and Belgium. From here on, the Germans would be outmanned and outgunned.

We knew that we would still encounter tough resistance. Units would get into tough spots, and more of us would lose our lives, but American Forces weren't going to lose any more battles. We knew that, very soon, the Germans would surrender and we would be going home. That knowledge, too, spurred us on to fight even harder.

—10—

To the Heart of the Reich

On 2 April 1945, our battalion left Camp Laon in France and traveled by truck and train to an area slightly northwest of Cologne. Our mission was to establish a defensive position on the west bank of the Rhine; send patrols across the river in the vicinity of Hitdorf and Rheindorf; determine the enemy's strength; and, at an appropriate time, cross the Rhine in strength and continue our push toward Berlin.

Initially, G Company sent a patrol across the river in two boats to probe the area and take prisoners. The patrol ran into opposition, one man was killed and three wounded, and the rest of the patrol was forced to withdraw across the river. Lt. Tom McLeod, a fellow South Carolinian, and two of his men from the 307th Engineers accompanied G Company on this mission.

The next night, H Company sent a patrol across the river, and it also was involved in a firefight. The patrol lost three men, who were reported missing in action.

The following day, we looked across the Rhine and saw a strange sight. A German officer and several enlisted men on the east bank of the Rhine were about to launch a boat. One of the men was carrying a pole, at the top of which a white flag flapped in the stiff wind. We watched as the men pulled on the oars, while the officer—a colonel, it turned out—stood in the bow of the ship like Washington crossing the Delaware. No one fired on them.

We wondered if the colonel was coming to surrender his command. Clearly, the Krauts were beaten, and we had heard rumors that German surrender was imminent. (In fact, VE-Day was still weeks away.)

When the Germans landed, the colonel, an older man with hollow cheeks and a soiled uniform, said he would like to speak to our commander, so we sent him back to Regimental Headquarters. He and his men were interrogated for two days and then released. He had not come to surrender, we later learned, but to request that we stop firing into the German hospital zone. Our regimental commander assured him that we would honor his request, despite the fact that the Germans at Anzio had deliberately turned their guns on our hospital tents and hospital ship.

On the night of 5 April, A Company established a bridgehead across the Rhine River in the town of Hitdorf. We had finally crossed the Rhine, an achievement that encouraged us to believe that the war would soon end.

The Germans, too, understood the significance of our presence on the sacred soil of the Fatherland, and they fought more fiercely than ever. On the night that A Company landed on the east bank of the Rhine, the Krauts threw everything they had—artillery and large numbers of infantry—at the invaders. A Company was forced to decrease the size of its bridgehead so that its men could defend themselves.

At that point, the strategists in our high command decided to send two platoons of I Company across the river to help A Company establish the bridgehead, then move southeast to Khindorf to seize and occupy the town. We left our 3d Platoon behind to occupy our position on the west bank.

At 0030 on 6 April, we launched nine boats containing men from the 1st and 2d Platoons. As company commander, I was on board one of the boats, which were made of metal, not canvas, for this crossing and moved more swiftly across the water.

We tried to make as little noise as possible, but the oars from nine vessels made enough of a splash to catch the ears of the Krauts. As we shoved off and began to row, four spotlights suddenly lit up on the opposite shore—four gleaming eyes that sent their beams all the way across the wide river and highlighted our boats. In an instant, we were the target of dense machine-gun and artillery fire. For a few moments, I thought I was back at Nijmegen. Then, an explosion flipped our boat into the air, and all of us on board went sprawling into the cold water.

As I swam to the surface, I was mentally checking my body for shrapnel wounds and was relieved to conclude that I hadn't been hit. I realized, however, that I wasn't out of danger. In addition to the continual rain of bullets, I found it extremely difficult to swim with boots, clothing, and equipment weighing me down. The other men, thrashing about in the water, were having the same difficulty.

"Swim back to the shore where we came from," I shouted and struck out in that direction. The west bank was much closer. Besides, much of our arsenal had sunk with our boat and we wouldn't have been equipped to fight, even if we could have made it to the far bank.

When I was about 50 feet from shore, the guy swimming next to me said, "Help! I can't make it!" Sergeant Johnson was swimming next to me, and I called to him, "Sergeant, you grab one shoulder and I'll grab the other, and we'll pull him ashore."

We grabbed him, but it was so dark, I couldn't see who it was. We reached the bank and dragged him out of the water. The three of us lay there for a minute as we sputtered and gasped for breath. Lying on my back, I turned to the man, who was lying on his face. "Who are you?" I asked.

"It's me, Captain," he said. "It's Martin."

"What were you doing on that boat?" I asked. "I told you to stay back at the command post."

"I know, Captain, but I didn't want you going without me. I was afraid you might need me."

"It looks like you needed me instead," I said.

The rest of the 1st and 2d Platoons had made it across. On our side of the river, the 3d Platoon was countering the German fire with mortars and all other weapons at its disposal. When he saw my boat had been sunk, Lieutenant Karnap, who had made it across, took over command on the German side. Leaving one squad to guard the boats, he formed the remainder of the two platoons and led them toward the center of the town to contact A Company.

As they moved along a road that paralleled a railroad track, the night suddenly lit up with the flashes of several machine-gun muzzles.

The nests were located along the railway. Karnap split his force into several small patrols, flanked the enemy, and either killed the machine gunners or drove them out of their positions.

While the 2d Squad of the 1st Platoon cleared the railroad area of snipers and pushed eastward to protect the flank of the platoons, the now decreased main force moved north and then west to the command post of A Company to get an estimate of the situation from its commander. It was grim. Men from the 2d Platoon of A Company had been cut off from the rest of the force and were holed up in the town church, where they were surrounded by Germans. The first order of business, therefore, was to break through the German lines and relieve the 2d Platoon. At the same time, I Company still had the mission of seizing and occupying Khindorf.

The commander of A Company, as ranking officer, gave the orders. The 2d Squad, 2d Platoon, was to move northward to cover the road that ran along the railroad track and also to cover the streets running east and west in the northern section of the town. At the same time, the 1st Squad, 1st Platoon, was to move southward and establish a roadblock on the main road entering the town from that direction. The 1st Squad, 2d Platoon, was to move northeast and establish a line of defense along the main road running north and south through the town. With the sole remaining squad (3d Squad, 2d Platoon), the commander of A Company set out toward the church to relieve the surrounded 2d Platoon of A Company.

No squad had an easy task that night. Each was constantly harassed by small groups of enemy troops, who fired at them from the second-story windows of houses and from dark alleys. While moving along its route, the 2d Squad, 2d Platoon, encountered a large enemy patrol that was attacking from the northern part of town. Instead of turning tail in the face of overwhelming odds, our men charged the enemy patrol, killed twelve men, wounded five, and drove the survivors out of town.

Though engaging in a fierce fight with the enemy, the 1st Squad, 2d Platoon, reached its objective. Hastily preparing a line of defense to the east, it repelled two enemy attacks of platoon strength (four times its size).

Meanwhile, the various squads of the 1st Platoon were battling their way forward. The men of the 1st Squad had reached the main road entering the town and were in the act of establishing a roadblock when a company of Germans, supported by two tanks, attacked their position. For awhile, they were in deep trouble as the tanks laid down a murderous barrage. Despite the squad's effort to prevent the Krauts from breaking through, the overwhelming size of the enemy force compelled its men to give ground.

Then, at the very minute when it seemed impossible to contain the German counterattack, the 2d Squad, 1st Platoon, reached the enemy flank and opened fire. The Krauts, believing they had been enticed into a death trap, turned and fled in wild confusion. They abandoned their weapons and scattered in every direction.

When the 3d Squad, 2d Platoon, reached its corner, the men were fired on by tanks and a platoon of infantry from the next block. Dividing into two units, on each side of the street, they closed with the enemy under cover of darkness. They fired their weapons from their hips and tossed Gammon and fragmentation grenades as they charged. In this furious assault by the nine men of the squad, they killed eighteen of the enemy, wounded that many more, and knocked out one of the tanks.

Reassembling, they crept toward the church to rescue the surrounded A Company platoon. When they were in sight of the churchyard, they were fired on by two enemy machine guns and several machine pistols. Our men immediately sought cover behind a building, while the enemy turned again to the trapped platoon. But our men didn't stay put. They stole down an alley in back of the house, then crawled along a hedge until they had penetrated the circle and were behind the Germans. On cue, they opened fire with their Thompson submachine guns and rifles. The result was carnage. They killed twenty-three of the enemy and wounded seven. Quickly entering the church, they removed the few remaining members of the platoon, all of whom were wounded, and carried them back to the command post of A Company.

On reaching the command post, Lieutenant Karnap learned that both companies were to withdraw from the beachhead before daylight. He sent a man to each position with orders for them to pull out. "But tell them to fight a delaying action," he said. "We need to buy time to evacuate the wounded and our prisoners."

The 3d Platoon of I Company, still occupying the west bank of the river, was reinforced by the 1st Section, Machine Gun Platoon of Battalion Headquarters. When the order came down to withdraw from the beachhead, the 3d Platoon took boats across to pick up the wounded and later the rest of the men.

It was like a little Dunkirk. The boats made trip after trip under heavy fire. When one boat was sunk by the German fire, several of the men from shore dived in and swam out to help the wounded. Incredibly, no one was lost during the evacuation.

I was never more proud of my men. Without my presence, they had carried out their assignments perfectly and displayed the instincts, nerves, and skills of seasoned veterans. I doubt that any unit in the entire European Theater could have done better than they did. Here's what they accomplished:

- A Company was able to withdraw its beachhead successfully.

- The enemy losses at the hands of I Company were estimated at one hundred killed, forty wounded, and one tank destroyed.

- The enemy was forced to pull troops away from its southern defensive positions to combat the actions of I Company.

- The losses to I Company were four men slightly wounded.

For the next several days, our battalion continued to exchange mortar fire with the Krauts. By 18 April, our patrols reported that the Krauts were still in Hitdorf and Rheindorf, even though we were regularly pounding them.

Sergeants Johnson and Muri found an abandoned American tank near our company area. We examined it and discovered that all it needed was a battery. We immediately scrounged up one, and I Company became mechanized.

Every day, we drove the tank from behind a building to the bank of the river, blasted away at the Krauts in Hitdorf, and then retreated behind the building. Johnson was the driver, Muri the tank commander, and I was the gunner. We made a great armored team.

I was standing in front of my command post one day when General Gavin walked by and asked how everything was going.

"Fine, sir, "I said. Just at that moment, an artillery shell came whistling in. I hit the ground as I was trained to do. When I looked up, the general was still standing.

"General," I said, "maybe we should move over behind that building, because the Kraut observer can see us right here." After a few minutes of conversation, he strolled casually down the road as if he were walking down Main Street in Smalltown, USA. He was absolutely fearless.

The next day, we spotted the Kraut artillery observer in the church steeple where he could watch our every move. The three of us cranked up the tank, zeroed in, and knocked the steeple off the church with the Kraut still inside. Afterward, things grew quieter. The artillery no longer had its "eyes."

On the night of 15 April, we noticed friendly troops across the river in front of our position. They had eleven tanks and two half-tracks, so we knew they were there in force. Friendly forces also reported that Hitdorf and Rheindorf were now clear of the enemy. Several days later, we received our orders.

Within a week or so, we moved to an assembly area near Hollenstoudt. We went by train to Breetze and across the Elbe River. We went through several towns and villages without resistance and stopped in Eldena. At this point, most German soldiers were looking for someone to accept their surrender.

It was no longer the end of the beginning, as Churchill had earlier said, nor even the beginning of the end. It was the end of the end—and both sides knew it.

After being ripped to pieces by bullets at Anzio and Nijmegen, we thought we were prepared for everything, immune to shock, and inured to horror. But these experiences, as grim as they were, didn't prepare us for what we found at Wobbelin, Germany. We were forewarned because, as we approached the town, we were all but overcome by the stench that hung over the buildings like a perpetual cloud and drifted out on the summer air into the surrounding fields. Several of the men gagged.

As we moved into the town, we looked for Germans to capture or kill. What we found instead was a gruesome and sickening sight—the remains of a concentration camp for Jews and other political prisoners. These people had been transferred from Auschwitz just before Poland was overrun by the Russians, and their German captors had abandoned them as we moved into town.

I had never seen human beings look so tortured and grotesque. They were skeletons, people with absolutely no flesh. Their bodies were no more than skin stretched over knobby bones that threatened to break through with the slightest movement. Their eyes were huge sunken pits in their skulls. Their teeth had rotted to yellow stumps, and most of their hair had fallen out.

We found them in squalid buildings. Many were too weak to walk or talk. I found one who spoke English, and he said that they had not eaten in days.

One building, about 30 feet by 60 feet, was stacked three deep with unburied bodies. An area adjacent to the building was bisected by a trench about 10 feet wide, 8 feet deep, and 100 feet long. The trench was half full of dead bodies. An abandoned bulldozer stood nearby. Apparently, it had been used to shovel the bodies into the ditch and cover them up, some of them still alive.

We immediately loaded the survivors into trucks and ambulances for delivery to the nearest hospital. Unfortunately, many of them never made it.

The city of Ludwigslust was just a few miles from the camp. We rounded up all of the town's citizens, along with the German POWs that we had captured, and ordered them to go to the camp, dig up the bodies, and bury them in individual graves in the town square.

One Jewish soldier recently assigned to my company had escaped from Austria after the German occupation. He had made his way to the United States, enlisted in the Army, and joined the paratroopers—with the single mission of finding his family and rescuing them. He had information that his mother, father, sister, and brother had been placed in a concentration camp at the time he escaped.

He found a Catholic priest in the Wobbelin camp and learned, to his horror, that his family had been imprisoned in this very camp. Only a week earlier, the priest said, his parents and his sister and brother had been thrown into the furnace and burned alive.

No one could fully comprehend the bitter sorrow of this young man. I guess I felt some part of it, however, when I held him in my arms and cried with him.

As it became increasingly obvious that the German army had disintegrated, we were poised to capture Berlin, the victory wreath of the war. We had visions of moving through the Brandenburg Gate and shooting holdouts along the way. Only when the capital of the Third Reich had fallen into our hands would we truly feel that our job was done.

Then, the word came down from Supreme Headquarters. We were to stop at the Elbe River and allow the Russians to take Berlin. We were bitterly disappointed, particularly because we knew we easily could have reached Berlin before the Russians. That command decision, undoubtedly made in Washington, would haunt the West for the next forty-five years.

Lieutenant Sims, in his account, picks up the narrative from the time we reached the Rhine until the last days of the war and his return home:

> While at Laon, France, the new company commander of H Company broke his leg so I again assumed command of the company and retained command until the war in Europe ended.
>
> On 4 April 1945, the well-rested 504th Parachute Infantry Regiment moved into the vicinity of Cologne and occupied defensive positions along the west bank of the Rhine River, north of Cologne. Our opponents were the Wehrmacht forces that had been trapped in what was called the "Ruhr Pocket." Mostly we conducted patrols across the river. We would slip over to the other side in assault boats to locate and reconnoiter enemy positions. Most patrols encountered German forces, but casualties were light.
>
> The Germans made several attempts to get patrols through my company position, but none succeeded. As the Ruhr Pocket continued to be compressed by U.S. units, our regiment ordered one

company to attack and seize Hitdorf on the east side of the Rhine River.

On 13 April, our patrols made contact with elements of the U.S. 97th Infantry Division as they advanced north along the east bank of the Rhine. Three days later, the Ruhr Pocket collapsed. We then crossed the Rhine and began a policing action northeast of Cologne to search for holdouts, ammunition, salvageable equipment, and displaced persons.

On 27 April, we moved to an area south of Hamburg and then to the east in pursuit of German units that continued to resist. By 1 May, we had reached the Elbe River, near the town of Blekede, where we crossed the river to continue our search. At that point and almost without exception, the Germans we encountered surrendered without a fight. A few entire regiments surrendered, and, in one case, an entire division.

During this operation, we cleared the towns of Dömitz, Ludwigslust, Hagenow, and Wittenberg. Our greatest problem became the 500-pound buried explosive charges that were detonated by gyroscopic sea-mine igniters and activated by the magnetic influence of passing vehicles.

I was nearby when an explosion lifted one of our tanks about 30 feet in the air, killing the entire crew. Our division engineers were able to locate a number of German engineers who had placed these explosives, so they were used to locate and disarm the remaining charges.

North of Ludwigslust, we came upon a concentration camp named Wobbelin. The treatment of the prisoners and conditions in the camp were the most gruesome violation of human rights that one could imagine.

We hoped to meet up with the Russian Army in this area, so our battalion sent out a jeep patrol to the east on 3 May, and 12 miles away, in the town of Eldenberg, the patrol met and were entertained by a company of Cossacks. During the next few days, there were a number of exchanges between our men and the Russians, with numerous parties.

By 5 May, the fighting was over for us. Although combat casualties for the 504th were light, we had a large number of injuries from accidental gunshots, falls from confiscated horses, motorcycle accidents, and accidents while driving German cars and trucks. Luckily, an order was issued, calling in most of these items in order to reduce injuries.

For a short period, the 504th performed as occupation troops in Germany. Then the regiment moved to a new camp near Nancy in France to prepare for a move to Berlin for occupational duty. I went on leave for a visit to Paris, and upon my return I found out that Lieutenant Karnap and I had more points under what was called "Green Project" than anyone else in the division. The greater the number of points, the quicker you went home.

So the two of us, after processing, were transported by military air from France to the United States. We landed in Dover, Delaware, on 15 September and went through customs. Customs officials gave us a hard time because of the German weapons we brought home, but in the end they let us through, weapons and all.

There were no WELCOME HOME signs or ceremonies—not even a "thank you" for a job well done. From Delaware, we traveled by bus to Indian Town Gap, Pennsylvania, for further processing. Still no welcome home.

After we finished processing, I departed for my home in Hamilton, Ohio. It was only when I got there did I receive a welcome—and that came from family members only.

After a day of sitting on the banks of the Elbe, I began to get itchy britches, so I got in a jeep and drove over to see Lieutenant Karnap and Sergeant Johnson, who were staring across the river.

"Let's take this jeep and see what's on the other side," I said.

Despite the fact that we would be disobeying General Eisenhower's orders, they jumped in the jeep with me, ready to go. After being in the Army for a couple of years, we had learned which orders we had to obey and which ones we could ignore. Had Colonel Tucker ordered me to stay on the west side of the Elbe, I would have obeyed. But an order from a five-star general in headquarters hundreds of miles away? Besides, what could they do to us? We would be going home soon.

We put a white flag on the jeep and took off. We passed through the first village and saw no Krauts, then on to the next and the next—still no Krauts. We drove 40 miles, and there was still no sign of the German army. Then, we rounded a curve and saw a long column of German vehicles winding down the road and coming straight at us. We continued until we met them head-on. We stopped. They stopped.

A German captain got out of the lead vehicle and approached me. Strangely, after years of fighting German soldiers and seeing them kill some of my best friends, I wasn't afraid of this man or the huge force behind him. We both knew that the war was over, that his side had been crushed, and that he and his men were now at our mercy. The fact that this caravan was moving in our direction told me everything.

"What do you want?" he asked in heavily accented English, as he tried to maintain an authority he knew he no longer commanded. We were not equals meeting under a flag of truce.

"I'm here to accept your surrender," I said.

He looked behind him at the line of troops and vehicles disappearing over the horizon, then looked back at me and the two men seated in the jeep—a lieutenant and a sergeant.

"Are you crazy?" he said.

"Not at all," I said. "I have a whole army of paratroopers and tanks behind me, and you have Russians right behind you. You're about to be sandbagged. Do you want to surrender to me or to the Russians?"

He stared at me for a long moment, as he considered my question.

"A moment," he said.

He went several vehicles back and talked to someone in a dust-coated Mercedes. After a couple of minutes, another officer got out of the car and accompanied the captain to where I was standing. As they drew near, I could see the second officer was a lieutenant general—Lt. Gen. Steimer, Commander, 3d Panzer Corps, it turned out.

With him, he had what was left of his command—hundreds of tanks, trucks, and flak wagons, as well as several thousand troops. We both knew that he could strike one last blow for the dying Third Reich and blow us off the face of the earth.

"How can you ask us to surrender?" he said in much better English than the captain's. "We only see three men—and none of you is a field grade officer."

Again, I explained his options. He nodded, retreated a few yards, and conferred with several of his senior officers. Then, he walked back toward me and withdrew his pistol as he approached. I held my breath. He handed me his pistol, with the barrel pointing toward him.

I said, "General, tell your troops to move forward as rapidly as possible. We'll set up checkpoints along the way to disarm them. If you'll climb in the jeep, I'll drive you back to our command post."

He agreed.

We drove back to Regimental Headquarters, where I delivered General Steimer to Colonel Tucker.

"I've accepted the general's surrender on behalf of the regiment," I told him.

Colonel Tucker, bewildered, asked me to step outside.

"Where did you get this guy?" he asked.

I told him.

"Burriss, what the hell were you doing over there? You had orders not to cross that river!"

I shrugged my shoulders.

"Do you want me to take him back?"

He glared at me for a moment, then showed just the trace of a smile.

"No," he said, "we'll keep him."

Colonel Tucker ordered us to set up checkpoints along the road to disarm the German troops, just as I had anticipated. Lieutenant Carmichael jumped into my jeep, and we took off to meet the column of surrendering Krauts. When we arrived, we pulled off the road and started waving them on—tanks, trucks, jeeps, half-tracks, and motorcycles.

This went on for a couple of hours and then we returned to our checkpoint, where our troops were ordering the Germans in the vehicles to throw out all their weapons and ammunition and to disable the big guns. Our men shouted these instructions and also warned the Germans that if anyone held on to a weapon, he would be executed.

Farther down the road toward Regimental Headquarters, we set up a checkpoint specifically to search for weapons. During the routine search of each German, most of whom were in the backs of trucks, one of our men found a pistol hidden in a boot. He shouted and held it up for the officer in charge to see.

"Take him off the truck and shoot him," the officer ordered.

Sure enough, three burly paratroopers hauled him down, dragged him screaming to the side of the road, and put a bullet through his head. The word quickly spread back down the line, and no one else attempted to smuggle in a weapon.

As the seemingly endless caravan rolled toward us, I heard a deafening explosion and turned in time to see a truck sailing through the air, then disintegrating as it crashed to the ground. It had struck a sea mine, the type used to blow up gigantic ships. The Germans had buried it under the road and had set the timer to detonate after so many trucks had passed over it. Poetic justice—they caught one of their own.

We sent a demolition team ahead with mine detectors to see if any more were buried in the road. Sure enough, they found several mines and disarmed them, otherwise more German prisoners of war might have been killed.

After the armored corps had passed through our position, I said to Lieutenant Carmichael, "Hogie, let's see if we can locate the Russians. They should have taken Berlin by now. Maybe we can at least get a look at it."

So off we went again in the jeep. Sure enough, after about 50 or 60 miles, we bumped into a Russian Cossack Division.

It was the strangest sight I had ever seen—a rough, tough, ragtag bunch who looked less like an army than a caravan of gypsies. They were in horse-drawn wagons and beat-up old trucks hitting on one or two cylinders. Their women, chickens, and dogs accompanied them. With the exception of a couple of officers, they looked and smelled as if they hadn't taken a bath in two months. But they greeted us with waves and smiles.

One colonel spoke fluent English, and we invited him and three more officers to return with us to Regimental Headquarters. They picked up several bottles of vodka, got into a car, and followed us to headquarters, where we had a huge, loud party. We had some problem with communication but none with drinking. Alcohol speaks a universal language and transcends international boundaries.

The next morning, I collared the Russian colonel.

"I've fought my way all across Europe," I said, "and I'd like to see Berlin."

"So would I!" he said. "My unit bypassed Berlin."

In this giddy, free-wheeling, almost postwar atmosphere, we decided to do it. We jumped into a car and took off—the Russian colonel, Lieutenant Karnap, Lieutenant Price, Sergeant Johnson, and I—toward Berlin.

As we drew near, Berlin rose over the horizon like the ruins of Pompeii—except that it was still smoking. As we entered the city, we saw nothing but huge piles of rubble—rock, brick, charred wooden beams, twisted steel. Every building was gutted, and few had four walls still standing. Occasionally, flames flickered and crackled among the mounds.

No one was on the streets, except a few burly Russian women in uniform and an occasional detachment of Russian soldiers patrolling the streets. With a map to guide us, we drove to where the Reichstag had stood and found the same thing there. In fact, we hiked to the top of the rubble heap and stood there for a few minutes and wondered if Hitler's corpse also lay beneath us.

"Well, we made it," I said, "after 2½ years of fighting."

The others nodded.

"I guess we're the first Americans to reach Berlin," Karnap said. We grinned and slapped our Russian comrade on the back. We could not foresee the tremendous tension that would soon build up between his nation and ours, a Cold War that, for a time, would be fought over control of this ruined city.

"It is a glorious victory," the Russian colonel said.

"Yes," I agreed, "but at what a price!"

A few days later, the war in Europe ended with the formal surrender of the provisional government of Germany. Hitler, as well as Josef Goebbels, his propaganda minister, and Heinrich Himmler, the head of the dreaded SS, had already committed suicide in the wake of the devastation. Göring was captured, later tried, and sentenced to death. He cheated the gallows by taking poison a few hours before his scheduled execution.

We weren't too concerned about the capture of the Nazi high command but much more interested in how soon we could go home. Washington set up a point system to determine who was eligible for discharge. Those of us who had landed in Sicily and fought in Italy, Belgium, Holland, and Germany had accumulated enough points to be released immediately, and it was so ordered. Our unit was shipped to a staging area in southern France to await transportation back to the United States.

There was still a war to be fought in the Far East, however, including a possible invasion of Japan. So that consideration took priority. All the men who had fought only a short time in Europe were scheduled to return to the States, enjoy a thirty-day leave, and then be sent to the Far East. Given the priority of the Pacific war, they were on board the first ships to head home.

Then, the Army Air Corps dropped atomic bombs on Hiroshima and Nagasaki, and suddenly the free world was celebrating VJ-Day. World War II was over. The men with low points, already en route home to fight again, were discharged before those of us with high points. We were left in France, bitching and cursing the system, as we awaited return of the ships that would take us home.

Some of the men, whether they had high or low points, were sent to Berlin to be "America's Guard of Honor," with orders to patrol the city. A lot of guys thought it was a privilege to be among the elite of the elite, but I was glad I didn't have to go. I wanted to get back to my wife and family in the worst sort of way.

I finally arrived in the States in September 1945 and reported to Fort Bragg, where Squee met me. I had wondered if we would be complete strangers, but after the first moment, I felt as if I had never been away. As we talked, I realized how rough it had been for her—waiting at home, dreading every mail delivery, not knowing from one day to the next whether I was dead or alive. Within a single month, she had experienced the loss of our son at birth; learned that her only brother, whom she loved dearly, had died in a Japanese POW camp; and received a message that I was missing in action in Sicily. (Of course, as soon as I learned that I had been reported missing, I persuaded the radio operator on the British ship headed for North Africa to cable her that I was safe.)

With our reunion, all that worry and heartache were finally behind us.

That was more than fifty years ago, but I still remember the pride and exhilaration of setting foot again on American soil and being with my family again. It is a feeling that younger Americans have never experienced because they have never had to fight to preserve the very existence of the nation, as we did in World War II. My generation fought and died in the unshakable belief that we were defending the greatest country on earth and that the survival of the United States ensured the survival of freedom and justice around the world. After all these years, I still maintain that belief.

Epilogue

I n 1994, I returned to the Netherlands at the invitation of the Dutch to participate in the fiftieth-anniversary reenactment of the Waal crossing. Our hosts were celebrating their liberation from Nazi rule, one of the grimmest periods in Dutch history. They wanted to thank the survivors of Operation Market Garden for our sacrifices and to acknowledge even greater sacrifices of the men who had given their lives so many years ago. I was touched by their gratitude, particularly given the passage of time. Most Americans had forgotten World War II. The people of the Netherlands remembered. We were told that tens of thousands of people were expected to attend. Five of us, all members of the 82d Airborne during World War II, were scheduled to repeat what we had done in 1944—make the same jump at the same time of day and land on the same field. I would be jumping three days shy of my seventy-fifth birthday, and I was looking forward to it.

On my way to the Netherlands, I reflected on those years—1941 to 1945—and was astonished at what, as a nation, we had been able to accomplish. When the Japanese bombed Pearl Harbor, our Army and Navy were undermanned and poorly equipped, and we had no separate branch known as the Air Force.

We faced two major military powers on opposite sides of the world. Germany and Japan each drew on proud military traditions and had been preparing for war for a decade. Both regimes were highly authoritarian and could command absolute obedience from both their civilian and their military populations. They had already conquered great nations and seemed all but invincible.

The United States was a democracy with a civilian mentality. Americans were not accustomed to being regimented and ordered about by some central authority. We didn't swear allegiance to führers or duces or emperors. If we were going to defeat the Germans and Japanese, we knew we would have to do it with civilian troops—men and boys from farms, small towns, and tenements of big cities. A peaceful conglomeration of draftees would have to be turned into a highly disciplined military force trained to kill other men and to do so without hesitation or remorse.

I was pretty typical of the men who went to war in 1941. At twenty-two, I was an easygoing, small-town boy who hadn't gotten into a fight in years. I knew little about international politics and less about military life. I certainly wasn't mad at people who lived halfway around the world—not at the beginning.

People who grew up during the 1960s and afterward saw mass demonstrations against the war in Vietnam. In addition, many young men said, "Hell no, we won't go," and moved to Canada. At the outset of World War II, only a handful refused to take up arms, and most of those were religious conscientious objectors, who believed that killing others, even in time of war, was wrong. Many of these men, however, willingly risked their lives as ambulance drivers and medical corpsmen.

In 1941, almost everyone wanted to enlist. The week after Pearl Harbor, long lines of men and boys stood in front of recruitment centers, and many who were unfit (4-F) tried to fool Army doctors so that they could put on uniforms and go into battle. I was certainly grateful that I had no physical disability and that I already held a reserve commission. I not only wanted to join the Army, but I wanted to see combat.

Suddenly, I found myself a second lieutenant in charge of thirty-five to forty enlisted men. Most of them were eighteen or nineteen years old, just out of high school, and had never held down a job or assumed any other responsibilities of adulthood. Few had fired a rifle, and none had tossed a live grenade at another human being or blasted a tank with a bazooka. Yet, we were all called upon to do just those things.

When we put on the uniform, we didn't think of the war as *our* war. We didn't start the fighting, and we felt no hatred for the individual

German soldier, but we soon understood that he had been sent to conquer us or to kill us if he could. Soon enough, it became personal for all of us, particularly when we saw our buddies cut in two by bullets or blown to pieces by artillery fire.

I first took the war personally when I received word that my child had died shortly after birth. At the time, I was crouching in a foxhole thousands of miles away because the Germans and Japanese wanted to run the world. That sense of commitment was further reinforced when I learned that my brother-in-law had died in a Japanese POW camp after surviving the Bataan Death March. He had planned to become a Presbyterian minister. We had named our first son after him.

Eventually, it became just as personal for virtually every American in uniform. And with most, it began in those early days of basic training followed by specialized training—a fierce, merciless regimen that was to prove itself superior on battlefield after battlefield, both in the Far East and in Europe.

Within days, American recruits began to pull together, to develop a sense of mission, and to set our sights on an enemy that threatened to attack our country and destroy our communities, our friends, and our families. By the time we had arrived overseas and encountered enemy troops for the first time, we had no compunctions about killing Germans and Italians, and we knew how to do it quickly and efficiently. That transformation seemed like a miracle. It was actually the result of extraordinarily fine training in tactics and the spirit of a nation ready to fight.

Caught unprepared at Pearl Harbor, Americans rallied quickly. During 1942, perhaps the most crucial period of the war, we all but caught up with the Germans and the Japanese in terms of mobilization, training, and the accumulation of weapons. By the middle of 1943, we were fighting the enemy to a standstill; by the end of the year, we were driving him back toward his own borders. It was an unprecedented reversal of fortune.

That reversal, however, was bought at a heavy price. In 1994, strapped in a jetliner crossing the Atlantic Ocean, I thought of what we had gone through during those years—the dangers and hardships that became, for a while, part of our daily routine. In retrospect, I found it hard to believe that, as young men, we had endured so much for so long and had still kept on fighting.

In the first place, when we went into combat and saw people getting killed, right and left—arms, legs, and heads blown off—we didn't turn tail and run. Most of us learned to live with death on a day-by-day, hour-by-hour, minute-by-minute basis. I can't really describe how it felt to crouch in a foxhole for two or three days and to know that at any second a bullet could whistle into my head and spill out my brains. I can only say that I began to look at the world in an entirely different way. I appreciated the simple pleasures of being alive—a hot meal, a clear sky, and, above all, silence. Fear settled into my consciousness like a dull ache, rather than grabbing me suddenly like a sharp pain. I went into emotional hibernation.

The typical company had a total of 119 men and eight officers. In my company, after Anzio, Nijmegen, and the Battle of the Bulge, fewer than 27 of them were still alive. Virtually all the survivors had been wounded, some of them five and six times. Yet, during $2\frac{1}{2}$ years of the heaviest combat of the war, I can recall only one man who broke and ran from a battle site. He was court-martialed and given thirty years in prison.

With all this horror, one might expect that those of us still standing would be broken in mind and spirit and to be prime candidates for the psychoanalyst's couch. This didn't happen either. I killed my first enemy troops—several Italian soldiers on the island of Sicily—without the slightest twinge of conscience. Since then, I have felt absolutely no guilt or trauma—no nightmares, no flashbacks, no post-stress syndrome, nor did any of the World War II veterans whom I have known. We were motivated by a just cause—freedom.

It wasn't just the aura of imminent death that plagued us. The life that we led in combat was so hard that, in retrospect, I find it difficult to believe that we survived it, much less that we fought and defeated a well-trained, well-supplied enemy. During fall, winter, and spring, the weather was often freezing, and sometimes the temperatures fell below zero. It rained or snowed constantly. Part of the time, we lived in foxholes half full of water, and the water sometimes froze at night. We were perpetually cold and wet, so most of us stayed a little sick all of the time. Yet, surprisingly, few men in my company dropped out of combat as the result of illness, and only a handful died of disease.

In addition, when we were under heavy bombardment or when we were pursuing the enemy, we could go without sleep or food for three or four days in a row. How did we manage to slog from point to point, haggard and hungry, and still man our rifles and machine guns and bazookas to ward off an enemy attack? After more than fifty years, I find the question more puzzling than I did at Anzio or Nijmegen during the heat of battle. We did it because we *had* to do it and because we were Americans who grew up with beliefs and values that contrasted dramatically with those of the enemy we were facing.

Crossing the Atlantic fifty years later, I was thinking about those beliefs. I remembered a question someone had asked me just a few days earlier: "Do you believe today's young men would be willing to take the same kinds of risks you took and endure the same kind of hardships your generation endured?"

I had shrugged my shoulders and said I didn't know. With several hours of flying time ahead of me, however, I gave the question some consideration. The more I thought about it, the more complicated the issue became. Before attempting an answer, I had to consider the differences between my generation and the current generation of Americans.

First, unlike today's generation, Americans were not living in prosperity prior to World War II. When the Japanese bombed Pearl Harbor, the nation was still mired in the Great Depression. Unemployment was high, pay was low, and few people could afford more than the bare necessities.

Our family was fairly typical. My father died during the 1930s and left my mother with three children. I was twelve years old, and I had a brother who was fifteen and a sister who was eighteen. We had no means of support, except $20 per month that an uncle sent. My brother and I pumped gas for nickels and dimes, and that extra income helped to buy necessities.

We lived on the edge of town, so we not only planted a garden but also kept and milked a cow. We wore clothes for a much longer period than young people would wear them today. My mother darned our socks as soon as we wore holes in them, and we used stick-on patches to cover up the rips and worn places on our pants and shirts.

In other words, we were used to hard times, and that fact might have conditioned us for war. Most young people today have led privileged lives compared with what we were used to during the 1930s and early 1940s. In fact, many people who live at the poverty level today have more luxuries than middle-income wage earners enjoyed sixty years ago.

Second, I believe that we had more spiritual resources then than we do now. We went to church every Sunday—rain or shine. Even as teenagers, we knelt beside our beds and prayed every night, and that habit stuck with me in the service. Wherever I was, whether in a foxhole at Anzio or sleeping on the ground in Holland, I still said my prayers and asked God to protect me and bring me back safely to my wife, family, and friends. It helped a lot.

We were used to hard times, and we were probably a more faith-bound generation. These conditions made the transition from peace to war easier for many of us to bear.

While considering these differences, however, I realized that I have more faith in the current generation than do many of my contemporaries. Thinking about my own children and grandchildren—about the kind of people I know them to be—I came to the conclusion that, even though their world is softer today than ours was and far more self-centered, they would be willing and able to run the same risks and endure the same hardships if they believed that their lives and families and their way of life were in danger of being wiped from the face of the earth.

If we were to go to war with a major world power, the young people of this nation could endure everything we endured and fight as bravely and as effectively as we fought. Or so I concluded as I flew back to Holland to reenact the past.

The Dutch officials in charge of the commemorative ceremonies wrote to say that in order to participate in the reenactment, we would have to log three recent jumps. I suppose they wanted to make certain that none of us would die of heart failure in midair.

So on a Saturday, a few weeks before the trip to Holland, my son Francis and I drove out to the site of a skydiving club near Columbia. Francis decided to come with me and learn what parachuting was all about. I hadn't jumped in more than 45 years. He had never jumped.

When we were airborne and over the drop site, the club jump master began sending chutists out the door. Each time a parachute opened,

he gave the "thumbs up" signal. When I got to the door, he sent me out and watched as I fell.

After 32 jumps as a paratrooper in World War II, for the first time I had a serious problem. My primary chute was wrapped around my arm and wouldn't open. As I fell, I weighed my options. If I went to my reserve chute, it might become tangled with the "streamer" that my primary chute had become. So I knew I had to untangle the primary chute from my arm.

I must have fallen 1,000 to 1,200 feet before I got the cords untangled. Meanwhile, in the plane, the jump master was peering out the door but not giving the "thumbs up" signal.

"Is he OK?" Francis yelled.

The jump master kept watching. Only when my chute blossomed did he turn his thumbs up. I'll say this for Francis—he went right out the door behind me.

We made one more jump that day and a third one on Sunday. At age seventy-four, I was qualified to jump again.

When I arrived at Nijmegen, local officials briefed me on the plans for the following day—19 September 1994. The five paratroopers who were going to jump would be flown over the original drop zone in single-engine Cessnas. We would bail out and land where we had landed fifty years earlier. Then, we would be picked up and transported to the bank of the Waal, where we would join members of the 3d Battalion of the 504th Regiment in a reenactment of the crossing.

"Will we have to row across in the same canvas boats?" I asked.

"No," an official said. "You'll be carried over in DUKWs and driven across the field to the dike, where we'll hold a memorial service."

DUKWs [pronounced "ducks"] are amphibous craft that would easily navigate the river with a full load. I was relieved. It had been hard enough to row those canvas boats when we were young. I didn't want to try it again at the age of seventy-five.

"How many people do you expect to attend?" I asked.

"Around 100,000," he said. "It will be a big holiday. All the school-children will be there and mayors from nearby towns."

The next morning, I was driven to the airport, where I was issued a parachute, courtesy of the Dutch, and met and shook hands with the four former troopers making the jump with me. I didn't know them because we had served in different outfits, but all of the outfits had been under Generals Ridgway and Gavin.

When the time came we suited up, strapped on our parachutes, and climbed into two Cessnas—two old troopers in one, three in the other, each plane with a jump master in addition to the pilot.

As soon as we were airborne, we encountered problems. Clouds and fog hung over the field at precisely the place where we intended to jump. Below were fifty thousand spectators and scores of food vendors, all looking skyward and trying to spot us. We certainly couldn't see them. Finally, after we made several passes, the pilot gave up.

"We'll go to an airport about 20 miles from the drop zone. Some Dutch paratroopers are jumping there as part of the celebration."

So we flew over the Dutch airfield, and the five of us bailed out. Several hundred civilians watched us drift down and applauded as we landed. There were no broken legs or skinned knees—pretty good for old-timers as out of practice as we were.

As soon as we were on the ground, a limousine picked us up and rushed us to the bank of the Waal River. After hearing who we were and what we had just done, the crowd gave a tremendous roar of approval. We then joined members of the 3d Battalion, 504th, whose ranks were likewise depleted. Private Schwartz's widow was also there. As I was talking to her, I couldn't help thinking that my widow might have been there as well.

The combined force filled up only two DUKWs. As 100,000 Dutch onlookers cheered and waved on a cold rainy day, we skimmed across the water—no paddling, no machine-gun fire, no artillery shells. We made the crossing in silence, each of us remembering how it had been on that day fifty years ago.

On the far shore, hundreds of schoolchildren were waiting to present us with flowers. Still standing in the DUKWs, we bent down and took them from red-cheeked, blue-eyed girls and boys who probably didn't fully understand what this ceremony was all about. The DUKWs then moved across the 900-yard green field, which looked exactly as it had in 1944. Again, it was easier to ride than run—and a lot more relaxing without enemy fire.

At the dike, where we had killed so many Germans, we stopped, climbed slowly and carefully out of the DUKWs, and assembled around a stone monument holding a bronze plaque that bore the names of all the men who had died there. The speeches began. I could recognize only a few of the words, but I understood the sentiments they expressed. Then every mayor in the Netherlands (or so it seemed) laid a wreath on the monument.

Finally, after the last speech, the regimental flag was dropped to half-mast, and we heard the clear, sad notes of taps. Grief, it seems, can lie dormant for half a century and then suddenly come alive again. There, on the green grass under a gray sky, surrounded by thousands of solemn Dutch faces, a diminished band of white-haired men—who had no time to stop and mourn their fallen comrades fifty years earlier—stood at attention in that historic place as tears streamed down their cheeks.

Just as the ceremony was ending, Francis Keefe and John Gallagher, two I Company veterans, came roaring up in a jeep.

"Burriss," they yelled, "the British tanks are waiting for us at the bridge. Been there over an hour."

I climbed into the jeep.

"Who's commanding the tanks?" I asked.

"Lord Carrington."

I wondered if Lord Carrington would remember what I had said to Captain Carrington half a century earlier. I hoped this meeting would be more cordial.

As we drove across the bridge, I looked up at the giant superstructure and remembered that a sniper, perched on one of the beams, had killed a man standing next to me. The bridge was still intact, well maintained and apparently none the worse for years of wear. I figured it could easily last another fifty years without replacement.

I looked up ahead, but I saw no tanks. A number of Dutch spectators were still staring down the road. We asked one of the men where the tanks had gone.

"On to Arnhem," he said. Apparently Lord Carrington had become impatient and moved on.

How ironic. After fifty years, they had finally done what General Horrocks promised they would do when we had planned the attack that fateful morning high above the Waal River. Did Lord Carrington forget that he had refused to do just that when the Poles and Red Devils were being slaughtered? Or was he simply trying to get it right this time, to make amends for the long-ago failure of the British to rescue their own doomed men? I never had the chance to ask him.

I don't know if the British tanks went all the way to Arnhem in 1994, and I don't care. I do know that Carrington's tanks were too late for the seven thousand British paratroopers who once waited for them in that battle-torn city and who now wait quietly and patiently in thousands and thousands of foreign graves.

Indeed, our own men, the ones who lost their lives in the war and those who have since died, are now waiting for the rest of us as our numbers diminish with each passing year. In twenty or twenty-five years, we all will be gone, joining our departed comrades in the great hereafter.

As one living witness who remembers, I'll be happy to be reunited with the men of the 3d Battalion. At Sicily, Anzio, the Battle of the Bulge, and Nijmegen, they fought as fiercely as any troops who ever went to war and died as bravely. I remember them with each passing day and still stand in awe of their courage and self-sacrifice.

I only hope that after we are all gone, future generations will recall that, when darkness had already descended on Europe and much of Asia, young men from cities, towns, and farms all over America willingly left their families and friends to fight and die on foreign soil in order to keep the world free. On that hope I end this book with the confidence that its recollections will help our children and grandchildren to understand why we had to defeat the Germans and the Japanese in World War II in order to preserve their freedom.

Appendix A

List of Contributors

Pfc. Larry Dunlop, H Company, 504th Parachute Infantry Regiment

Sgt. Albert Essig, I Company, 504th Parachute Infantry Regiment

1st Lt. Roy Hanna, Headquarters Company, 3d Battalion, 504th Parachute Infantry Regiment

Pvt. Al Hermanson, 376th Field Artillery Battalion

Capt. Henry B. Keep, S3, 3d Battalion, 504th Parachute Infantry Regiment

Capt. Delbert Kuehl, Headquarters and Headquarters Company, 504th Parachute Infantry Regiment

2d Lt. James Magellas, 504th Parachute Infantry Regiment

Pvt. Francis W. McLane, I Company, 504th Parachute Infantry Regiment

1st Lt. Edward J. Sims, H Company, 504th Parachute Infantry Regiment

Sgt. Robert Tallon, Headquarters Company, 3d Battalion, 504th Parachute Infantry Regiment

Sgt. Albert Tarbel, H Company, 504th Parachute Infantry Regiment

Appendix B

Casualties of the
504th Parachute Infantry Regiment
during World War II in Europe

Name	Rank	Where	Date	How
Adams, Dale	Cpl	Holland	20 Sep 44	KIA
Allison, Norland W.	Pvt	Anzio	5 Mar 44	KIA
Altemus, William E.	S/Sgt	Holland	13 Oct 44	DOW
Amaral, George R.	Pvt	Sicily	10 Jul 43	KIA
Armstrong, Clyde H.	Pfc	Germany	23 May 45	KODY
Atherton, Kenneth O.	Pvt	Sicily	11 Jul 43	KIA
Bains, Alvin	Pvt	Belgium	21 Dec 44	KIA
Baldwin, Leon E.	S/Sgt	Holland	27 Sep 44	MIA
Barker, Alexander L.	Sgt	Holland	27 Sep 44	KIA
Baxter, George A.	Pvt	Anzio	23 Jan 44	KIA
Beall, William R.	Maj	Italy	24 Sep 43	KIA
Beaty, Leonard W.	Cpl	Holland	27 Sep 44	KIA
Bei, Anthony	Pvt	Holland	20 Sep 44	KIA
Briggs, Richard H.	2d Lt	Sicily	10 Jul 43	MIA
Brown, Charles	Cpl	Holland	28 Sep 44	POW
Busby, Harry F.	1st Lt	Holland	20 Sep 44	KIA
Campbell, Dale E.	Pvt	Holland	20 Sep 44	KIA
Chesko, Leonard S.	Pfc	Anzio	6 Feb 44	KIA
Clemons, Caine J.	Pfc	Holland	20 Sep 44	KIA
Colishion, Peter L.	Pvt	Holland	20 Sep 44	KIA
Collins, Arthur E.	Pvt	Sicily	28 Jul 43	KIA
Collins, Dennis	Pvt	Holland	27 Sep 44	KIA
Collins, Edward P.	Cpl	Holland	12 Oct 44	KIA
Colman, Robert C.	Pvt	Holland	27 Sep 44	POW
Conley, Henry F.	Pvt	Sicily	10 Jul 43	KIA
Cooper, Garland E.	Pfc	Holland	27 Sep 44	KIA
Cortez, Valentino M.	Pvt	Holland	27 Sep 44	POW
Couture, John F.	Pvt	Holland	3 Nov 44	KIA

Name	Rank	Where	Date	How
Crockette, Vernel E.	Pvt	Sicily	10 Jul 43	KIA
Curry, Cornelius E.	Pvt	Holland	27 Sep 44	KIA
Dew, Robert G.	Sgt	Holland	27 Sep 44	MIA
Digan, Edward C.	2d Lt	Sicily	13 Jul 43	KIA
Downs, Francis L.	Pvt	Holland	20 Sep 44	KIA
Esposito, Nicholas G.	Pfc	Holland	21 Sep 44	KIA
Etheredge, Adnirum J.	T/5	Italy	11 Dec 43	KIA
Ferrill, Willis J.	1st Lt	Anzio	23 Jan 44	KIA
Fetzer, Robert L.	Pvt	Anzio	8 Feb 44	KIA
Fort, William G.	S/Sgt	Sicily	10 Jul 43	POW
Frazier, James R.	Pvt	Sicily	10 Jul 43	MIA
Funk, Le Vern J.	Pvt	Anzio	10 Jul 43	MIA
Gannon, Robert E.	Pfc	Anzio	26 Jan 44	POW
Gauntey, Davis L.	Pfc	Holland	27 Sep 44	KIA
Gerle	Lt	Itlay	11 Dec 43	KIA
Gewont, Walker J.	Pvt	Sicily	10 Jul 43	POW
Gilmore, Rollo	Pfc	Germany	3 Feb 45	MIA
Gilson, Frank W.	1st Lt	Italy	12 Dec 43	KIA
Gondela, Thadeus S.	Pfc	Holland	20 Sep 44	KIA
Goodman, Chester R.	Pvt	Italy	11 Dec 43	KIA
Goodman, Harry W.	Pfc	Anzio	9 Feb 44	KIA
Grooms, Darrell D.	Pvt	Holland	27 Sep 44	KIA
Gross, Leonard E.	Cpl	Italy	11 Dec 43	KIA
Hall, John W. Jr.	Pvt	Holland	20 Sep 44	KIA
Hamblet, Warren O.	Pfc	Italy	12 Sep 43	KIA
Hamilton, Joseph V.	Pfc	Holland	12 Oct 44	KIA
Hartgraves, William D.	Sgt	Sicily	10 Jul 43	MIA
Hartman, William S.	Cpl	Holland	23 Sep 44	DOW
Hayden, Paul E.	Pfc	Belgium	21 Dec 44	KIA
Heiden, Norman H.	Pfc	Holland	23 Sep 44	KIA
Herman, James R.	Pvt	Belgium	8 Jan 45	DOW
Higginbotham, John T.	Pvt	Sicily	10 Jul 43	MIA
Hill, George B.	Pvt	Sicily	10 Jul 43	KIA
Hollingsworth, Buford	Pvt	Sicily	11 Jul 43	MIA
Jacoby, Harold	Pvt	Holland	27 Sep 44	KIA
Johnson, Donald	Pvt	Belgium	24 Dec 44	KIA
Johnson, Harold R.	Sgt	Holland	23 Sep 44	DOW
Johnston, Warren R.	Pvt	Holland	21 Sep 44	KIA
Kanapkis, Edward	T/4	Sicily	10 Jul 43	KIA
Katonik, Paul J.	Pvt	Holland	20 Sep 44	KIA

Name	Rank	Where	Date	How
Kaufman, Herbert C.	Capt	Sicily	11 Jul 43	KIA
Kennedy, Edward W.	1st Lt	Holland	1 Nov 44	DOW
Knight, Gerald W.	Pfc	Holland	28 Sep 44	MIA
Komula, Walter I.	Pfc	Anzio	9 Feb 44	KIA
Konetzko, Alphose L.	Pfc	Holland	2 Oct 44	KIA
Labinsky, Myron F.	Cpl	Sicily	11 Jul 43	KIA
Livingston, Edie H.	Pvt	Normandy	6 Jun 44	POW
Lucero, Ernest F.	Pfc	Italy	12 Dec 43	KIA
Lumpkin, Edward B.	Pvt	Italy	11 Dec 43	KIA
Maloney, John K.	Sgt	Anzio	7 Feb 44	KIA
Massey, Charles T.	S/Sgt	Sicily	10 Jul 43	KIA
McVitty, Clyde C.	Pvt	Anzio	9 Feb 44	KIA
Messina, John S.	Ist Lt	Sicily	13 Jul 43	KIA
Mulstay, Donald F.	Sgt	Italy	11 Dec 43	KIA
Muniz, Thomas A.	Pvt	Italy	22 Dec 43	KIA
Muston, Raymond L.	Pvt	N Africa	27 May 43	DODY
Muszynski, Walter J.	Pvt	Holland	20 Sep 44	KIA
Nelson, Edward P. Jr.	Pfc	Italy	23 Sep 43	KIA
Northrop, Charles E.	Cpl	Anzio	26 Jan 44	POW
Pappalardo, Joseph S.	Pvt	Sicily	10 Jul 43	MIA
Pascavage, Tony	Cpl	Italy	11 Dec 43	KIA
Pearce, Charles W.	Pvt	Holland	27 Sep 44	POW
Pfeffer, Frank	Pvt	Anzio	6 Feb 44	KIA
Philbeck, James C.	Pfc	Anzio	26 Jan 44	POW
Pietrala, Edmond J.	Pfc	Anzio	24 Jan 44	KIA
Pomaibo, William	Pvt	Sicily	10 Jul 43	KIA
Preston, Andrew J.	Pvt	Belgium	7 Jan 43	POW
Rice, William A.	Pvt	Sicily	10 Jul 43	MIA
Ritch, Wallace	1/Sgt	Sicily	10 Jul 43	MIA
Robbins, Grady L.	Sgt	Holland	21 Sep 44	KIA
Samolis, Casimer	Pvt	Italy	14 Dec 43	KIA
Schultz, Alvin R.	Pvt	Anzio	24 Jan 44	KIA
Schultz, Harvey W.	Pvt	Holland	23 Sep 44	DOW
Seitzinger, Jack M.	Pvt	Holland	20 Sep 44	KIA
Shelby, Talbot P.	Pvt	Holland	28 Sep 44	POW
Shelden, Harold K.	Pfc	Holland	21 Sep 44	KIA
Simmons, Leroy M.	Pvt	Belgium	25 Dec 44	KIA
Smith, Davis R.	Pvt	Belgium	9 Jan 45	DOW
Smith, Winfred K.	T/5	Holland	20 Sep 44	KIA
Snyder, Charles J.	2d Lt	Holland	28 Sep 44	KIA

Name	Rank	Where	Date	How
Stanford, Davis S.	Cpl	Holland	27 Sep 44	MIA
Stefaniak, Leon L.	Pvt	Sicily	10 Jul 43	KIA
Storm, William J.	Cpl	Holland	12 Oct 44	KIA
Sullivan, George L.	Pvt	Italy	23 Sep 43	DOW
Swellander, Delbert W.	Pvt	Anzio	4 Mar 44	KIA
Swift, Andrew T.	Pvt	Holland	27 Sep 44	KIA
Switzer, Carl M.	Pvt	Sicily	10 Jul 43	KIA
Taplin, Rex D.	Pvt	Italy	20 Dec 43	KIA
Walls, Harry C. Jr.	Pvt	Sicily	10 Jul 43	KIA
White, Melvin B.	S/Sgt	Anzio	15 Feb 44	DOW
White, William H.	S/Sgt	Holland	30 Oct 44	KIA
Whitmire, Solon W.	Pvt	Holland	27 Sep 44	DOW
Willson, Victor J. Jr.	Pvt	Holland	27 Sep 44	MIA
Zentgraf, Frederick	Pvt	Holland	20 Sep 44	KIA

Key:
    DODY, died on active duty
    DOW, died of wounds
    KIA, killed in action
    KODY, killed on active duty
    MIA, missing in action
    POW, prisoner of war

Index

About the Author

T. Moffatt Burriss was born in Anderson, South Carolina, and graduated from Clemson College in 1940. He was teaching at Orangeburg (South Carolina) High School when World War II broke out. With a reserve commission in the Army, he volunteered for duty in the paratroopers and fought in Sicily, at Anzio, in the Battle of the Bulge, in the assault on Nijmegen, and in the invasion of Germany.

He was awarded the Silver Star, the Bronze Star with Oak Leaf Cluster and Combat "V," the Purple Heart, the Presidential Unit Citation with two Oak Leaf Clusters, the French Fourragère, the Belgian Fourragère, and the Dutch Lanyard.

After World War II, Burriss returned to South Carolina and became a building contractor. He also served for fifteen years in the South Carolina House of Representatives. For nine of those years, he was Republican Minority Leader.

He lives in Columbia, South Carolina.